**365 Days of Devotions**

# That Is SO Me

## Other books in the growing Faithgirlz!™ library

*The Faithgirlz!™ Bible*

*NIV Faithgirlz!™ Backpack Bible*

*My Faithgirlz!™ Journal*

## The Sophie Series

*Sophie's World*

*Sophie's Secret*

*Sophie Under Pressure*

*Sophie Steps Up*

*Sophie's First Dance*

*Sophie's Stormy Summer*

*Sophie's Friendship Fiasco*

*Sophie and the New Girl*

*Sophie Flakes Out*

*Sophie Loves Jimmy*

*Sophie's Drama*

*Sophie Gets Real*

## Nonfiction

*Everybody Tells Me to Be Myself but I Don't Know Who I Am*

*Girl Politics*

*Body Talk*

*No Boys Allowed: Devotions for Girls*

*Girlz Rock: Devotions for Girls*

*Chick Chat: Devotions for Girls*

*Shine On, Girl!: Devotions for Girls*

## Check out www.faithgirlz.com

the beauty of believing

# 365 Days of Devotions

That Is SO Me

**Flip-Flops, Faith, and Friends**

Nancy Rue

ZONDER**kidz**

ZONDERVAN.com/
**AUTHORTRACKER**
follow your favorite authors

We want to hear from you. Please send your comments
about this book to us in care of zreview@zondervan.com. Thank you.

ZONDERKIDZ

*That Is SO Me*
Copyright © 2010 by Nancy Rue

This title is also available as a Zondervan ebook. Visit www.zondervan.com/ebooks.

Requests for information should be addressed to:

Zonderkidz, *Grand Rapids, Michigan 49530*

---

Library of Congress Cataloging-in-Publication Data

Rue, Nancy N.
    That is SO me : 365 days of devotions / Nancy Rue.
       p.  cm. — (Faithgirlz!)
    ISBN  978-0-310-71475-0 (softcover)
    1. Girls—Religious life—Juvenile literature.  2. Preteens—Religious life—Juvenile
literature.  3. Christianity—Biblical teaching—Juvenile literature.  4. Devotional
calendars—Juvenile literature.  I. Title.
BV4551.3.R84   2010
242'.62—dc22
                                    2010020345

---

Published in association with the literary agency of Alive Communications, Inc., 7680 Goddard Street #200, Colorado Springs, CO 80920

Zonderkidz is a trademark of Zondervan.

*Editor: Kathleen Kerr*
*Art direction: Cindy Davis*
*Cover design: Sarah Molegraaf*
*Interior design: Sherri L. Hoffman*

*Printed in the United States of America*

---

10 11 12 13 14 15 /DCI/ 23 22 21 20 19 18 17 16 15 14 13 12 11 10 9 8 7 6 5 4 3 2 1

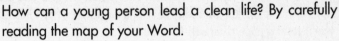

# What's Up with This Book?

How can a young person lead a clean life? By carefully reading the map of your Word.

*Psalm 119:9 MSG*

If someone asked you, "What is SO you?" you might answer with something like this:

- Wearing flip-flops (with sparkles, of course).
- Playing soccer ALL weekend.
- Watching a Pixar movie marathon.
- Reading *Anne of Green Gables* for, like, the twentieth time.

The answer you probably *wouldn't* give would be, "Reading the Bible"—not unless you were trying to impress your Sunday school teacher. It's not that you don't believe in the Bible and know it's important, but, let's face it, most of the time it doesn't seem to have anything to do with you, right? Take this verse, for instance:

*Hear the word of the Lord. This is what the Lord says: About this time tomorrow, a seah of flour will sell for a shekel and two seahs of barley for a shekel at the gate of Samaria.*

*2 Kings 7:1*

First of all, what's a *seah*? Or a *shekel*? And why do you care how much flour and barley cost four thousand years ago? How does any of that relate to YOU, when your biggest challenge at this point is understanding fractions or figuring out why your best friend is mad at you *now*?

Actually, a verse like that *doesn't* have a whole lot to do with you. But there are plenty in the Bible that do. Check this one out:

*The Lord detests lying lips, but he delights in [people] who are truthful.*

*Proverbs 12:22*

Doesn't every girl you know need to be reminded of that when the gossip in the restroom gets juicy?

The Bible is really full of verses, stories, and explanations that are SO you, right now, in your tween-hood. All you need is a little help finding the parts that are all about you and some pointing-in-the-right-direction so you can put them to work. This book will give you both.

Here's how it works. Each day that you sit down with *That Is SO Me* you'll read a page that will include:

- A verse or two from the Bible.
- A few paragraphs that will help you get how those verses are about you.
- A section called "Do That Little Thing" with a suggestion that will help you put the verse to use.

The days of the week will look like this:

- Sunday – "Do That Little Thing" – This is a quiz, but there are never any right or wrong answers. You just pick out what's true for you.
- Monday – "Find Out" – You'll ask one or two grown-ups you know who love God to help you figure something out.
- Tuesday – "Just Think" – This gives you something to toss around in your mind, daydream about, and imagine.
- Wednesday – "God? Can We Talk?" – This will suggest some things for you to talk to God about in your quiet time together.
- Thursday – "Listen Up!" – Maybe the hardest one, this will ask you to get really quiet and listen for God's voice. You won't necessarily hear words, but you might have a thought or feeling you didn't have before. Sometimes the answers will come later, through something that happens or something somebody says.
- Friday – "You Can SO Do This" – This will challenge you to take action on something you've learned during the week.
- Saturday – "Shout-Out" – This will be your chance to give God a shout-out, sharing something that he's done in your life during the week. It might feel funky to you at first, but it might turn out to be one of your favorite parts.

If you just read and do the activity every day, by the end of a year you'll totally get that this treasure called the Bible is your guide for living an awesome life—a life where things aren't quite so confusing, problems are easier to solve, and people are not as hard to get along with as you thought. That's a lot.

If you do MORE than that—if you copy down some of your favorite verses and keep them with you, or talk to your friends about the stuff you're learning, or do those "little things" most of the time—you're not only going to "get" the Bible, you're going to "live" the Bible.

You might start out just reading the page-a-day because your grandmother gave you this book and your mom says you have to do some kind of daily devotional—and that's okay. Once you hear your own questions as you read and see situations you are facing and feel an "Oh, I get it!" in your brain that sends you off to fix something that's been driving you nuts for weeks—once that happens, this book and your Bible will probably go with you to sleepovers and summer camp and Grandma's house. (And won't she think she's all that for giving it to you in the first place?)

What's even cooler is that not only are you going to get to know the Bible as your handbook for living, you're going to get to know God. The Bible is, after all, the record of God talking to his people and his people listening (or not listening) and obeying (or not obeying). That's why it's called the Word, and it can answer four important questions for you. Questions like these:

- Who is this God everybody talks about?
- Who am I in God's eyes?
- What does it look like to be who God called me to be?
- How can I be the "God-made me" in a world that's so mixed up?

For that reason, *That Is SO Me* is divided into four parts, each one covering thirteen weeks, or ninety-one days, or 2,184 hours, or—well, you get the idea—so you can explore those four questions and find the answers. Of course, when you completely lose your mind and become a teenager you'll have a lot MORE questions, but by then you'll be a *That Is SO Me* graduate who knows how to find the right-now stuff in the Bible, how to understand it, and how to use it.

Before you start, there are a few things you'll want to do to get ready:

- Pick a time in your day when you can spend 20 or 30 minutes with this book and not be interrupted. If that sounds impossible with your family's schedule, talk to one of your parents and see if they can help you carve out a half hour when your pesky little brother is taking a bath or before you have to turn your light out at night.
- Find a place where you can be alone and won't be distracted by everything in life. Pick a spot where you won't be able to see or hear the TV, the Instant Message beep on your computer, the leftover pizza that's calling your name ... If space like that is a joke at your house, again, ask one of your parents to help you locate a little haven. It's the absolute best when you can keep your Bible, this book, and your favorite pen there and don't have to hunt for them every time.
- Talk to God ahead of time about how you're doing with this idea of a WHOLE YEAR of devotions. Whether you think it's the coolest thing on the planet or you would rather memorize the multiplication tables than do this every single day, put that out there for God and ask for whatever help you need. If you've never really talked to him before, now's a great time to start, just by saying, out loud or in your mind, "God? Can we talk?" (The answer will be *yes!*)

That's all there is to it—except for one more thing that may be niggling at you, especially if you've never been excited about reading the Bible or don't really know much about it. You may be wondering, "How do I know the answers to my questions are really in there?" It's perfectly okay to think about that. Doubt is an important part of faith, because if you never honestly ask the questions that are truly bothering you, you'll never find out what you want to know.

Paul, who you'll read about in the weeks ahead, was totally devoted to Jesus and changed his whole life because he asked him to. He understood about those little nagging doubts, and he has helped people with them for centuries by writing this:

*There's nothing like the written Word of God for showing you the way. Every part of scripture is God-breathed and useful one way or another—showing us truth, exposing our rebellion, correcting our mistakes, training us to live God's way. Through the Word we are put together and shaped up for the tasks God has for us.*

*2 Timothy 3:15–17* MSG

Who doesn't rebel and make mistakes and wonder exactly how to live? You have nothing to lose by seeing what the Bible has to say about those things and trying out the solutions. Chances are good that you will find yourself reading and praying and doing—and suddenly saying, "That is SO me!"

# PART I

# Who Is This God Everybody Talks About?

God looks down from heaven ... to see if there are any who understand, any who seek God.

Psalm 53:2

When you were a little kid, coloring those pictures in Sunday school of all the children sitting on Jesus' lap, it was easy to answer the question: Who is God?

"He's kinda like my daddy, only bigger."

"God is love. It says so in the song."

"He's up in heaven." Blinking of big eyes, followed by, "That's all."

And then you went on to nibble a graham cracker or, depending on your taste, the purple crayon you'd just used to color Jesus' hair.

Now that you're no longer that sweet little baby, it isn't so simple to say who God is, is it, girlfriend? Especially when you're in trouble, or you're lonely, or things are happening that lead you to believe that whoever God is, he's lost *your* address.

All the more reason to explore who God is right now—you need him. And with so many changes starting to happen in your life, this is a good time to get a clear and true picture, because that is the one thing that won't change. Crayons ready? Let's go.

## God, Major Creator

In the beginning God created the heavens and the earth.

Genesis 1:1

Yeah, duh," you may be saying. "Anybody who's ever opened a Bible knows that."

True. How many pictures have you colored in Sunday school classes since you were in Pre-K of the same thing—a skinny strip of blue sky across the top of the paper and lollipop-shaped trees and cats with enormous heads? Can you remember handing them proudly to your mom and saying, "God made everything," and then skipping off to get your juice box?

This week, now that you're a more mature individual, you'll do something different with the truth that God created the heavens and the earth—something that will help you appreciate how creative God is and how you, being made in God's image, are creative too. Prepare to be impressed.

13

# Sunday

God said, "Let there be light," and there was light.

Genesis 1:3

That was Day One, the first day that ever existed. Before that, it was basically always night. Can you even imagine that? Think about a time when you woke up in the middle of the night. Freaky, huh? Maybe you had trouble seeing across your room. Perhaps things took on frightening shapes in the darkness—there was most definitely a creature crouching on the chair, ready to pounce on you. Wasn't it the biggest relief on the planet to turn the light on and see that it was only your dirty clothes piled on the chair?

But what if you could never turn on a light? Wouldn't it be the scariest thing a person can think of? That wasn't the kind of world God imagined. The first thing God did was create light—for us to see by, to chase away fear. Bask in the light today. Whisper a prayer of thanks to God that you have eight hours that are monsters-under-the-bed-free.

## Do That Little Thing: QUIZ

Star the statement that fits you.

My way of being creative is to:

_____ do something artsy, like draw or make music.
_____ dream up fun stuff to do, like trips and parties.
_____ imagine things, like pictures in clouds.
_____ figure stuff out, like the fastest way to finish my math homework.

Any time you take a thought and do something (hopefully good) with it, you're being creative. God's thought was to make light out of darkness. You are put here to do that too — to make light out of darkness with your creativity. Read on tomorrow to find out how.

# Monday

God said, "Let there be an expanse between the waters to separate water from water."

Genesis 1:6

Not only was everything dark before God created the world, it was all under water! Up to the brim, with no way out. It just keeps getting scarier, doesn't it? Seriously, imagine there was no sky. You couldn't look up in wonder at the moon. Or see pigs and dolphins and ice cream cones in the clouds. Or watch those clouds turn gray while you pray for snow so school would close.

Even our imaginations can't touch what it must have been like before Day Two. What we *can* do is think about the gift that sky is. It's our weather forecaster, our mood lifter, our memory jogger (how many times have you looked up in the air until the answer came to you?), our idea of heaven, and our creativity inspirer.

Spend some time today looking up. Somebody will probably tell you that you're weird—so what else is new? There is nothing strange about gazing into the heavens and asking God a question or two, or daydreaming something wonderful, or letting the blueness calm you. It's one of the main reasons God put the sky there in the first place. Celebrate that.

## Do That Little Thing: FIND OUT

Ask your mom or dad or some other adult who loves you how you create light and space in their lives. If that question stumps them (it's hard for them to think like that when they're busy driving the family van or taking out the trash), ask if you ever make their day a little sunnier or give them the feeling that there really is room to laugh and play after all. What you hear will show you how you are already working creatively in God's world.

# Tuesday

God said, "Let the water under the sky be gathered to one place, and let dry ground appear."

Genesis 1:9

Without land, not only would we be waterlogged, we'd miss out on some of the best things in life—like, anything that comes from "vegetation." No apple pie. No lemonade. No chocolate (cocoa beans, anyone?). You'd never climb a tree or spit watermelon seeds on the Fourth of July. You wouldn't even be reading this book, since paper is made from trees.

It's more fun to imagine God dreaming up all the different kinds of land and the stuff to grow on it. The cactus-dotted deserts of the Southwest. The towering redwood forests of the West Coast. The blackberry-covered hills of the Pacific Northwest. The golden-haired wheat fields of the Midwest. The palm-tree-swaying beaches of the South. The cranberry bogs of the Northeast. The more you read and think about God creating the world, step by gorgeous, detailed step, the more amazing it gets.

Raid the produce drawers in your refrigerator today and find something to eat that came from the land. Sit down on some earth, eat that snack, and savor it. It can be a very cool experience that brings you closer to God-thoughts.

## Do That Little Thing: JUST THINK

What would it be like to have an all-natural day? If you ate only food that was grown without preservatives (carrots instead of Cheetos, for example)? If you walked to school instead of taking the bus? If you played outside rather than keeping your nose in a video game? Do one of those things today. You'll see that God really did give us all that we needed when he created the world. The earth is his gift to you. Use it well.

# Wednesday

God said, "Let there be lights in the expanse of the sky to separate the day from the night."

Genesis 1:14

God got a lot done on the fourth day. Sun. Moon. Stars. Sunrises.
Sunsets. Tides. Tans. Freckles. From a universe of heavenly
bodies to the collection of sunspots on your nose, God took care of
the rhythm of life. He created a beat that we don't always pay attention to, but that keeps us going day after day.

You go to sleep at night and wake up in the morning. Spring
blossoms and warms into sunny summer, and then the earth starts
to sleep in one big blaze of color called autumn and finally fades into
winter, only to start all over again. And through those seasons you
pick flowers and eat peaches and carve pumpkins and throw snow-
balls and grow and grow and grow, across the seasons of your own
life. Baby girl to toddler to little girlfriend to unstoppable tween to
out-of-your-mind teenager to grown-up to grandma.

If you quiet your mind, you can almost hear the steady ebb and
flow of it all. That's God at work. So no matter whether you understand your math homework or not, whether you got invited to the
major sleepover of the year or didn't, whether you ever learn to do a
cartwheel—everything really is all right.

## Do That Little Thing: GOD? CAN WE TALK?

For this first "God? Can We Talk?" just close your eyes and let yourself depend on God for help with that little problem that's growing
like a seed inside you. Get used to doing that—because the God
who hung the moon can certainly advise you on what to do with an
annoying little brother.

# Thursday

God said, "Let the land produce living creatures according to their kinds."

Genesis 1:24

How fun is it to imagine God making up animals? Did he chuckle when he created the rhinoceros' face? Weep with joy at the cuteness of a baby panda? All you have to do is draw your own imaginary creatures or concoct them out of modeling clay to get a glimmer of God's experience.

Not only is God creative—he's organized. He put the animals into categories—like livestock, creatures that move along the ground, and wild animals. Each group has its purpose—although some of us have trouble figuring out just why we have to have snakes—and each is part of the balance God so delicately created. The bigger animals eat the smaller ones, which must be where those pesky snakes come in.

Everything that lives and breathes and has being does so because God created a system that keeps the world alive. Just think, then, what he's doing right now in your life to keep you in balance. You get sleepy, so you crawl into bed. You feel hungry, so you scope out the snack situation in the pantry. You experience sadness and you burst into tears. You are part of God's perfectly balanced circle of life. Doesn't that make you feel a little more secure?

## Do That Little Thing: LISTEN UP!

Listen to some animals making their life sounds, maybe the crickets setting up a racket after dark or pigeons cooing in the park. Think about how God feels about them. He cares about every feather, fin, and fur tuft. Consider that kind of love — and then read on tomorrow to learn how much *more* God loves *you*.

# Friday

God created man in his own image, in the image of God he created him; male and female he created them.

Genesis 1:27

Finally, God made people. He simply spoke, and there they were, male and female, as beautiful and balanced and perfect as everything else he created.

"Uh, hello," you may be saying. "I don't think I'm *that* beautiful and balanced—and I am definitely not perfect. What's up with that?"

The Scripture says God made "man" (meaning humans, not just guys) in his own image. We're not sure if that means we look like God, but we know every human being is worthy of honor and respect, and no one has the right to take a life away.

Since we're made in God's image, we have the same responsibility God has—to take care of the world. We must be pretty awesome if God trusts us to care for the creatures he so carefully thought up and crafted and put in his handmade world. God thinks very highly of you. You must be special.

So hug your Bible and thank God for both the job and the instructions for how to do it. Then hug your dog, cat, bird, or snake if you have one. You might just wave at your fish. They can be hard to hold onto.

## Do That Little Thing: YOU CAN *SO* DO THIS

Choose one of these to do.

- Feed the family pet(s) tonight.
- Give something special to a family pet (that isn't going to make him or her throw up later!).
- Provide for a wild animal (bird feeder or bread for the ducks in the pond).
- Volunteer to do something for a neighbor's pet — like hang out with a dog that's tied up in a backyard.

# Saturday

> By the seventh day God had finished the work he had been doing; so on the seventh day he rested from all his work. And God blessed the seventh day and made it holy.
>
> Genesis 2:2–3

How could God be tired if he's God?

God didn't rest because he was worn out from creating the world. He relaxed because the world was done, and it was perfect, and he could simply sit back and enjoy.

Not only did God curl up and savor the world, he made the day holy, which means "set apart." It was a day like no other before it (which wasn't that hard, since there had only been six others!) and God loved it.

You can do as God does, just in a human way. When you've done something you think God is smiling on, enjoy what you've created. Set that time apart, even just a few minutes, and thank God for it. Life is made up of many holy moments. Share as many of them as you can with God.

## Do That Little Thing: SHOUT-OUT

Share a holy moment with a friend by celebrating that God created her. Make her a card or a picture or a cupcake with all the love you can pour into it. Tell her you're glad she is who she is and that she's your bud. Make it a moment set apart for the two of you. She is, after all, one of God's creations.

## God, the Boss of Everyone

> Now the Lord God had planted a garden in the east, in
> Eden; and there he put the man he had formed.
>
> Genesis 2:8

And that's when the trouble started!
God put the tree of the knowledge of good and evil in the
middle of the Garden and told the man to take care of it. God said
he was free to eat from any tree but that one. If the man ate the fruit
from that tree, he would "surely die."

Anybody could follow those instructions, right? Who needs the
knowledge of good and evil when your life is perfect? And besides—
who wants to die?

God even provided the man with his best gift yet—a woman to
be by his side. Those two had it made. They could even run around
naked and think nothing of it, because they had nothing to be
ashamed of. Until ...

Well, until they messed it up.

This week you're going to see God dealing with what he created—namely, us—and showing more of who he is. You can really
tell a lot about a person by the way he reacts when somebody messes
with him. That's how you'll discover this next part of God's character. Watch what God did when those lucky people in the Garden
threw it all away and made things really tough for those who came
after them.

# Sunday

> "You will not surely die," the serpent said to the woman. "For God knows that when you eat of it your eyes will be opened, and you will be like God, knowing good and evil."
>
> Genesis 3:4–5

B efore you get all superior and say you wouldn't have fallen for the serpent talking trash about God, imagine the scene.

You're hanging out in the perfect Garden in your perfect body with absolutely nothing to do but eat. All the fruit you've been allowed to munch on has been delicious, but at this point, you've sort of been there, done that. And then along comes a talking snake.

You're impressed with how smart he is. He is "more crafty than any of the wild animals the Lord God had made." And he recognizes how smart *you* are — smart enough to keep up with God, who obviously wants to keep you depending on him instead of thinking for yourself.

It worked on that woman and, don't kid yourself, it would probably work on any of us. Haven't you ever thought God didn't know what he was doing — like when things didn't go your way, even when you prayed SO hard? The serpent is still at work in the world, which is why it's important for us to know God, exactly as he is. More on that tomorrow. Meanwhile, let's take a closer look at you.

## Do That Little Thing: QUIZ

Put a check next to each of the following things that you have done.

____ Thought God was wrong.
____ Knew what was the right thing to do but didn't do it.
____ Disobeyed a God-rule you thought was stupid.
____ Rolled your eyes during a sermon.
____ Decided you were doing fine without church.

There's a little bit of that first man and woman in all of us, huh?

# Monday

Then the eyes of both of them were opened, and they realized they were naked.

Genesis 3:7

The woman fell for the serpent's bit about being as smart as God and pigged out on the fruit of the forbidden tree. All her husband had to see was her chowing down and he joined right in.

And then the serpent's promises fell through. They now saw evil—hello, him!—as God did, but that included the evil in themselves. Suddenly their naked bodies weren't so perfect. Before, it was fun to romp through the Garden without clothes. Now, not so much. Now they knew they weren't God. Out came the fig leaves and they started sewing, because they were ashamed.

The serpent promised they wouldn't die if they ate the fruit, and in fact, they didn't drop over at the first bite. But shame slowly kills over time, because shame separates you from God. It makes you want to hide, as the man and his wife did—like they could hide from God, right? And when you hide yourself, you can't possibly be all you were made to be or do what you were made to do or even enjoy what's been given just for you.

We all have to deal with shame, because we know about evil and sometimes we jump right in. But we can't hide from God. He always finds us. And don't worry: God knows how to handle us.

## Do That Little Thing: FIND OUT

Ask your mom or dad to tell you about the first thing you did that got you into trouble when you were little. Accept that even before you really knew about good and evil, you could do either one. That's why you need the God who does what he did next in the story.

# Tuesday

The man said, "The woman you put here with me — she gave me some fruit from the tree, and I ate it."

Genesis 3:12

Now isn't that just like a guy? Nobody shoved that piece of fruit down his throat, but when God wanted to know what was going on, he said it was *her* fault.

Haven't all of us shifted the blame onto somebody else, even when we know we've made our own choice? What really matters is what God did when the man and the woman 'fessed up to what they'd done (which, of course, God already knew about because, well, he's God).

The first thing God did was turn to the serpent and give him what was coming to him: he had to crawl on his belly and eat dust forever. Ewwww, huh? And then he made it so women and their kids would always hate snakes. That accounts for the creepy feeling you get even when you see a python on TV.

God knew the source of the evil, and he took away some of its power. It's still there, and it will sneak up on you and "strike [your] heel." But you can also "crush [its] head" (verse 15). God made it so that you can stamp out that evil whenever it tries to get to you. The man and woman wanted the knowledge of good and evil, and they got it, but they also received a way to protect themselves. See how great God is?

## Do That Little Thing: JUST THINK

When has evil tried to creep up on you — and you caught it in time?

Thank God for nudging you and reminding you that even though evil can slither up on you, you can still crush it with your heel.

# Wednesday

Cursed is the ground because of you; through painful toil you will eat of it all the days of your life.

Genesis 3:17

God could have just wiped out the man and woman and started over with a new pair, or he could have turned THEM into snakes. Instead, he had mercy on them.

That doesn't mean he let them off. He kicked them out of the perfect Garden, but he didn't destroy them. He loved them too much. Just like any good parent, he taught them the consequences of being rotten kids. Since then people have had to work for their food, and work hard, with all kinds of obstacles ("thorns and this-tles," vs. 18) coming up to get in the way. It's no longer a perfect world—did you notice?

But there was still hope in what God did. He said we *would* eat the food we have to work hard for. It might be "painful toil" (verse 17) sometimes, but we are not evil like the serpent. We have it rough because evil exists, but we are still allowed to be an important part of God's creation. Now that's a God ya gotta love.

## Do That Little Thing: GOD? CAN WE TALK?

Close your eyes and think for a few minutes about the work God has you doing these days — besides "getting an education" and "helping around the house." Maybe being nice to that girl everybody else teases? Not whining about your lack of an iPod, because you know money's tight right now? Ask God to give you a hand with it. God can do that, you know. If he didn't want to help, he would have done a whole lot worse than just put us to work a long, long time ago.

# Thursday

> The Lord God said, "The man has now become like one of us, knowing good and evil."
>
> Genesis 3:22

Nobody would have blamed God if he had just sent Adam and Eve out of the Garden of Eden naked. But he seemed to have checked out the pathetic outfits they'd tried to stitch together from leaves and decided no children of his were going out into the world dressed like that. He made them a wardrobe out of animal skins, and he did it himself. He didn't pack them off without everything they needed.

And then he said, "The man has now become like one of us." Who was he talking to? Didn't you get the idea that God was creating the world on his own?

Being a King, God had a heavenly court, what you might imagine as angels. They are mentioned several more times in the Bible, where God talks to them and runs things past them. Here he tells them that although man — that's all of us — now knows about good and evil, man can't live forever like they do. Eventually, all people are going to die. We're all separated from God in a way he didn't intend. That must be so sad for God — to love us so much and yet be apart from us because we drift away. Makes you want to try to stay close, doesn't it?

## Do That Little Thing: LISTEN UP!

Meet yourself someplace where you and God can be alone. Listen to the silence. You may hear what's going on inside of you — those still, small thoughts that get shouted down by all the commotion of your everyday life. They tell you that God is right there, no matter how separate you may feel when you're running all around doing homework and playing soccer and fighting with your brother. You might not be in a perfect garden, but God is still taking care of you.

# Friday

> Then the Lord said to Cain ... "But if you do not do what is right, sin is crouching at your door; it desires to have you, but you must master it."
>
> Genesis 4:6–7

Adam and Eve had two kids—boys, Cain and Abel. When Abel made an altar he put a lot of thought into honoring the Lord, and Cain just threw something together. They obviously hadn't learned from their parents' experience with disobeying God, but then most of us *do* have to make our own mistakes, don't we?

God didn't like Cain's offering as well as he did Abel's, and Cain got mad. He had been careless and thoughtless about what he took to God, so what did he expect? But he was like most of us, ready to blame somebody else. (He must have gotten that from his parents.) God said Cain just had to do what was right and he'd be accepted, simple as that. If he didn't, sin would be crouching right at his door, just like that serpent, ready to strike.

It still is. Don't you deal with sin every day? Every time you have a chance to cheat on that test you didn't study for? Every time you could tell a little fib to get yourself out of trouble? Every time you're tempted to rattle off a memorized prayer before you fall asleep instead of hanging out with God when you're wide awake and really talking to him? God says to you as he did to Cain, do what's right and you'll master sin. It's as simple as that.

## Do That Little Thing: YOU CAN *SO* DO THIS

Choose one of these to do this week or come up with one of your own — something that will require thirty minutes of real focus on God. Do it with a heart full of love for him, in thanksgiving for the chances he gives you to do the right thing.

- Lie on your back, look up at the sky, and just talk to God like you would to a friend.
- Draw or paint an image of how you feel about God.
- Give God a concert.
- Write a prayer.
- Dance for God.
- Invite God to play with you.

# Saturday

> Then the Lord put a mark on Cain so that no one who found him would kill him.
>
> Genesis 4:15

Cain didn't take God's warning. He let his anger get the best of him and he killed his brother Abel. THEN he thought he could keep God from finding out. Were these people stupid, or what? And when God asked, "Where is your brother Abel?" Cain said, "I don't know ... Am I my brother's keeper?"

Not only did Cain kill his brother, he tried to cover it up by being a smart mouth. But God didn't do to Cain what Cain did to his brother. He just said, "When you work the ground, it will no longer yield its crops for you. You will be a restless wanderer on the earth" (verse 12).

But Cain was hardheaded, that guy. He complained about the punishment, said when he was wandering around, somebody was sure to kill him. Anybody else but God would have said, "Are you *serious?* I'm letting you off without striking you dead right here, and you're whining about it?" But God put a mark on Cain so nobody would take him out.

One more time: somebody messes up royally; God finds out; God gives the natural consequences; but he still protects, still takes care, still loves. This is your God.

## Do That Little Thing: SHOUT-OUT

Warning: this could be painful. Think about a time when your parents gave you consequences for something you did wrong, consequences you now realize were fair (even though you may have whined about them at the time). They were behaving like God, in his image. So go to them and thank them.

Told you it could be painful!

# God: Up Close and Personal

I will make you into a great nation and I will bless you.

Genesis 12:2

So far you've seen God create an incredible world and make it possible for us to live here, even though the first people unleashed evil into it. You know that God loves us and isn't going to leave us all by ourselves.

And yet from that Bad Boy Cain on, the people we read about in the Bible kept forgetting that. No matter how many chances God gave them, they couldn't keep their minds right for seven seconds. That's when God showed the next part of himself: his desire to have a personal relationship with his people. He decided to create a group who would center their whole lives around him. Maybe then they would remember how to really live in his world.

For that, God needed a leader on earth, and he chose a guy named Abram, later changed to Abraham. You'll read parts of his story this week, and you'll see how important it was and still is to God to have his people pay attention to him and do exactly as he tells them. As you read, remember that Abraham is like the father of all of us, because he was the one God called on to create the new nation that you as a child of God belong to. You know how in school you learned that George Washington was called the "father of our country"? Abraham is the "father of our faith." He's a good person to get to know.

# Sunday

Leave your country, your people and your father's household and go to the land I will show you.

Genesis 12:1

Abram and his wife, Sarai, were in Mesopotamia, ready to settle down, when God told Abram he wanted him to set off on a pilgrimage to a better world where he (God) would be honored. You might think, "Hey, a road trip—I'm there!"

But travel was rough in those days. People had to carry everything they owned with them, including tents to live in, and there were dangers along the way, from wild animals to desert robbers. And God didn't spell out for Abram exactly where he was going to end up. He just said, "I will make you into a great nation, and I will bless you ... and all peoples on earth will be blessed through you." All of it came true, over many centuries, but Abram didn't know that. All he had was God's word. That was the thing about Abram—he never questioned God, not like a lot of the other Bible characters you'll meet. If God said do it, he just went for it.

Could you be quicker to obey God when you know how to behave? Could you argue less with your mom, your dad, your teacher? Ask questions and have opinions, but when it comes to the wisdom of the people in charge of you and the authority of God, it's a good idea to be like Abram and move now, ask questions later.

## Do That Little Thing: QUIZ

Think you wouldn't be as quick as Abram to chuck it all and move on? Have you ever:

- gone home when friends decided to make prank phone calls or send ugly emails?
- left the restroom when the gossip started?
- turned the channel even when everybody else was screaming to see that violent video?

Don't sell yourself short. There's a little Abram in you. You know God too.

# Monday

"Look up at the heavens and count the stars — if indeed you can count them." Then he said to him, "So shall your offspring be."

Genesis 15:5

It had now been awhile since God promised Abram he would be the father of a great nation, and Abram was beginning to wonder. His wife Sarai was way past the age when women have kids, and she'd never had a baby—so where was this "nation" supposed to come from? Even Abram, with all his faith, was bound to ask that sooner or later.

God didn't get upset with him. In fact, he did something that really showed Abram that he wanted a relationship with him. He entered into a covenant with him. That means he made a promise to him and sealed it with an oath, just like when a person in court swears on the Bible to tell the truth. He got down to the details, saying he would be Abram's protecting king, more precious to him than all of Abram's wealth. When Abram still wasn't sure, God took him outside and told him to look up at the heavens. In that part of the world, Abram could see more than eight thousand stars without a telescope (which they didn't have then). God told him that was how many people would come from him.

Abram believed him, because Abram was a righteous man. Finally, somebody got it. Who better to be the father of God's new nation? Makes believing sound like a good choice, doesn't it?

## Do That Little Thing: FIND OUT

Ask a person who has moved around a lot (or remember yourself if the person is you!) what it's like to leave home. Then think about Abram picking up and leaving everything, no questions asked, to obey God. Pray that you'll be as willing when God calls on you to give up something familiar for him.

# Tuesday

God said "… your wife Sarah will bear you a son, and you will call him Isaac. I will establish my covenant with him."

Genesis 17:19

Sarai, Abram's wife, did not believe that God was going to let her have a child of her own. She was getting older by the minute! So she made her servant Hagar have Abram's baby, a boy named Ishmael.

Then Sarai got jealous of Hagar and sent her and her son off in the desert to die. Mind you, it was *her* idea to let Hagar bear Abraham's child. God took care of Hagar and Ishmael, and promised once again that Abram AND Sarai were going to start God's nation of faithful people. He sealed the covenant by changing Abram's name to Abraham, "father of many," and Sarai's name to Sarah, for "princess." It was obvious that SHE, not Hagar, was to be the mother of the kings that God promised Abraham's descendants would be.

God told Abraham to name his son Isaac, which means "he laughs." Well, yeah, since Abraham fell facedown and hee-hawed when he heard about becoming a father. But even Abraham's laughter was a sign of faith. Ask somebody even just sixty or seventy years old if they would want to become a new parent right now, and see if they think it's funny. Probably not. Abraham didn't tell God he was crazy or cruel. He just laughed and went with it.

How many times could you just do that, instead of deciding that God clearly doesn't know what he's doing? It's so much easier to giggle than to argue!

## Do That Little Thing: JUST THINK

Is there some impossible situation in your life right now that you could just throw your head back and cackle over? A brother or sister who drives you nuts? Or a teacher who makes outrageous demands? Try laughing about it. It could set you free for what God has planned.

# Wednesday

The Lord said to Abraham, "Why did Sarah laugh and say, 'Will I really have a child, now that I am old?' Is anything too hard for the Lord?"

Genesis 18:13–14

When Sarah found out she was going to have a baby, she thought it was pretty funny too. She didn't realize that the three men who had come to visit and reveal this news were part of God's council. It was a huge honor for Abraham to be in on what they had to say. When Sarah laughed in disbelief, it was time for God to say, "What's up with the laughing? Is anything too hard for me?"

The answer was — and is — no. Sarah knew nothing was impossible for God, which was why she lied and said she didn't laugh. Why did she even try that? It didn't work for Adam, Eve, or Cain!

But Sarah knew that if it DID happen, if she DID have a baby, it would be a great gift. She said, "After I am worn out ... will I now have this pleasure?" She didn't see giving birth in her nineties as a burden — she thought it would be wonderful to have a child of her own to love and hold, and especially watch him grow to be the leader of a great nation. There was a lot of faith in that.

## Do That Little Thing: GOD? CAN WE TALK?

Remember that impossible situation you thought about yesterday? Bring that to mind again. Describe to God just what a "pleasure" it would be to have the matter solved. God wants to know your dreams, and he'll listen. After all, you're God's covenant friend too.

# Thursday

> Sarah said, "God has brought me laughter, and everyone who hears about this will laugh with me ... Who would have said to Abraham that Sarah would nurse children?"
>
> Genesis 21:6–7

Sarah must have been a fun person. She laughed about everything. Imagine her, all white-haired and wrinkled, gazing at a perfect baby son in her arms and laughing softly into his little face. It must have seemed like a dream to her, so she celebrated with her laughter, and she wanted everybody to join in, to know that it was God who brought her such happiness.

Finally, Sarah got it. This was God's work. Who else could have done such an impossible thing? Who else would let her nurse a baby when most women her age were leaning on canes, watching their granddaughters feed their own infants? It took her awhile, but then, not everybody was as faithful and unquestioning and obedient as Abraham. The point is, she finally understood.

But when Isaac was two or three, Sarah worried that Ishmael, Abraham's son by Hagar, would get some of Isaac's inheritance. She sent Hagar and Ishmael (who was in his teens by then) away again. And once again, God took care of them. In fact, he promised that Ishmael would have a ton of descendants of his own. Abraham was happy because Ishmael was his kid too. God took total care of Abraham and his family so that Abraham could carry out the work God gave him to do. And all Abraham had to do was obey.

## Do That Little Thing: LISTEN UP!

Go to your quiet place, whisper to God that you want to do exactly as he says, and then listen. You might remember that girl you were sort of rude to at school yesterday or that chore you promised your mom you'd do that you haven't quite gotten to. Your next job for God won't be to pick up and move or become the mother of nations — but it will be just as important. So go and do.

# **Friday**

Some time later God tested Abraham.

Genesis 22:1

There was one more test Abraham had to pass, and this one was a toughie.

God said, "Take your son, your only son, Isaac, whom you love, and go to the region of Moriah. Sacrifice him there as a burnt offering."

*What?* God wanted him to set fire to his precious son on an altar, like he would a lamb or a calf? *Seriously?*

God had to make sure Abraham was willing to make the supreme sacrifice of obedience to him, or he couldn't trust him to be the father of the people who were to shape his special world.

You may be thinking, "Hasn't Abraham proven himself enough? Wasn't it kind of cruel of God to put him through this?" But just as always, Abraham did exactly as he was told. It's not hard to imagine tears pouring down Abraham's face when he bound his son and put him on the altar and raised the knife.

That's the kind of obedience that separates the people who say they believe in God and want to serve him, and the people who really do. God no longer asks his children to go this far, but he can ask a lot. Are you ready for that?

## Do That Little Thing: YOU CAN *SO* DO THIS

What could you let go of this week that would make God smile? Your turn in the front seat since your brother loves sitting up there so much? The brownie in your lunch to that girl who is having a really bad day? Your chance to score your fifteenth goal to the teammate who hasn't scored one all season? Do that little thing.

# Saturday

I know that you fear God, because you have not withheld from me your son, your only son.

Genesis 22:12

God did NOT let Abraham sacrifice Isaac. At the very moment when he "reached out his hand and took the knife to slay his son," an angel called down to him from heaven and said, "Do not lay a hand on the boy ... Do not do anything to him."

Man—that was close! Just when you thought God had finally asked too much, he came through.

You can imagine Abraham practically melting into a puddle of relief as he put his knife away, untied his son and—probably—hugged him for a long time. And Abraham wasn't the only one who was relieved. Think of how Isaac must have felt. Yeah, his dad definitely had some explaining to do.

It probably helped that Abraham could share with him how much they were both going to benefit from Abraham's willingness to obey. God said, yet again, "I will surely bless you and make your descendants as numerous as the stars in the sky and as the sand on the seashore." And it was all because Isaac's father had obeyed.

## Do That Little Thing: SHOUT-OUT

Can you think of a way that God has blessed you this week—whether you deserved it or not? Did you make a friend? Have some special private time with your mom? Suddenly get fractions when they've been a total mystery to you for weeks?

Whatever has happened that has blessed you, tell somebody. Let them know you give God the credit. Show God off. You'll be even more blessed.

# God: Your Travel Guide

> Isaac prayed to the Lord ... The Lord answered his prayer.
> Genesis 25:21

Don't you wish it were that easy? You pray to the Lord, and the Lord answers. Life is good. How simple would that be?

Not as simple as you might think, actually. The people you're going to read about this week didn't just pray and then sit back with a milkshake and fries and wait for God to come through. They couldn't ask God for help and then do whatever *they* thought would make it happen, either. Between the praying and the answering, people like Isaac (remember, he was Abraham's son) and Jacob, Abraham's grandson, and Joseph, Jacob's son, had to follow God as their guide.

So, no, God has never been like a fairy godmother (or godfather!). Instead, he's been there — and still is — to nudge his children, show them the way, and then prod them along. It isn't always easy, as you'll see in this week's stories. But it sure makes terrific people out of us.

# Sunday

She said, "Why is this happening to me?" So she went to inquire of the Lord.

Genesis 25:22

Isaac, Abraham's son, married Rebekah. Like her mother-in-law Sarah, Rebekah couldn't seem to have children, so Isaac prayed to the Lord, and the Lord saw to it that Rebekah became pregnant, not with just one baby, but two.

Rebekah was thrilled, of course, until the twins turned her womb into a boxing ring and started duking it out in there. It must have been incredibly painful, enough for her to ask God, "Why is this happening to me?"

That's Step One in using God as Guide: ask him the tough questions. It can be anything from, "Why am I so lame in spelling?" to "Is there any special reason why I have to have asthma?" "Was it something I said?"

Rebekah didn't hesitate.

She got an answer too. God told her that the two boys she was carrying were each going to be the father of a separate nation, and that the older one would serve the younger one. That was unusual, since at that time it was always the other way around. Rebekah must have known there was going to be trouble, and she was right. Jacob and Esau fought about everything and eventually split up and didn't see each other for years. That's Step Two: the information God gives you may not always be happy stuff, but at least you will be prepared for the hard things.

## Do That Little Thing: QUIZ

Fill in any of the blanks you want to.

- Why does _____ always happen to me?
- Why do I always have to be the one to _____?
- Why won't anyone let me _____?
- Why can't I learn to_____?
- Why doesn't _____ like me?

Go to your quiet place and ask God those questions. Don't expect answers right away, but do expect to feel a little better just talking about them.

The Lord said to Jacob, "Go back to the land of your fathers and to your relatives, and I will be with you."

Genesis 31:3

Jacob, the younger of the twins, followed God as his guide. Many times, God's intentions must have seemed like a mystery to him.

He married the woman of his dreams, Rachel, but only after his father-in-law tricked him into marrying her older sister, Leah, first. He had a bunch of sons and a daughter by Leah, but Rachel went for years before she was able to give Jacob a son (Joseph). Laban, his father-in-law whom he worked for, was always trying to cheat him, and Laban's sons spread rumors that Jacob used their dad to become wealthy.

Jacob could have decided God didn't like him anymore and tried to go it on his own, but he continued to follow God's guidance. God finally said, "I have seen all that Laban has been doing to you. Now leave this land at once and go back to your native land."

Laban wasn't the nicest guy on the planet, so Jacob packed his wives and kids and all their belongings on camels and took off with his own livestock without telling Laban he was leaving, just as God said to. Then God went to *Laban* in a dream and told him to "be careful not to say anything to Jacob, either good or bad" (verse 24).

That makes Step Three pretty plain: Listen to God and do what he says, even if it's scary. God will take care of the details you have no control over. It's sort of a relief, isn't it?

## Do That Little Thing: FIND OUT

Ask someone you respect if he or she has ever done something she knew God wanted her to do, even if it was scary.

# Tuesday

Your name will no longer be Jacob, but Israel, because you have struggled with God and with men and have overcome.

Genesis 32:28

Going back to his homeland, Jacob was going to have to face his brother, Esau, whom he hadn't spoken to in years. Jacob was afraid Esau would take out his whole family. Following God's guidance, though, he sent some livestock ahead with his servants as a gift for Esau.

But wouldn't you know, when Jacob was alone in camp that night, some guy jumped him and started wrestling with him. Jacob had been fighting people all his life, first Esau (like, from before birth!) and then Laban, and now some stranger. Jacob kept on even after the guy knocked Jacob's hip out of joint. Finally, Jacob said he would only let go if the guy would bless him. That's when the man revealed that he was God himself, in the form of an angel!

What did that mean for Jacob? Jacob could be afraid and struggle, but God would always be stronger than he was. And because he hung in there, God was going to take him to his homeland and put him in charge of it.

You might be scared and fight God sometimes, but he'll always be strong for you. So take Step Four: ask God to bless you, even when you've been wrestling with him. You can expect to *be* blessed when you let God be your guide.

## Do That Little Thing: JUST THINK

Wrestle with God. Seriously. Tell him about something that's going on in your life that just doesn't make sense to you. You might not understand right away, but do one thing before you go — ask God to bless you, and he will.

# Wednesday

When his brothers saw that their father loved him more than any of them, they hated him and could not speak a kind word to him.

Genesis 37:4

Talk about sibling rivalry! A lot of kids *think* their dad loves the other kid in the family more than him, but Jacob really *did*. He even gave Joseph a fancy coat, something he never did for the other eleven boys and one girl. You can hardly blame the siblings for being hateful to Joseph, especially when he had dreams about ruling over the rest of them and was, shall we say, unwise enough to tell them about it!

One day, when they got Joseph alone, they sold him to a passing group of Ishmaelites. They dipped his coat in goat's blood and showed it to their father, telling him that Joseph had been eaten by a wild animal.

They were probably hoping that Jacob would finally have some love for them with Joseph out of the way, but Jacob vowed to mourn for his lost son for the rest of his life. Yeah, that plan backfired.

No, it wasn't fair of Jacob to give only Joseph the great clothes. And it wasn't very sensitive of Joseph to brag to his brothers. But the brothers could have gone to God for guidance instead of selling him off. As much as you may have wanted to pawn your little brother off on a busload of tourists from time to time, you know there's a better way! Knowing that is Step Five in following God as Guide.

## Do That Little Thing: LISTEN UP!

Tell God about something you don't think is fair, and then get quiet. If you listen hard enough, you may get that settled feeling that says, "Just be patient. I have it all worked out."

# Thursday

When his master saw that the Lord was with him and that the Lord gave him success in everything he did, Joseph found favor in his eyes and became his attendant.

Genesis 39:3–4

After his brothers did him dirty, Joseph could have given up and become a little street kid, thinking God had abandoned him. But Joseph stayed focused on God as his guide, and it paid off.

Look at *how* it paid off. Potiphar—the pharaoh's guy who bought Joseph from the Ishmaelites his brothers sold him to (whew!)—saw that Joseph was totally connected to God. Potiphar figured if God was good to Joseph, he was going to be good to him too. He put him in charge of his whole household and trusted him to take care of everything he owned, which was a lot of stuff. God blessed Potiphar's house and family and fields too.

That's how it works with God. If other people see God in your life because you're following him as your guide, they can't help being affected as well. That girl in your class might not know she likes you because you're a God-follower, but when she comes to your house and sees how lovingly your family members treat each other (most of the time!), she may go home and be nicer to her brother or mother. God loves to spread the blessings around—through you. That's Step Six.

## Do That Little Thing: LISTEN UP!

It might be hard to tell how God's blessings on you might trickle down to somebody else. But God may point someone out to you if you ask who might need a little of him to rub off of you. Then wait. You may find yourself spreading around a God-blessing.

# Friday

> While Joseph was there in the prison, the Lord was with him;
> he showed him kindness and granted him favor in the eyes of
> the prison warden.
>
> Genesis 39:20–21

Nuh-uh. After everything he'd already been through, Joseph did *not* end up in prison. Yeah, he did. Joseph was a total babe, and Potiphar's wife had a thing for him. When Joseph wouldn't flirt back with her — hello, she was the boss's wife! — she told Potiphar Joseph had tried to kiss *her*. She must have put on a convincing act because Potiphar believed her and threw Joseph in prison.

Definitely not fair, but nobody's lived a perfect life since Adam and Eve blew it in the Garden of Eden. Bad, unfair stuff happens. We learn from Joseph not to give up, but to keep on doing what God asks, and he'll take care of us.

First, Potiphar didn't dump Joseph into a scary maximum security prison, but in the "place where the king's prisoners were confined." It could have been a lot worse.

And as soon as the prison warden got to know Joseph, he saw that he was a quality person and put him in charge of the other prisoners. Joseph interpreted dreams for the guys, just as he'd done for his brothers, and finally the Pharaoh himself called on Joseph for help with a troubling dream he was having. The Pharaoh decided he was so wise, he put Joseph in charge of his palace. It hardly gets any better than that! And all because Joseph kept believing that God was his guide. Step Seven: keep believing, no matter what happens.

## Do That Little Thing: YOU CAN *SO* DO THIS!

Think of one situation in your life right now that is really a bummer — so bad that it doesn't seem like God could be in there anywhere. Write your bummer situation here:

_____

_____

_____

_____

_____

_____

_____

_____

_____

_____

_____

Now, look for God in it. Find the tiny spot. Take that first step with the tiny glimmer of a God-blessing and see what happens.

# Saturday

Joseph was the governor of the land, the one who sold grain to all its people. So when Joseph's brothers arrived, they bowed down to him.

Genesis 42:6

Yes! Those evil brothers finally got what was coming to them. Now Joseph could rule over them. Following God as guide really paid off, right?

His brothers—and his father—were starving because of the famine that had fallen over the whole land. Joseph had made sure there was plenty of food stored up in Egypt, which was why Jacob sent the other sons there. They didn't know Joseph was governor. Jacob didn't even know he was still alive.

But Joseph didn't make life miserable for them as they'd done to him. God was still Joseph's guide, and God never guides anybody to get revenge, even if it would make perfect sense to the world. Joseph said this to his brothers: "Do not be distressed and do not be angry with yourselves for selling me here, because it was to save lives that God sent me ahead of you" (Gen. 45:5).

Man. And then he brought Jacob in and took care of them for the rest of their lives. Even on his deathbed—when he was 110 years old—Joseph told his brothers who were left, "God will surely come to your aid and take you up out of this land to the land he promised on oath to Abraham, Isaac and Jacob" (Gen. 50:24).

That's Step Eight: Forgive, no matter what.

## Do That Little Thing: SHOUT-OUT

Think of one person you were nice to this week that you didn't WANT to be nice to. Then turn to somebody you love and tell them that you're so glad God kept you from being hateful. It was, after all, God's love that made *you* behave lovingly. Somebody needs to hear that.

# God, You Want Me to What?

Now, go. I am sending you to Pharaoh to bring my people the Israelites out of Egypt.

Exodus 3:10

What's it like on the last day of school when the final bell rings? The doors fly open and kids burst out of the building like they're being released from prison. That's called an "exodus." Now picture thousands of people making an "exodus" from a country where they have lived as SLAVES for generations (which is even worse than being in school!).

Long after Joseph and his brothers died, the Israelites continued to live in Egypt and have babies, who then had babies of their own, until there were so many of them that the new pharaoh was afraid they'd take over his whole country. He turned them into slaves and even ordered that every baby boy born to an Israelite be thrown into the Nile river.

One little Israelite baby boy made it, though—Moses. His mom hid him in a basket along the river bank, where he was found by Pharaoh's daughter. She kept him and raised him in the palace, until one day Moses saw an Egyptian beating one of the Israelites and murdered the guy. Once the word of that got out, Moses ran away and lived apart from his people to avoid being killed himself.

Meanwhile, the cruel treatment of his people went on. This week you'll learn the rest of Moses' story, and find out about God's big expectations of his people. WARNING: he expects a BUNCH, so get ready.

> God heard their groaning and he remembered his covenant
> with Abraham, with Isaac and with Jacob. So God looked on
> the Israelites and was concerned about them.
>
> Exodus 2:24–25

It may seem like God had forgotten his people while they spent 430 years making bricks with their bare hands and building cities for the Pharaoh while getting barely a crumb for themselves. But just because there's suffering doesn't mean God isn't there, making preparations to save people from the things that make them miserable. Check out what God was doing during that time:

- He practically filled Egypt with Israelites. That took time.
- God had Moses grow up in the palace so he would know how the Pharaoh thought and operated, which later made him the perfect person to go and work with him on letting the Israelites go. Growing up takes time too.
- Moses had time to show that he cared about his original people (he did, after all, knock off an Egyptian who was trying to kill one of them), and to leave and start a family of his own, again with his own people. That stuff doesn't just happen overnight.

God was definitely there all the time, and he expected his people to wait until the time was right. That's one of the hardest things God expects us to do: wait on him. But as you're going to find out this week, it's so worth it.

## Do That Little Thing: QUIZ
Put a check next to any of these things you might be waiting on God for right now. Add any that aren't here if you want.

\_\_\_\_ I'd like to be allowed to do more older-kid stuff.

\_\_\_\_ I wish I looked older.

\_\_\_\_ I want _____ grade to hurry up and be over.

\_\_\_\_ I want my little brother/sister to grow up so he/she will stop annoying me.

# Monday

> Moses said to God, "Who am I, that I should go to Pharaoh
> and bring the Israelites out of Egypt?"
>
> Exodus 3:11

Talk about scary. Moses was just tending his father-in-law's flock of sheep when suddenly a bush burst into flames but didn't burn up. In fact, it talked—and told Moses it was God.

But the truly terrifying part was when God said to Moses, "Now, go. I am sending you to Pharaoh to bring my people the Israelites out of Egypt" (Exodus 3:10). The Pharaoh was powerful enough to have anybody—or everybody—snuffed out if he got ticked off enough. And that same Pharaoh had reason to be mad at Moses. The Israelite had killed an Egyptian and then took off, after all the royal family had done for him. When God told Moses to go to the palace and say, "All right, Pharaoh, give 'em up, let's go," it was enough to make Moses say, "Me? You want *me* to do what?"

The first thing we human beings do when asked to do the seemingly impossible is say, "I can't. You don't understand: I'm not the one for the job." We might get away with that with just plain people, but not with God. He simply says, as he did to Moses, "I will be with you" (Exodus 3:12). So what does God expect? He expects us to believe that he knows who the right person is for the job. He is, after all, God.

## Do That Little Thing: FIND OUT

Ask a grown-up about a time when he or she had to do something that seemed impossible. Find out what his or her first response was.

You'll probably be surprised to find out that even grown-ups say, "Who, me?" more often than you think.

# Tuesday

Ever since I went to Pharaoh to speak in your name, he has brought trouble upon this people, and you have not rescued your people at all.

Exodus 5:23

God reassured Moses, right there in the burning bush, that he would be with him when he went to the Pharaoh. But even after he gave Moses clear instructions to go to the leaders of the Israelites and tell them to approach Pharaoh and promised him it was all going to turn out okay—Moses still wasn't convinced.

After all, he wasn't the sharpest tack in the box when it came to public speaking. It was all he could do to say, "O Lord, please send someone else to do it" (Exodus 4:13). So God told Moses he could take his brother Aaron with him, who could wow people with his words. When Moses and Aaron went to Pharaoh, though, he pretty much laughed in their faces and made the Israelites work even harder. Some of them went to Moses and Aaron and told them to back off— they were better off before they started making noises with the Pharaoh. Moses went to God and said, "What are you *doing*? Why aren't you working with me here? What do you expect me to do?"

God said Moses had to trust that this was the way to do it. God makes the same thing clear to us. He expects us to speak his Word and trust that he knows what he's doing, even when it doesn't seem like it.

Told you it was going to be a lot.

## Do That Little Thing: JUST THINK

It's okay to think about a time when you didn't think God knew what he was doing, because that takes you straight to God to ask him. Write it right here. There are some examples to help you (they might even fit you!).

God, I didn't think you knew what you were doing when:

_____

Examples: *Someone died. Someone got really sick. Someone was in an accident. I didn't get chosen, and I really was the best. A really mean girl got away with, well, being really mean.*

If you've never talked to God about that before, do it now. He'll listen.

# Wednesday

Didn't we say to you in Egypt, "Leave us alone; let us serve the Egyptians"? It would have been better for us to serve the Egyptians than to die in the desert!

Exodus 14:12

Just as he promised, God turned Pharaoh's heart, and he let the Israelites go. And then he complicated things. He told Moses to lead them around in circles so Pharaoh would think he could come after them and take them back. That's exactly what happened.

What in the world was God thinking? That he really wanted a big finish to this thing, so the Israelites would see how powerful he was, how much he loved them, and how much he wanted to do for them. God gave Moses the power to part the Red Sea so they could walk across on dry land, and then drowned the Egyptians when they tried it. Now *that* was dramatic.

The Israelites were so freaked out when they saw Pharaoh coming with his 600 chariots and all his men marching after them, they turned on Moses and said, "Now we're going to die, thanks to you. At least when we were slaves we were still alive. Hello!"

This time Moses knew what God expected of him, and he said to the people, "Do not be afraid. Stand firm and you will see the deliverance the Lord will bring you today" (Exodus 14:13). God expects you to keep following him, no matter how bad things look. If you don't, you might miss the big finish!

## Do That Little Thing: GOD? CAN WE TALK?

Look at some of the situations you've written down or thought about this week. Do you need a cloud by day and a pillar of fire by night to get you through one of those? There's one of each, because God is there for you 24/7/365. So go to your quiet place and ask God to show you what step to take next. Just one right next thing. Just a tiny move toward a solution. Just ask. Then keep your eyes open.

# Thursday

If you listen carefully to the voice of the Lord your God and do what is right in his eyes ... I will not bring on you any of the diseases I brought on the Egyptians, for I am the Lord, who heals you.

Exodus 15:26

Whew! The Israelites made it across the Red Sea, and God saw to it that they wouldn't be bothered by those Egyptians ever again. You'd think they'd be grateful.

Not! Within three days they were whining because they were thirsty and the water in the town of Marah didn't taste good.

You would expect God to lose his temper and just leave the thankless bunch of whiners in the desert to shrivel up—but he didn't. He had Moses throw a piece of wood into the water, which made it sweet. Then he told the people what *he* expected of *them*: listen to what I say and do what I tell you is right, and I will heal you.

And God didn't leave anything for them to guess. Chapters 20 through 31 of Exodus are full of his instructions. He even told them how to wash their hands, for Pete's sake.

It really is that simple for us too. But as you'll see as you read on, simple doesn't mean easy. It's a good thing God is understanding!

## Do That Little Thing: LISTEN UP!

Before we can know what God wants us to do, we have to listen. He's already spoken to us through the Bible, which is why it's called the "Word." So today, go to your quiet place and choose one of these passages that fits what you may be thinking about today (see the "issues" in parentheses) or choose one of your own. Read it out loud and listen to it. Just listen.

- Exodus 14:5–31 (Someone has broken a promise to me.)
- Psalm 70 (I'm not getting an answer to my prayers as fast as I want.)
- Ephesians 4:25–27 (I'm so frustrated and jealous I'm about to explode.)
- Mark 9:17–27 (I'm just not sure God can or will help me with this impossible problem.)

# Friday

All who are skilled among you are to come and make everything the Lord has commanded.

Exodus 35:10

If God just expected the Israelites to follow a bunch of rules, he could have left them in Egypt where there were plenty of rules. He wanted them to recognize that *he* was making all the good things happen for them, and that meant they needed to worship him. Because they were such a clueless bunch, he gave them specific instructions for how to do that, starting with the *place* where they were to gather on the Sabbath.

God was still leading them to the Promised Land, a trip that was going to take forty years. So their tabernacle had to be sort of portable, but it couldn't be tacky and thrown together. God knew it would mean a lot more to them if they each had a part in building it, and he had a job for each of them. Everything was to be made by the people, right down to the tent pegs.

This was to be done only by those who were willing. God still expects us to take part in building his church, whether it's babysitting in the nursery or making cheer-up cards for the old folks or singing in the kids' choir—not because we have to, but because we're willing to share our skills and ourselves.

That actually sounds like the fun part. And with so many "right things to do," it's great to have one that is pure joy, all the way.

## Do That Little Thing: YOU CAN *SO* DO THIS!

So—what's one tiny thing you can do for *your* church? Or if you don't have a church, what could you do for your family or your special group of friends? Check off the things you might do to help "build the tabernacle." Then, do ONE of those things this week.

\_\_\_\_ Join the children's choir, or just sing out in church.

\_\_\_\_ Seek out people who look sad and say hi or just smile at them.

\_\_\_\_ Help the Sunday school teacher or the youth pastor or my mom with the little jobs.

\_\_\_\_ Run errands.

\_\_\_\_ Suggest how to make Sunday school more interesting or how to raise money for projects or how to help fix a problem.

# Saturday

In the future, when your son asks you, "What is the meaning of the stipulations, decrees and laws the Lord our God has commanded you?" tell him.

Deuteronomy 6:20–21

Don't you sometimes wonder why there have to be so many rules (stipulations, decrees, and laws)? The first several books of the Bible are definitely full of them—how to do everything from cook beans to go to the bathroom. Even kids back in the desert with Moses were asking, "What is UP with all these RULES?"

God told parents to explain it this way:

- We were slaves but God set us free.
- God has given us all kinds of wonderful signs to show that he's there taking care of us.
- Following the rules God gives will keep us going, keep us alive.
- Doing all these things brings us closer to God, where we can enjoy his blessings and his love.

It's the same for you. The more you try to do the right thing, the God-thing, and you know it's what God wants you to do, the closer you feel to him. And the closer you feel, the freer you are from even thinking about doing the wrong thing. And the more you do the right thing, the happier your life is. Nobody but God could have put together a system like that. So God expects us to accept the rules, but he sure gives us a lot when we do.

## Do That Little Thing: SHOUT-OUT

Pick the "rule" that you're having the most trouble following right now.

- Showing God respect with my words (not swearing or using "God" for anything else but his name).
- Making Sunday a devoted-to-God day (not using it to cram in all my homework or complain about going to church).
- Showing respect for my parents or teachers (not talking back, not lying to them, not complaining about everything they ask me to do).

- Telling the truth (not gossiping, not cheating, not exaggerating, not fibbing to get out of trouble).
- Treating people fairly (not excluding people, not bullying in any way, sharing).
- Being grateful for what I have (not being envious or jealous, not whining for stuff I think I have to have).

Follow the rule, just for today. Then tell somebody how good it feels to do it God's way.

# The God of Second Chances

> O Sovereign Lord, do not destroy your people, your own
> inheritance that you redeemed.
>
> Deuteronomy 9:26

The Israelites put Moses through a nightmare with all their whining and complaining. And THEN, before he could even get the Ten Commandments down the mountain to them, they started worshiping some idol they made for themselves—after all Moses had done for them—after all GOD had done for them.

No wonder God told Moses he was going to blot them out and start over. But Moses begged God not to destroy them. And God listened.

If God would give THEM a second chance, just think what he'll do for you. This week you'll find out how that works so that you can start to see it happen in your own life. You may not be as ungrateful and rebellious as those Israelites, but you WILL make mistakes just about every day. This week is for you!

# Sunday

I stayed there on the mountain forty days and nights ... and God listened to me ... God decided not to destroy you.

Deuteronomy 10:10 MSG

The Israelites were TOTALLY blessed to have Moses with them. Anybody else probably would have let God do away with them. But after Moses pitched a fit and broke the tablets with the Ten Commandments on them, he went all out trying to save the people. He stayed up on the mountain before God for forty days and forty nights with no food or water and prayed for those ungrateful people who had created a golden calf to worship.

Now this is God we're talking about. He didn't have to listen to Moses, but he gave in and told Moses to make new tablets and a wooden chest to put them in. He'd give his people another chance.

Remember this about the second chances:

- God gave them another try because Moses was faithful. Keep strong Christians on your side, because you won't always know when you're messing things up.
- God didn't give them another chance because THEY deserved it. He did it because it was HIS will. You can't earn that forgiveness. It's a gift from God.
- If God hadn't given them a chance to try again, his whole plan would have gone down the tubes. You are part of God's big plan, so he would rather see you grow from your mistakes than be ruined by them.

## Do That Little Thing: QUIZ

Make a list of the chances-to-make-it-right that have happened to you since your last birthday. For example: *I flunked my vocabulary test because I didn't study. Instead of grounding me, my mom helped me study and the next week I got a 98.*

# Monday

The Israelites acted unfaithfully in regard to the devoted things.

Joshua 7:1

Moses died before the Israelites crossed into the Promised Land. At least he didn't have to see how they were good for a while — and then totally messed things up again.

God put Joshua in charge, who was devoted to God and did everything God told him. But did the people keep God's commandments about how the moving tabernacle was to be handled? You guessed it. NO.

This time it seemed like God wasn't going to give them a second chance. The Israelite army went up against a weaker army and got beaten. Joshua fell face-down in front of the ark and wailed, "Now everybody's going to think we're a bunch of losers, and they'll all be out to get us."

God told Joshua to stand up and face the truth. The Israelites were defeated because somebody had stolen stuff from the tabernacle of God and were using it for themselves. What did they expect?

God doesn't give second chances to people who refuse to do it his way. If you want another try — if you don't want to be defeated by your own sin — you have to admit you were wrong and do what God wants you to do. As long as you do that, God will turn your mistakes around. He wants to do that for you.

## Do That Little Thing: FIND OUT

Ask your friends if they ever made or saw a mistake that affected a whole group. Maybe a brother or sister acting up on a family outing made everybody miserable, like one kid acting out in class and keeping the entire class from getting a privilege. Did that person get turned around and headed in the right direction? Or did he or she get punished? Which works better — learning or being grounded? See how God works?

# Tuesday

As for me and my household, we will serve the Lord.

Joshua 24:15

Joshua was another one of the good guys. He led the Israelites in fighting all the enemies they had to defeat so they could have the land God promised them. Then, one day, Joshua told the people that he was old and would be leaving them on their own.

The Israelites had enough trouble doing what was right when they had a great leader telling them what to do all the time! But it was time for them to show God that they could follow him with their hearts. Joshua did a huge review of all the ways God had provided for them, and then he went over what their part was going to be—AGAIN: "Fear the Lord and serve him with all faithfulness" (Joshua 24:14).

On that day, Joshua said, they should *choose* whom they would serve—gods they made up, or the real God. You have a choice, too. Whether your friends or family decide to serve God by doing what's right in his eyes or not, you can decide to follow him. If you've said you would before and haven't exactly followed through, now is a good time to commit again. After all, God gives second chances.

## Do That Little Thing: JUST THINK

Think about when you made your decision to follow God. If you haven't done that, think about whether you'd like to right now. Even if you just say, "God, I've decided that as for me, I will serve you," that's huge. It gives you all the chances you need.

Eventually that entire generation died and was buried. Then another generation grew up that didn't know anything of God or the work he had done for Israel.

Judges 2:10 MSG

A nd guess what? The very next verse starts off with, "The people of Israel did evil in God's sight." Couldn't these people get a clue?

Maybe they started off right, and maybe some of them even tried to follow God all their lives. But obviously they left out one important thing: they didn't pass on to the next generation the wisdom of God and the wonderful things he'd done.

That would be like nobody telling you what a great God we serve. No one showing you how to worship him. The important grown-ups in your life neglecting to teach you how to live a life that pleases God. Can you imagine yourself knowing nothing about God? Nothing?

Grown-up God-believers have a big responsibility to teach kids everything they know about having a relationship with God. What does that mean for you?

- You can go to the adults in your life — like your parents, your grandparents, your pastors — and let them know that you want to learn as much as you can about how to live a true God-life.
- You can make sure the little ones in your life get the benefit of what you know of God. Sing them the songs. Read or tell them the Bible stories. Help them out when they get mixed up.

Keep passing on the Word. It keeps *our* next verse from being, "They did evil in God's sight."

## Do That Little Thing: GOD? CAN WE TALK?

Get by yourself with God for a very private talk. In a journal or with your words or drawings, open up about the ways you might have slipped away from him lately — the blessing you keep forgetting to ask at lunchtime, the ugly stuff you've been blurting out to your sister, etc. This is not a guilt trip; it's just a cleansing talk with God — to clear the way for you to do better tomorrow.

# Thursday

Go in the strength you have.

Judges 6:14

The Israelites were doing so much bad stuff, God handed them over to their enemies, the Midianites — not a nice group of people. Naturally they cried out to God, so he sent them a prophet to explain all over AGAIN what they needed to do and be.

That prophet was Gideon, and he was truly bummed out. The angel of the Lord said to him, "The Lord is with you, mighty warrior" (Judges 6:12). Gideon said, "If the Lord is with us, why has all this happened to us?" To us it seems obvious why, but God told Gideon to go with the strength he had, and he would strike down those evil Midianites. He said he'd be with him.

After the Israelites strayed from him so many times you've probably lost track, God was still willing to give them one more chance, through Gideon, who was from the weakest clan and was the smallest and youngest guy in his family.

You, hopefully, don't have to do battle with large bands of enemies, although it may seem like it at times. When those times come, God wants you to use whatever you have, and he will be with you, giving you that one-more-chance. It may be your gift for calming people down or your big laugh that makes everyone forget why they were even mad in the first place. Go in the strength you have. God will be with you.

## Do That Little Thing: LISTEN UP!

Tell God where you feel weak. You might feel like the wimpiest girl on the softball team, or the slowest math student in class, or the shyest girl in your Sunday school. Then just listen. You might feel God pumping you up, just a little, just enough to go in the strength you have. Give it a chance.

# Friday

Do not be angry beyond measure, O Lord; do not remember our sins forever.

Isaiah 64:9

It finally happened. The Israelites got so far from God that their fiercest enemies, the big bad Babylonians, took them away from their beloved country and made them live in a strange land. Imagine being ripped from your home and family and being put someplace where you couldn't do any of the things that were familiar to you—couldn't even worship God. Homesick doesn't even begin to describe the feeling.

We can say, "Well, they deserved it." It wasn't like the prophet Isaiah didn't warn them about everything they were doing wrong. But the story has a sort-of-happy ending. The people finally, finally got it. They realized that it wasn't God abandoning them that made them miserable. It was their own bad stuff!

God brought them back home because they prayed so hard to him and admitted that it was their fault. That's when God lets people try again, when they say, "I have messed up big time. Please help me, God. Please forgive me."

That doesn't mean it's going to be all okay in a snap. It means the journey to a new place—a new part of you—can begin.

## Do That Little Thing: YOU CAN *SO* DO THIS!

Choose a way to share what you know about God with a little kid. Maybe a fun praise song, or a favorite Bible story. Do a puppet show version, or even make your own book as a gift, complete with drawings. Be a God-lover in your speech and actions as you spend time together. And give that little person a second chance if she doesn't get it the first time!

# Saturday

Behold, I will create new heavens and a new earth. The former things will not be remembered, nor will they come to mind.

Isaiah 65:17

Have you ever asked someone to forgive you, and she did? But then she reminded you every chance she got what it was you did that she had to forgive you for? How much did you hate that?

Maybe you've been on the other side of that too. You TOLD someone you forgave her, but you couldn't seem to resist the chance to bring it up every now and then. Why do we do that? Usually it's just to make sure that even though we say all is forgiven, it had better not happen again.

Our Father doesn't hold a grudge or expect you to carry guilt inside you for the rest of your life over every mistake you've made. It's over, and you are free to go on living tomorrow better than you have today. And if you make a mistake tomorrow—which you surely will because you're a human being—you can go to God without feeling as if you've already had all your chances. God has forgotten about those!

It's sort of hard to believe, but you CAN believe it, and to show it, simply celebrate it. Every time you go to God for a new start, rejoice with a grin because God loves you enough to forget your past. It just doesn't get any better than that.

## Do That Little Thing: SHOUT-OUT

When was the very last time you went to God and said, "I am SO sorry I did that, Father"? Write it here. If you've never done that, do it now, and then write it here!

_____

_____

_____

_____

_____

Now invite someone to have a jubilation cookie with you, and tell her this one's for the God who forgets. That should lead to an interesting conversation. God will love it.

## God Hires Losers

> He raises the poor from the dust and lifts the needy from the ash heap; he seats them with princes and has them inherit a throne of honor.
>
> 1 Samuel 2:8

We've seen God use some amazing people as we've studied together these past six weeks. Abraham, Jacob, Joseph, Moses, and Joshua were pretty impressive. No wonder God chose them for his big missions. He is, after all, a God with big expectations.

But God doesn't just use larger-than-life men to work for him. He can actually use anyone who is willing to say, "Send me, God." This week you're going to learn about two of those unexpected people—just ordinary folks God called on because they were exactly the ones to do the job. Reading about Samuel and David will hopefully show you that you, too, will have a job to do for the Father—and probably more than one in your lifetime. And there's no time like right now to see how that works. Enjoy your discoveries.

# Sunday

The Lord, the God of Israel, declares: "I promised that your house and your father's house would minister before me forever." But now the Lord declares: "Far be it from me!"

1 Samuel 2:30

If you had a closet full of clothes that didn't fit you any more, wouldn't you clean out all the old stuff before you put the new outfits in there? That's what God had to do in his temple when a man named Eli was the head priest.

Way back in Moses' time, when the Israelites were still traveling across the desert to the Promised Land, God promised that all the descendants of Aaron, Moses' brother, would be priests, which was a huge honor. At the time of this story, that descendant was Eli, who was a man of God doing an excellent job.

As a priest, that is. As a father—not so good. Eli's sons treated people's offerings to the Lord like they were at a barbecue, and that's just for starters. Eli warned them that they were going to come to a bad end, but like a lot of kids, they paid no attention to their father.

God had to "clean out the closet" and get them out of there so he could put in someone he could trust when Eli died. That's the way it is with God. He has certain things that have to get done, and if one person won't do them, he'll find someone else who will do them even better. Wouldn't you like to be the one God can count on?

## Do That Little Thing: QUIZ

What things could you get rid of to make room for what God might have in store for you? Check off any of these, and add your own if you want. Then get the inner broom ready!

\_\_\_\_ gossiping
\_\_\_\_ watching a LOT of TV
\_\_\_\_ excluding people
\_\_\_\_ not-so-good grades
\_\_\_\_ spending WAY too much time playing computer games
\_\_\_\_ staying in trouble with my parents for not following rules
\_\_\_\_ _____

# Monday

Speak, for your servant is listening.

1 Samuel 3:10

What if God had something in mind for you from the time you were born — even before? What if you started to train for it right after you stopped drinking out of a baby bottle?

That's what happened to Samuel. Before he was even born, his mother promised that he would be brought up in the temple by Eli. Right after he was weaned (his mom stopped breast-feeding him) she took him to Eli, and Samuel was the one God chose to take the place of the wicked sons, which meant he had to start early learning about the duties of a priest.

But God had something even bigger in mind for Samuel. He revealed to him, in person, what was going to happen to Eli's sons. It was a huge thing, a thing Samuel then had to tell Eli, a thing that made him very sad. Eli had let God down by not disciplining his sons for the wrong they'd done in the temple, and God wasn't going to let that go.

Big hard stuff for Samuel, and yet he did it. He was only about twelve years old when God began this work in him. After that, "The Lord was with Samuel as he grew up, and he let none of his words fall to the ground" (I Sam. 3:19). Everybody realized that Samuel was a prophet, a person God revealed himself to.

Wow.

## Do That Little Thing: FIND OUT
Ask some God-loving grown-ups when they first sensed God talking to them. They don't have to be prophets — God speaks to everyone who listens. Just find folks who listened and have them tell you their stories.

# Tuesday

He cried out to the Lord on Israel's behalf, and the Lord answered him.

1 Samuel 7:9

We've heard this before. Israel messes up and somebody has to go to God for them. This time was a little different, however. Somebody made God really unhappy by looking into the Ark of the Covenant (the wooden chest that held the tablets with the Ten Commandments) when he had strictly forbidden it. But the people mourned that mistake and for twenty years, while God kept the ark away from them, they "sought after the Lord" (1 Samuel 7:2). Samuel said if they were returning to God with all their hearts (verse 3), they had to get rid of all their foreign gods and serve only him.

At first it seemed that their plan was backfiring, because while they fasted and prayed, the Philistines, one of their worst enemies, gathered to attack them. But the Israelites didn't freak out and start defending themselves. They begged Samuel to keep praying — which he did. And God sent a major clap of thunder that freaked the *Philistines* out and sent them running. The Israelites were able to take them down. And for the rest of Samuel's lifetime, "the hand of the Lord was against the Philistines" (verse 13), and Israel was able to protect some of the surrounding nations and restore peace.

All this happened because a young man paid attention to God and didn't think he was too unimportant to speak up. Samuel rocked, don't you think?

## Do That Little Thing: JUST THINK

Close your eyes — or take your drawing tool in hand — and picture yourself at the age you are right now, sharing some piece of what you absolutely know about God with someone who needs to know it too. Imagine yourself writing a note or having a talk or passing it along with a hug. Whatever comes to mind, follow it. And if it seems like the next right thing to do — do it.

# Wednesday

Your kingdom will not endure; the Lord has sought out a man after his own heart and appointed him leader of his people, because you have not kept the Lord's command.

1 Samuel 13:14

Do you know a kid who's really smart, could probably be number one in the class except that he doesn't do his homework, won't follow the rules, and drives the teacher nuts? It's hard to be patient with a kid who has it all and just throws it away.

God wasn't patient with it. He chose as king a man named Saul, and at first it seemed like it was going to work out. "The Spirit of God came on him in power," and he rescued the whole city of Jabesh from the Ammonites.

But the first time God asked Saul to *wait* for him to act, Saul tried to take matters into his own hands. He just couldn't wait with faith. God went to Samuel and told him it really made him sad. Saul denied what he had done, kept telling Samuel that he DID do what God told him, which only made things worse.

Sure, in the end, he begged for forgiveness, and he was forgiven. But God still took the kingdom away from him. He wanted somebody "after his own heart." We'll talk about that guy tomorrow.

## Do That Little Thing: GOD? CAN WE TALK?

Take a deep breath, and remember first that God loves you way more than anyone else loves you, which is a lot. Keeping that in mind, talk to God about one way you think you might have let him down. It doesn't even have to be something big. God just wants your honesty, and now is the perfect time to learn it. It makes you a girl after God's own heart.

# Thursday

The Lord said, "Rise and anoint him; he is the one."

1 Samuel 16:12

God's next choice for king was about the last guy who would have come to anybody's mind. He told Samuel to go to Jesse's house because he had chosen one of Jesse's sons to rule next. Samuel was pretty freaked out since Saul was still king and might have Sam's head chopped off if he found out. But as always, Samuel trusted that God knew what he was doing.

The scene at Jesse's was sort of like the story of Cinderella when the Prince came to the stepmother's house to find the girl whose foot fit the glass slipper. Jesse kept bringing out sons, but each time Samuel said, no, that wasn't the one God had chosen. Pretty soon he was out of kids, except for the youngest who was out tending sheep—not a high-level position.

The minute the youngest son walked in it was as if the owner of the glass slipper had been found. The Lord said to Samuel, "Rise and anoint him; he is the one." This was David, and from the moment Samuel poured oil on his head, the Spirit of the Lord was on him.

There's just no telling whom God is going to choose for what job. It pays to be ready!

## Do That Little Thing: LISTEN UP!

Ask God to show you a person who seems to be doing God's work even though he or she doesn't "fit" what we think of as a great leader or super star. Could it be the lady in the cafeteria who always smiles at you when you're having a rough day? The bus driver who doesn't have to yell to get people to behave on the bus? The mom who always has the neighborhood kids at her house and makes everybody feel like part of the family?

When such a person comes to mind, thank God for him or her. Then ask how you could be just a little bit like that yourself.

Let no one lose heart on account of this Philistine; your servant will go and fight him.

1 Samuel 17:32

How many times have you heard it? "You have to wait until you're older."

Does it make you feel like putting your hands on your hips and telling the world, "Hello! I'm not a CHILD!"

Actually, you *are* a child, but you're a growing-up one, and sometimes the adults in your life don't recognize just how fast you're growing.

That happened to David. He didn't take the throne right away. Meanwhile, Saul, who was still officially king, called for someone to play the harp for him to soothe his troubled soul. David evidently rocked on the harp because Saul hired him as his full-time harpist.

About that time, the biggest Philistine soldier—we're talking nine feet tall—told Israel to pick one guy to fight him. If the Israelite won, the Philistines would be their subjects; if he won, it would be the other way around. Hello! Who was going to volunteer for that duty? Actually, David did. He got his slingshot and headed for the camp where Goliath, the giant, was waiting. His brothers told him he was conceited, thinking he could take on Goliath, and David said what any youngest kid would say: "Now what have I done? Can't I even speak?" (1 Samuel 17:29). David whipped out his slingshot and took Goliath down with one shot right between the eyes. He knew what he was supposed to do, and he didn't let anybody stop him.

## Do That Little Thing: YOU CAN *SO* DO THIS!

The story of David and Goliath doesn't teach you to take on every bully on the playground. It shows you that whatever it is God has asked YOU to do, you are not too small or too young to do it. Look back at the things you've talked to him about in "Do That Little Thing" this week. Choose one, and just do it. You're ready.

# Saturday

For the sake of your word and according to your will, you have done this great thing.

2 Samuel 7:21

Have you ever just thought about how good your life is? You have a family, a place to live, everything you need (though maybe not everything you WANT!)—and you're probably discovering your gifts and talents, making friends, discovering new stuff. It's easy to say, "Hey, I deserve this. I'm a good person. I do what I'm supposed to do (most of the time!). Yeah, this is the way life is supposed to be."

David had a great life too. He had been promoted from shepherd boy to king, for starters. God took down all his enemies and made it so that everybody thought David was all that. He promised that David's people would be taken care of, and he showed him that David's line (all the sons and grandsons and great-grandsons, etc. who came after him) would endure forever. It doesn't get any better than that.

And David sat in God's presence and said, "Who am I, O Sovereign Lord, and what is my family, that you have brought me this far?" (verse 18). David knew he didn't earn God's gifts to him, that God had done all this because he wanted to, not only for David, but for the whole nation of Israel. Without a bunch of thoughts about how good he was, he had more space for listening to God. Makes you want to get all humble, doesn't it?

## Do That Little Thing: SHOUT-OUT

Tell somebody how great your life is — because God is making it that way. The best people to tell are your parents, one or both, or whoever takes care of you. Thank them for all they've given you, and ask them if they'll thank God with you. They may even come up with blessings you haven't thought of. That screams for a celebration!

## A God of Your Very Own

I trust in you, O Lord; I say, "You are my God."

Psalm 31:14

When you talk about God, do you ever say, "*my* God," as in "I love my God," or "I pray to my God"? You can. It doesn't mean you're being selfish — "This is my God and nobody else's!" It means you consider God to be personal. Belonging close. Being in you. Your God.

We've been talking a lot in the past weeks about God doing big things to show us who he is. Being the Creator, the One in Charge, the Guide with great expectations, the God of Second Chances, who can make even the lowly great. God is big enough for the whole world.

But God is also close enough to be in your world. He cares about — and knows about — every little freckle on your cute face, every crinkle of your smile, every nose hair — well, you get the idea. If God is that up-close-and-personal, he wants you to know him that way too.

So get ready to snuggle in with God. This week will show you how to know God not just from the big picture, but from the personal snapshot he wants to show you.

# Sunday

When I am afraid, I will trust in you. In God, whose word I praise, in God I trust.

Psalm 56:3–4

Worries and fears can whisper in your head. It's completely normal to feel anxious when you're having trouble with a subject at school or when your best friend isn't acting so much like a friend.

It's also normal to get upset when you hear about crimes on the news or your parents having a (loud) disagreement. God made us with a built-in system for alerting us to danger. It's that dry mouth, sweaty palms, butterflies-in-the-stomach feeling you get that spurs you on to either run away or fight back.

It helps to go to someone you feel safe with and talk it out or just get a hug, but that someone might not always be available — like if you wake up frightened in the middle of the night or you're staring, frozen, at your math test in the middle of class.

God is always, always there as your Personal Protector. You can close your eyes and breathe him slowly in, calming yourself in the knowledge that he is right inside you with protection from your fears. Nothing can come between you and him, not even your worst nightmare!

## Do That Little Thing: QUIZ

Make a list of all your fears. Just write them down or draw a picture for each one. Don't think you're afraid of anything? Challenge yourself to think of just one. Don't have enough room here to squeeze them all in? Pull out a whole notebook! If you get a little (or a lot) anxious while you're writing, tell God you trust him. You don't have to be alone when you're afraid. Not ever.

> I will praise the Lord, who counsels me; even at night my heart instructs me ... You have made known to me the path of life.
>
> Psalm 16: 7, 11

Wouldn't it be great to have your own personal tutor who was at your beck and call 24/7? If you were having trouble with long division, you could just turn and say, "Could I get a little help here, please?"

That's probably not going to happen — unless your daddy gets a giant promotion! But when it comes to the other things in life that you need help with, you do have a Personal Teacher. That would be, of course, God.

Friend issues, family stuff — God has all the answers there. Difficulties with anger or lying or temptation — God can help you handle that. Tough times with a teacher, a coach, a babysitter — God knows all about tough times. There isn't anything God doesn't have an answer for.

It takes some practice to rely on God for individual instruction. It means figuring out what's bothering you, which God can help you with, then finding that quiet place and taking the time to be with God and talk it out. And listening — through the Bible, through wise people, through acting on what you think God is telling you and seeing how it works. That takes more work than just venting to your friend and trying to move on without really solving the problem.

You can go to wise people, even your BFF. Just go to God first, because he will often lead you to just the right people at just the right time. All you have to do is ask.

## Do That Little Thing: FIND OUT

Ask people what they think makes a good teacher. Write it down (or carry a little tape recorder). Later, go over the list and think of God as the Teacher with all those qualities (unless you have something like "Gives everybody an A whether they deserve it or not!") Isn't that Teacher the one you want to consult on a daily basis? How about now?

# Tuesday

The Lord is close to the brokenhearted and saves those who are crushed in spirit.

Psalm 34:18

Do you remember the last time you were brokenhearted? It hurt, didn't it, when your best friend dumped you? Or your grandpa died. Or your dad didn't get home for your birthday. It actually feels like your chest has been split in two, especially when you cry, as most of us do when our spirits are crushed by some hurtful life-thing.

A broken heart is also lonely. It can feel as if you're all by yourself in your pain. Being held while you bawl your eyes out is a great healer. But at those moments when you don't even know what to do with your arms, you are so alone.

And yet, "The Lord is close to the brokenhearted" (Psalm 34:18). Even before you start to cry, even before you realize how hurt you are, God is already there with the heavenly Kleenex, the almighty hug. And when you throw yourself down on your bed or throw tennis balls against the fence, you can feel God whispering that he's so sorry you're in pain. He doesn't let you skip the tears and the hurting chest and the heaviness of a broken heart. But he does let you rely on him to lead you through your feelings and gives you space to feel them. That's especially important if other people tell you not to cry.

Best of all: he will heal your broken heart. God eases into the raw places and not only makes you feel better, he makes you stronger.

## Do That Little Thing: JUST THINK

As painful as it might be, think, just for a minute, about the last time your heart was broken. If you didn't go to God for comfort then, go now. If you did, thank him now for the comfort he gave you. You might still have some slivers of hurt, which is perfectly normal. God will soothe your slivers just as he did the big break. God's like that.

I confess my iniquity; I am troubled by my sin.

Psalm 38:18

You can probably guess an iniquity isn't good. Think Mean Girl who deliberately turns all her friends against one former friend just because she feels like it, and you've pretty much got iniquity down.

Even if you're not guilty of iniquity, you probably have other sins to confess. We all do because we all make choices, and sometimes we make the wrong ones. We can do our best, but because we're people, we will never be completely sin-free.

That's why God is our Personal Confessor. You may not have thought about this before, but doesn't it feel better when you realize you've hurt someone to go to that person and say you're sorry? Since every sin we commit is committed against God as well as someone else (or ourselves), it makes sense to go to him first and blurt it all out. It clears your head so you can go to the *person* you need to confess to.

Other people aren't always forgiving when you go to them to unburden your guilt. God always is. You may still have to suffer some consequences for your actions, but you don't have to stay guilty and feel horrible about yourself forever and ever. God, the Personal Confessor, erases it from your record.

## Do That Little Thing: GOD? CAN WE TALK?

Since saying what you've done wrong can be hard to squeeze out of your mouth, you might want a little help talking to God this time. Use this little outline if you want — or just let loose if that works for you.

Dear _____ (Your favorite way of addressing God),

I am writing this letter to read out loud to you because it's hard for me to admit to this thing I've done that is way wrong.

Okay, here goes. I am really troubled by the fact that I _____
_____. I don't know if it's considered "iniquity" but I know it's sin, and I'm so sorry I did it.

Will you please forgive me? And will you help me go to _____ (person's name) and ask for his/her forgiveness too?

And if I don't get it, will you help me with the broken heart I'm going to have?

Thank you for being my Personal Confessor. I know I'm going to sin again, but I promise I will come to you the minute I realize it. And I pray that you will help me never to make THIS mistake again.

I love you.

_____

(Your name)

# Thursday

Two things have I heard: that you, O God, are strong, and that you, O Lord, are loving.

Psalm 62:11 – 12

Have you figured this one out yet?

You're supposed to be nice to people, but you shouldn't let them walk all over you either. You're supposed to include the kids nobody else wants to hang out with, but sometimes those are the kids who get in trouble, and that's bad for you.

It's like walking a tightrope sometimes. It requires way more balance than most of us have. Fortunately, God is your Personal Balance.

God asks us to love our neighbors as much as we love ourselves, but sometimes loving somebody means you have to do something that person isn't going to like. For example, your best friend is amazing, but she's gotten pretty bossy lately. You have to tell her you're tired of being pushed around and you'd like to get back on even terms again.

It's pretty clear, until you're in the middle of the situation. Just get quiet and ask God how you can be both loving and strong. Somebody might wonder why you're standing there with your eyes closed. If anybody asks, just say you're trying to get your balance.

## Do That Little Thing: LISTEN UP!

Find a place where you can draw a straight line a few feet long or make one with string. Stand on it, one foot in front of the other. If you can keep your balance that way, prop one foot against the opposite ankle like a bicycle kickstand. Then slide it up to your calf. Keep going until you lose your balance.

Now ask God where that losing-your-balance place is in your life. Where are you struggling with being both loving and strong? Close your eyes while you balance and just listen. His answers will come. Maybe now, maybe later, but they will come. Since God is perfect balance itself, he can keep you standing tall.

# Friday

Because he turned his ear to me, I will call on him as long as I live.

Psalm 116:2

Think about the things you've learned in school lately: how to do long division, how to multiply fractions, how to write a paragraph that actually makes sense. Now think about other skills you've mastered: riding a two-wheeler, ice skating, making a killer milkshake. Once you learn how to do those things, you don't have to keep going back to whoever taught you and say, "Could you show me that again?"

But when it comes to getting along with people, controlling some of your own little urges, or figuring out the next right thing to do, you never just "get it" once and for all. Learning those things is part of the long journey you'll take all your life, because the kinds of situations you have to deal with change as you get older. For instance, you learned that pitching a fit wasn't going to get you your way when you were two (Okay, maybe three ... or four ...). Now you have to learn how to compromise so everyone gets a little bit of satisfaction. Later you'll learn what things NOT to compromise on.

The harder life gets — and it will — the more help you'll need from God. Keep getting closer now, so turning to him for guidance will be as natural as pitching that fit used to be.

## Do That Little Thing: YOU CAN *SO* DO THIS!

Pick one thing God seems to be asking you to grow in right now. Something like not exaggerating, or obeying your mom the first time, or stopping the rumor that's spreading at school.

Now — practice going to God for a growth spurt. Pray about one little thing you could do to get just an inch better. Once it's clear to you, do it. God will be there. He wants you bigger too.

# Saturday

How can a young man keep his way pure? By living according to your word. I seek you with all my heart; do not let me stray from your commands.

Psalm 119:9–10

Olympic skaters and gymnasts have their own individual coaches. Those professionals are with them constantly, long before the big event, working them for hours every day to get them ready.

And that doesn't just mean perfecting their skating program or their floor routine. Personal trainers have their athletes out there running and doing pushups and lifting weights—things their audiences will never see them do, but which are totally necessary if they're going to be in shape for competition.

Living your life isn't like preparing for some big event, because your events are happening all the time. But in order to be in shape for all the things that are going to come your way, you, too, need a Personal Trainer. Guess who?

God is there to train you to have great relationships, to serve him to the fullest, to make a difference in this world. Those are things other people will see and probably admire you for. But to do those things, God will put you through some things no one else may ever see. Things like praying long and hard, listening until it seems like the answers will never come, confessing with big tears on your face, obeying in little things nobody will think to praise you for.

Sign up for his training program, and you'll be ready for anything.

## Do That Little Thing: SHOUT-OUT

Think of one thing God has trained you to do, like:

- keeping my mouth firmly closed when I'm about to say something ugly.
- ignoring my siblings when they try to push my buttons.
- stopping a rumor instead of spreading it.
- smiling at the kids nobody else pays attention to.
- stating my case to my dad calmly instead of whining.

Tell someone about God training you to do that. It may help someone else turn to God as her Personal Trainer.

# WEEK 9

## God: Maker and Keeper of Promises

> God is not a man, that he should lie, nor a son of man, that he should change his mind. Does he speak and then not act? Does he promise and not fulfill?
>
> Numbers 23:19

I *promise*.

Those are two of the best words you can hear, aren't they? Especially when they're attached to something lovely —

- I promise we will get ice cream on the way home.
- I promise we will go to the movies this Saturday.
- I promise I will be there, in the front row, at your dance recital.

Other promises you don't even have to hear. You know that the day you were born your parents made a promise to love you and take care of you. On the first day of school, your teacher is promising to give you the best education possible. When you get in the car or on the bus to go to school, you hope the driver has made a promise to get you there in one piece!

Kept promises make you feel secure and safe. Broken promises — the ones people don't come through on — can really shake your world. When something you were depending on doesn't happen, it makes you wonder what you *can* count on.

People are human, and from time to time they *are* going to let you down. But God never makes a promise he doesn't keep, and his promises are huge. So get ready for a hopeful week, a week of promise made by our Promise-Keeper God.

> The Lord himself will give you a sign: The virgin will be with child and will give birth to a son, and will call him Immanuel.
>
> Isaiah 7:14

Immanuel. That's a pretty big name for a little baby. And its meaning is even bigger. Immanuel means "God with us."

Through Isaiah (one of God's big-time prophets), God promised that he was going to send a person who was actually himself in human form, so he could be *with* us. The people just weren't getting how they were supposed to live godly lives (ya think?), so God promised he would come on down here himself and show them, act it out for them.

To make sure people would know when the promise was being fulfilled, God set it up so that there would be no mistake. This was to be no ordinary birth. Immanuel would be born to a young woman who wasn't even married yet, and hadn't even been with a man ever.

Only God could keep a promise like that, and he did, when Jesus was born. "All this took place," the Bible says, "to fulfill what the Lord had said through the prophet" (Matthew 1:22). Keep reading this week to see how God kept his promise in every detail.

## Do That Little Thing: QUIZ

Take a quick look at how you think about promises right now. Remember to be honest as you check the answer that sounds most like you.

You promise your parents that you'll spend Friday night going out for pizza and a movie with your brothers and sisters — and then your friend asks you to spend the night at her house. You:

____ a. Ask your friend if she would mind if you stayed at her house a different night.

____ b. Spend the night at your friend's house and ask your parents if they'll do the pizza/movie outing again sometime when you can go too.

Choice *a* is the way God works with promises. Even if you didn't check that one, it's something to work toward. Promise God that you'll try, huh?

# Monday

> You, Bethlehem ... though you are small among the clans of Judah, out of you will come for me one who will be ruler over Israel.
>
> Micah 5:2

Have you ever seen one of those t-shirts that says, "WHERE IN THE WORLD IS _____?" and has the name of some itty-bitty place that doesn't even have a Wal-Mart? Like Bucksnort, Tennessee?

That was the attitude people back in Old Testament times had about Bethlehem. It was one of the smallest, puniest villages in Israel. But God promised (through the prophet Micah) that the One he was sending to save his poor, outcast people would come from that little bend-in-the-road place. He would honor them by having his Son come from among them.

Far away to the East, some magi (men who studied the stars) believed they saw a message in the stars. They arrived in Jerusalem and asked around, "Where is the one who has been born king of the Jews?" Now, there was already a king in Jerusalem, a very bad dude named Herod, who was freaked out at the suggestion that somebody else was going to kick him off the throne. In a panic, he called his advisors and asked them where this king, this Christ, was to be born. "In Bethlehem in Judea," they replied, "for this is what the prophet has written" (Matt. 2:5). Little did he know that Jesus Christ had already been born there and that Jesus was already King. God had kept his promise.

## Do That Little Thing: FIND OUT

Go to a grown-up who does a lot to take care of you. Ask that person what promises she has made to you, even if she's never actually spoken them out loud. Then thank that promise-maker in your life for caring so much about you.

Promise?

# Tuesday

The glory of the Lord will be revealed, and all mankind together will see it. For the mouth of the Lord has spoken.

Isaiah 40:5

When would it be good to see the glory of the Lord revealed? Maybe when you've messed up and your parents have come down on you and you feel like a loser? It would be nice if God would reveal his forgiving glory right about then.

That's what God promised to do when he sent Isaiah to speak to his people. They had been sent away to Babylon, away from the country they loved. They brought a lot of that on themselves because they didn't listen to God (just like you don't listen to your parents sometimes). But God knew what they needed if they were ever going to stay close to him.

"Comfort my people," God said to Isaiah (40:1). He told him to assure the people that their punishment was over, and their sin had been paid for.

That's like your mom or dad saying, "I think you've learned your lesson. Let's put it behind us." God has promised that to you. He sent Jesus to show us how to live as people who don't have to walk around feeling like losers because they make mistakes. People who can bubble over with love because they aren't under punishment for every little wrong thing they do. Yep. The glory of the Lord has been revealed.

## Do That Little Thing: JUST THINK

Think about what comforts you when you're upset or afraid or feeling bad about yourself. Make a quick list — anything from your favorite cat to a hunk of chocolate.

Now think about being comforted by God, especially when the kitty and the candy bar aren't available. How could you find that comfort? Go to your quiet place and talk it out with God. Imagine him rubbing your back as you cry into your pillow. Sing a praise song until you feel better. Just think. And then do.

Promise?

# Wednesday

Here is my servant, whom I uphold, my chosen one in whom I delight; I will put my Spirit on him and he will bring justice to the nations.

Isaiah 42:1

G o girl!"
"I'm proud of you, honey."
"You know something? You rock!"

It feels so good when a person you look up to is proud of you. You probably sit up taller and get a big ol' grin on your face. And best of all, you want to do even better.

What if GOD said that about you? He actually does sometimes. Can't you feel God's pleasure when you help your little brother with his homework, even though he has recently flushed yours down the toilet? Don't you experience God's pride when you refuse to spread that rumor that would really get you some attention? God loves it when we do it his way. He delights in us.

We're all constantly doing things that disappoint him. But being the great Maker of Promises, God promised us that he would send someone in whom he delighted every minute of every day. Someone who could show us how to be better in the delighting-God department, so that the world we live in would be more fair.

God announced that this Someone was here in a loud, clear voice when Jesus was baptized. He said from heaven, "This is my Son, whom I love; with him I am well pleased" (Matthew 3:17). Jesus is here, showing us how to please God too.

## Do That Little Thing: GOD? CAN WE TALK?

Go to your quiet place and curl up for a talk with God. Ask him how you've delighted him lately. Then ask him how you might have disappointed him, even just a little. Finally, ask him to show you how to make that right, or for help in just letting it go and moving on to do better next time. Have a good talk.

# Thursday

Then will the eyes of the blind be opened.

Isaiah 35:5

Which is a more comforting promise to hear?

- "I promise we'll do some fun things during your spring break."
- "I promise that during your spring break we'll go to the movies Tuesday and to the lake on Saturday."

That second one is way more reassuring that certain things are going to happen.

The suffering people of Israel wanted details too. So God didn't just say, "It's going to be all right." He gave very particular ways in which he was going to make things better. He said Immanuel would:

- strengthen feeble hands (Isaiah 35:3).
- steady weak knees (vs. 3).
- strengthen fearful hearts (vs. 4).
- open blind eyes (vs. 5).
- unstop deaf ears (vs. 5).
- help the mute (people who can't talk) to shout (vs. 6).

And they all happened. "Then [Jesus] touched their eyes," the Bible tells us in Matthew 9:29. "And their sight was restored" (vs. 30). And that was just one of the many healings he performed.

God still heals today. No, not everyone who is blind gets to see again, and not every deaf person suddenly has miraculous hearing. But everyone—everyone—can be close to God and feel his comfort and his love. That's the best healing of all.

## Do That Little Thing: LISTEN UP!

In your mind, listen to your own needs for healing. Where could God help you? Maybe you have a physical condition to deal with, like asthma or ADD. Or maybe you need healing for a bad habit, such as lying or whining. Or maybe you have some fears — about reading out loud or meeting new people or being in the dark. Whatever it is, let God reassure you that you can be healed — whether it's to be free of it or to work on it or to accept it. God promised. He'll make good on that.

# Friday

From that time on Jesus began to explain to his disciples that he must go to Jerusalem and suffer many things...and on the third day be raised to life.

Matthew 16:21

Some things can be hard to hear and accept.

"Honey, I'm sorry, but Grandpa is going to die."

"We have to move. Daddy has a new job."

You want to cry, throw a fit, and demand that things change right NOW! Can you imagine how the disciples felt when Jesus told them he was going to be killed? Peter, for one, wasn't having it. He took Jesus aside and said, "No way! I'm not going to let this happen to you!" Jesus wasn't having *that*. He knew it was going to be hard on them, but it had to be. It was what God had promised.

God "promised" to have his son killed? That doesn't sound like much of a promise! It's definitely the hard-to-hear kind. But God had also promised that the glory of the Lord would be revealed. Jesus was going to come back from the dead. And sure enough, on the third day after he was killed, an angel said to the women who went to his tomb, "Do not be afraid ... he has risen, *just as he said*" (Matthew 28:5–6, emphasis added).

The tough promises can have very happy endings.

## Do That Little Thing: YOU CAN *SO* DO THIS!

Is there something hard that you need to tell someone? Do you need to take a friend aside and tell her that her gossiping is wrong? Do you need to 'fess up to your mom that you haven't exactly been doing your homework? It can be so hard you get a lump in your throat just thinking about it, but talk to God about it (lump and all) and then go do it. Speak tenderly, but do it.

# Saturday

I will pour out my Spirit on all people ... Even on my servants, both men and women, I will pour out my Spirit in those days.
Joel 2:28–29

The disciples could believe in Jesus because – hello! – he was right there with them. But we don't see Jesus in the flesh or hear him talking to us like a person. We can't follow him around to watch him turn a kid's lunch into a whole banquet. And yet we just know he still lives, in us, through us, around us. What's that about?

It's about the Holy Spirit, another thing God promised through a prophet (Joel this time). He said he would pour out his spirit on ALL people. That was a huge promise back then because there were strict rules about who was better than whom. But God promised he would allow his spirit to pour over absolutely everyone, so that all could be forgiven and comforted and know they were loved.

Many, many years later, after Jesus had gone back up to heaven, great tongues of fire rested on the disciples and "All of them were filled with the Holy Spirit" (Acts 2:4). When people wanted to know what was going on (were the disciples drunk, they wondered?), Peter reminded them of Joel's prophecy. "The promise," he told them, "is for you and your children and for all who are far off — for all whom the Lord our God will call" (Acts 2:39). The promise is still there. For you. For everyone.

## Do That Little Thing: SHOUT-OUT

Do you know somebody who needs to hear about the Holy Spirit? A friend who doesn't have a church, a girl who isn't living the way God tells us to live, a grown-up who just seems sad. Find one small way to share the Holy Spirit with that person, something as simple as, "Whenever I'm — lonely, tempted, or sad — I just remember that God's Spirit is in me." The Holy Spirit will do the rest. God promises that.

# Who Jesus Says God Is

If you knew me, you would know my Father also.

John 8:19

D o people ever say to you, "You're just like your mother," or "You're so much like your dad!"? Has anyone ever told you that you and your best friend are like twins, or that you totally take after your grandmother (grandfather, Great-Aunt Ethel ...)?

No two people are exactly alike, of course. And sometimes when your mom says, "You act just like your father!" she doesn't exactly mean it as a compliment. But there is probably somebody in your life who is a lot like you. To know him or her is a lot like knowing you, at least in some ways.

Here's another thought. Have you ever met a friend's mother and suddenly realized, "Oh, I get why she acts like that. Her mom does the same thing!"

That's what Jesus was talking about when he said, "If you knew me, you would know my Father also." Although you are in some ways different from that person who is a lot like you, Jesus and God our Father are identical. God sent Jesus as himself, to show us exactly who he is and how he works.

It just doesn't get any clearer than that. This week, let's look at who Jesus says God is. In his Jesus-way, our Lord used images, things we're familiar with, to explain something that is bigger than we are and often hard to wrap out minds around. So get your imagination—and maybe even your drawing materials—ready. When Jesus says, "I am," he'll be telling you who God is. You're gonna want to know!

# Sunday

I am the bread of life. He who comes to me will never go hungry.

John 6:35

What if you heard something so cool you couldn't believe it? Like maybe one of your classmates told you that the teacher decided not to give that big test after all. Would you believe it immediately and do a cartwheel in the hall? Or would you have to have more proof? Would you ask three or four (or a dozen) other kids just to be sure? Would you ask for it in writing?

That's what happened after Jesus used a few loaves of bread and a couple of fishes to feed five thousand people. People experienced it in their own stomachs—and yet folks who heard about it still wanted more proof that Jesus was acting on God's behalf.

Twelve baskets of leftovers wasn't enough?

They wanted something REALLY big, a sign that was REALLY obvious, like the manna from heaven that God gave their forefathers. Jesus said he'd brought something better—himself. When he said "I am the bread of heaven," he didn't mean for everybody to come up and take bites out of him to fill their tummies. He was saying they needed to have their souls nourished with comfort and freedom and strength.

Anybody could give them bread. Only Jesus could assure them that God wanted them to have more than that. God wanted them to live forever in his love.

## Do That Little Thing: QUIZ

Name your three most favorite things to eat, things that make you feel good and give you energy:

_____

_____

_____

Now check off three things God can "feed" you that would also make you feel good:

____ comfort
____ freedom
____ strength
____ wisdom
____ love
____ forgiveness

Pray for those today, and be prepared to be filled up.

# **Monday**

Whoever believes in me ... streams of living water will flow
from within him.

John 7:38

Imagine you're taking a walk in the woods or on a farm and you
come across a pond. This little body of water doesn't have a stream
feeding it, so the water has gotten all murky and you can't see
through it. There's green gunk growing on the top, and a couple of
dead fish are floating on that, setting up a nasty stink. You can't get
away from the pond fast enough, and then a squad of mosquitoes
bombards you and goes to town on your bare arms.

EWWW!

You definitely wouldn't drink that water. You'd go to a stream
where the water was moving and clear and wasn't a maternity ward
for insects.

People in Jesus' day had to gather their water from streams, or in
the villages from wells, which are fed by streams. Jesus met a woman
at a well one day and used the image of fresh, life-giving water to
help her understand who he was.

This woman was from Samaria. Jews weren't supposed to talk to
Samaritans because they considered them to be unclean, yet Jesus
asked this lady for a cup of water. And he said to her, "If you knew
who I was, *you* would ask *me* for water. And not water from a nasty
pond, but living water. Water that will get your life moving, make
you feel free and loving and forgiving. You'd never be thirsty for
those things again."

Makes you want to drink up Jesus, doesn't it?

## Do That Little Thing: FIND OUT

Go to three different adults you know are close to God. Ask each one
of them: *What do you think when you hear "A spring of water, well-
ing up"?* See if they compare that to Jesus. You might give each one
of them a drawing you've done of your own image of that welling-up
spring as a thank-you.

# Tuesday

I am the light of the world. Whoever follows me will never walk in darkness, but will have the light of life.

John 8:12

What does the word "darkness" make you think of? Waking up in the middle of the night after a bad dream? Having the lights go out in the middle of a thunderstorm?

Sometimes darkness can be fun, like when you're hiding just before someone's surprise party. But most of the time darkness is a bummer because—hello!—you can't see where you're going.

Jesus said anyone willing to stick with him wouldn't have to wonder where the next step in life was going to lead, because they would always be able to see the way. With the light of Jesus you would:

- see that laughing at the girl everyone said was nerdy would be wrong.
- know that teasing a friend about her stutter or her taste in shoes would hurt her feelings.
- understand why your parents won't let you watch R-rated movies.

It will always get dark with fear or sadness or anger in your life. But with Jesus as your flashlight there will also be light to understand by, and you will be calm and happy and loving again. Jesus definitely shines.

## Do That Little Thing: JUST THINK

Divide a piece of paper into two columns. Color one column a dark color (but not so dark that you can't write on it). Color the other a light, bright color. On the dark side, make a list of things that seem dark in your life. Then across from each one in the light column, write one of these Jesus-things that would bring light to that darkness:

- love
- comfort
- forgiveness
- clear thinking
- self-control
- gratitude

# Wednesday

I am the gate for the sheep.

John 10:7

Let's clear up the sheep-pens-gates thing.

Sheep were quite valuable, so sheep owners built pens for them with walls to keep them from wandering away. There was only one opening, and that had a gate. Anybody entering any other way, like by climbing over the fence, was obviously up to no good (John 10:1).

Several shepherds kept their sheep in the same pen and hired one watchman to guard them. When a shepherd came in and called to his own flock, they knew who he was. The other sheep, who didn't belong to him, would just go on doing whatever it is sheep do (verse 3).

So Jesus is the way for God to come in and call to us. We belong to him. We recognize his voice in the Gospels. The gate swings open and you can follow wherever Jesus leads you in your life.

Just watch out for people who try to get you to follow them instead of Jesus. They may:

- make fun of you for going to church.
- say things like, "Oh, come on, do it. Who's going to know?"
- try to convince you that God doesn't care about the way you dress.

Just keep your eyes on that gate. Jesus is right there calling your name—way louder than those other voices. Follow his.

## Do That Little Thing: GOD? CAN WE TALK?

Tell God about any "thieves and robbers" who seem to be trying to climb over the "wall." You can make a list or just pray over each one. Ask God to keep them out and help you stay focused on the gate where Jesus is calling your name. Remember that some of the "thieves and robbers" might just be a little confused, and you may even be able to invite them into the pen with you, where they, too, can hear Jesus calling.

# Thursday

> I am the good shepherd. The good shepherd lays down his life for the sheep.
>
> John 10:11

Today, Jesus talks about what happens after the sheep pass through the gate and go outside.

- A shepherd in that part of the world didn't "drive" his sheep. He went on ahead and the sheep followed his voice.
- He would lead them to pastures where they could totally pig out and have everything they needed.
- Sometimes wild animals got to the sheep. There were cliffs and ledges they could fall off of. Sometimes they just got separated from the flock and were lost and scared. The shepherd would do anything to rescue a sheep, even if it meant giving up his own life.

It works the same way with the God Jesus came to show us.

- He doesn't force anybody to go with him. He doesn't "drive" people. He goes out ahead and those who know him follow him.
- If they follow him, they'll have everything they need.
- There will still be dangers. Sometimes people fall into bad stuff. Sometimes they just wander away from God, but he will do whatever it takes to get them back.

That's a shepherd worth following.

## Do That Little Thing: LISTEN UP!

Imagine yourself as a little lamb — cute and fluffy and white, but clueless. You can't go anywhere unless a shepherd leads you.

Don't *baaaa*, but get quiet and imagine that shepherd's voice. Gentle. Comforting. Strong. Wise. That will give you a pretty good idea what Jesus may have sounded like. Enjoy it. Let it comfort you and strengthen you and clear your mind. Then frolic, Little Lamb. You are taken care of.

# Friday

I am the resurrection and the life. He who believes in me will
live, even though he dies.

John 11:25

Has anyone you loved died? Maybe a precious grandparent or a
pet you treasured? It's so hard because that person or furry com-
panion is never coming back.

But what if the one who has passed on came back to life? There
just might not be anything better than that.

Jesus had three friends who were brother and sisters to each
other: Mary, Martha, and Lazarus. He loved them like family. While
Jesus was out of town, Lazarus got very sick, and Mary and Martha
sent for Jesus, knowing how he healed people.

Instead of hurrying back, he told his disciples that Lazarus' illness wasn't going to end in death and this would be a good chance
to show who God was.

Lazarus died, and by the time Jesus got there, he'd been in his
tomb for four days. Jesus told them to take him to the tomb and roll
away the stone. At first they hesitated. After four days, Lazarus was
going to be pretty smelly. But Jesus simply said, "Lazarus, come out!"
(John 11:43) And Lazarus walked out, still wrapped up in the burial
cloths, looking a little like a mummy.

What was that all about? Jesus showed that God even has power
over death. He assured them that we'll all leave this earth, but he is
the coming-back-to-life after our time here is over. A life that goes
on forever with him.

## Do That Little Thing: YOU CAN *SO* DO THIS!

Today, write a letter — or draw a picture if you'd rather — to a Christian you loved who has left this earth. Tell that loved one how happy
you are that he or she is with God now, living forever the way Jesus
promised. The person you're writing to doesn't need your letter, but
it will surely make you feel more at peace about his or her passing.
God wants that for you.

# Saturday

I am the true vine, and my Father is the gardener.

John 15:1

You may know even less about gardening than you did about sheep. Let's do a little landscaping lesson.

Grapes were a major crop back in those days, and grapes grow on vines.

- In order to have healthy grapes, you need a healthy vine, a true vine that is strong and has good roots in the ground.
- Other branches grow from the vine.
- You can't just let the branches grow all tangled and every which-way. The ones that are out of control and straggly have to be cut back by the gardener, so that when they grow back they will produce more grapes.
- Obviously if a branch is cut off from the vine, it isn't going to bear any fruit. It will eventually die.

So what does that mean God-wise?

- "Bear fruit" for God, which means make a difference with who you are and what you do.
- Be attached to Jesus, the main vine, in order to "bear fruit."
- If you get out of control, start growing way out apart from the Jesus-vine, God, the gardener, is going to cut you back so you'll be closer and bear more fruit.

So, God, get out your pruning shears. We're ready!

## Do That Little Thing: SHOUT-OUT

Get yourself a bunch of grapes (or some other fruit). In a group of people you love and trust, give each person a grape or other piece of fruit and say, "Just a little treat for you." If anyone asks why, tell them it's a God-thing. If they want to know more, share how God's pruning you, bringing you closer to the true vine. If nobody asks, at least you've shared some of God's fruit, and no gift is ever wasted.

## God, The Forgiver

> Praise the Lord, O my soul, and forget not all his benefits —
> who forgives all your sins and heals all your diseases, who
> redeems your life from the pit and crowns you with love
> and compassion.
>
> Psalm 103:2–4

Have you ever heard grown-ups talk about a job with benefits? They're referring to having health insurance and a retirement plan and a paid vacation (now that last part you can relate to, right?). Benefits are all the goodies a person gets in addition to a regular paycheck for doing a job.

Benefits are great, so it would only make sense that believing in God has benefits too. The psalm at the top of the page lists them. God:

- forgives you when you mess up.
- heals you when you're sick, inside or out.
- brings you out of the funky moods you fall into.
- gives you all the love and compassion you need.

This week we're going to look into that first benefit: forgiveness. And we're not talking just about second chances, but about that deep-down reassurance that you're okay with God. That benefit is even better than a vacation.

# Sunday

Who is this who even forgives sins?

Luke 7:49

The people asking that question were teachers of the Jewish law. They knew that only God could forgive someone, and they were shocked that Jesus was claiming to be God.

Well, yeah.

This whole conversation came about because some guys brought a man to Jesus who was paralyzed. There were so many people gathered in Peter's house where Jesus was staying they couldn't get in to see him, so they made an opening in the clay roof and lowered him in through that. They were determined! They wouldn't have gone to all that trouble if they hadn't truly believed Jesus could heal their friend.

And this man needed healing in a major way. But first, Jesus said, "Son, your sins are forgiven" (Mark 2:5). He was telling him that it's more important to be right with God than to be able to walk. Even if he hadn't gotten the man to his feet again, Jesus changed his life by showing him that God wipes away all memory of past ugliness and wrong-doing and gives a fresh new start. Then Jesus gave him a bonus and said, "Get up, take your mat and go home" (verse 11), and the man walked out "in full view of them all" (verse 12).

The lesson? The most important thing God does is forgive us. Everything else is just dessert.

## Do That Little Thing: QUIZ

Have you ever:

____ talked about another girl behind her back?
____ yelled at one of your siblings?
____ talked back to one of your parents?
____ been tempted to cheat (or maybe even given in to that temptation)?
____ wished somebody mean would trip or drop her backpack in a puddle?

If you checked off any of those, here's good news: you've been forgiven. Pick up your "mat" and start walking, back to being the good person you are.

# Monday

Forgive us our sins.

Luke 11:4

In yesterday's story, we saw Jesus forgive when people weren't even asking for it. Now we get the next step: knowing that you need forgiveness and asking God for it.

Why? If God already knows you need to be forgiven, why even say it?

Think about when you've done something you shouldn't have and realized it maybe before anyone else did. Did you go to the person and tell her? If so, was that person kind of impressed that you would be mature enough to come forward and try to make things right? Want to know a secret? A lot of the time, adults already know what you've done, and they wait for you to come to them so that *you* can show that you're growing up.

It's the same with God, only better. God knows every not-so-good thing you do. He just loves it when *you* know it, too, and realize you need his help. Asking for forgiveness brings you closer to him. That's why he's the Great Forgiver.

## Do That Little Thing: FIND OUT

Ask some God-lovers that you look up to how they confess their sins to God. Write down the things you find out, or just remember them. Then try one. Feel God smile.

# Tuesday

God did not send his Son into the world to condemn the world, but to save the world through him.

John 3:17

Have you ever watched a funny TV show or movie in which a policeman was having WAY too much fun catching people breaking the law and dragging them into jail?

Maybe you have even taken a certain amount of pleasure in telling on somebody you didn't like—just to see that person get in big trouble. Even just watching the mean girl go down can bring an inner smile.

God doesn't operate that way. He doesn't get joy out of busting his children. It isn't Jesus' job to walk around pointing the finger at us and telling us we're NOT going to spend all of eternity with God if we don't shape up. He came to *save*, not to rub our faces in how rotten and disobedient and guilty we are. We do enough of that to each other!

That's a God you can feel safe talking to honestly, telling your sins to, and asking for forgiveness. You aren't going to hear: "What in the world were you thinking? What a moron!" You are going to know: "I forgive you. Now, let's start over."

## Do That Little Thing: JUST THINK

Think of someone you know who seems to love being critical, pointing out other people's faults. Tell yourself, out loud if you have to: "That is not how God is." Now think of someone who is always encouraging, always helping people become better. Tell yourself, out loud if you want: "That is how God is, only better." Then go thank that person.

# Wednesday

"Neither do I condemn you," Jesus declared. "Go now and leave your life of sin."

John 8:11

Wow. A *life* of sin. It's one thing to make a mistake once in a while, even once a day—but to live a whole life around a bad thing, yikes.

That's the way it was with a woman some bigwigs brought to Jesus. She'd been caught doing something very wrong, which she had evidently been doing repeatedly for some time. Under the law of Moses, she should have been stoned to death.

Mind you, the teachers and Pharisees didn't really care whether the woman was punished. They were just trying to trap Jesus, because he'd been talking about forgiveness and love instead of law. If he said to let her go, he'd be going against the law. If he said to go ahead and stone her, he'd be going against what he'd been teaching. They thought they were so clever.

Jesus turned that around on them. He said, "If any of you is without sin, let him be the first to throw a stone at her." What could they do? If anybody hurled a rock at her, that person would be saying, "I'm as perfect as God."

Is it any surprise that they all dropped their stones and went away pouting? And then Jesus forgave the lady and told her to leave her life of sin and start over. When God forgives, he takes away the sin. He expects that we won't go out looking for it again. Forgiveness is a gift. We must use it well.

## Do That Little Thing: GOD? CAN WE TALK?

Talk to God about anything that you seem to keep doing wrong over and over, again and again. Whether it's arguing with your mom even when you've promised not to, or only doing your homework halfway even though your teacher has given you multiple chances — take it to God and ask him to forgive this pattern you've formed. And then ask him to help you leave it, for always. He will. That's just the way he is.

# Thursday

*Father, forgive them, for they do not know what they are doing.*
Luke 23:34

It's not hard to forgive the little things. Like when your best friend tells you that you have a booger coming out of your nose, right in front of a bunch of boys. It makes you mad for a while, but you can forgive and even forget and move on.

But what about those times when somebody does something really major to you or to someone you love? A careless driver hits your dog with his car. A group of girls makes your life miserable at school. It's really hard to say, "I forgive you. I don't wish you would fall down and break your face."

It's hard because you're human. Fortunately, God isn't. He forgives even the worst sins.

And it has never been worse than people nailing Jesus to a cross and letting him die there in pain and shame. Doing that to the Son of God—it's just hard to imagine God forgiving that.

Jesus looked down at the people who had spit on him and beaten him up and said, "Father, forgive them. They do not know what they are doing." It wasn't that they didn't realize they were hurting him. They just didn't know he was really God. That's how God forgives even the worst—because he understands us. Isn't that the best?

## Do That Little Thing: LISTEN UP!

Whisper to God the worst thing you have ever done. It doesn't matter if nobody else thinks it's particularly horrible — it matters to you. Then let it go and listen. Somewhere, sometime, somehow, you will know that God forgives. He just does, because he's God.

# Friday

It is not the healthy who need a doctor, but the sick ... I have not come to call the righteous, but sinners.

Matthew 9:12-13

Jesus didn't always hang out with the best people. He chose to have supper with "tax collectors and sinners," which today would be like going to a local bar and sitting next to the loan sharks and drunks. The teachers of the law would never be around people like that.

But Jesus told them that those were the very people he *should* be hanging out with. They were only going to accept God's forgiveness if they knew they were truly loved. Jesus had to get in there and eat with them and tell them jokes and ask them questions about their wives and kids. Once they knew him, they'd realize that he was telling them the truth. They would trust that God forgives.

Did they deserve all that attention? Not if we human beings have anything to do with it. But God doesn't forgive us because we deserve to be forgiven. He forgives us because he loves us and wants us to have better lives. So he gets in there and finds us in the middle of our lying and our cheating and our hissy fits, and says, "Listen to me. I love you, and I want to forgive you. How about it?"

How about it, indeed.

## Do That Little Thing: YOU CAN *SO* DO THIS!

Pick out that one person you know who is not, shall we say, the "best." She might be the girl who cusses her head off on the school bus. Or the player on the other soccer team who cheats and always gets away with it. The next chance you get, just smile at that person — a forgiving, loving smile. Then see what happens.

# Saturday

I tell you, her many sins have been forgiven — for she loved much.

Luke 7:47

Jesus really must have been a delightful person to be with—even the Pharisees invited him over for dinner. One night when he was at one of their houses, a woman heard that he was there and basically crashed the party.

She had lived a "sinful life." Can't you just imagine the Pharisees looking down their noses at her and feeling all superior? They probably didn't notice that she was bawling her eyes out. What they did see was that she brought in a jar of perfume and knelt behind Jesus. While he was eating, not disturbing him at all, she wet his feet with her tears and wiped them with her hair. Her *hair*, okay? And then she kissed his feet and poured perfume on them.

Jesus had probably been walking around in sandals all day, on dusty, unpaved streets where animals pooped and people dumped their garbage. And there she was, getting down and dirty with her own hair.

The host of the party saw it as a case of Jesus not knowing what kind of woman she was. Jesus saw it as a chance to show that the people who have totally messed up, repented, and been forgiven really know what kind of gift they have received, and they are going to spend the rest of their lives thanking God and serving him. Even if it means using their tears and their kisses—and their hair.

## Do That Little Thing: SHOUT-OUT

Find a grown-up you trust and tell that person about the big-time mess-up you named on Thursday. Then tell that person how grateful you are that God has forgiven you. You might even want to celebrate together. Chocolate is as good as perfume!

## Dr. God, the Great Healer

> Jesus went through all the towns and villages, teaching in their synagogues, preaching the good news of the kingdom and healing every disease and sickness. When he saw the crowds, he had compassion on them, because they were harassed and helpless.
>
> Matthew 9:35–36

You talk about busy—in just two chapters of Matthew (chapters 8 and 9), Jesus healed:

- a centurion's servant.
- Peter's mother-in-law.
- a whole crew of demon-possessed people.
- a paralyzed guy.
- a little girl who had already been declared dead.
- a woman who had been bleeding for twelve years.
- two blind men.
- a man who couldn't talk.

And that was just the beginning. Obviously healing is a huge part of who God is. Yet we all know good people who pray to God everyday and try to live godly lives, but who are still sick or blind or hopeless. What's that about?

Jesus showed us. Let's find out this week as we look at God, our Great Healer. Be ready for some healing yourself.

# Sunday

"Be quiet!" said Jesus sternly. "Come out of him!"

Mark 1:25

Jesus was commanding an evil spirit. Hmmm. That sounds kind of freaky, doesn't it?

Evil spirits can be pretty sneaky, and you can see them without realizing what they are. A person who gets hooked on drugs or alcohol is affected by the evil force of addiction. People in the news who "go crazy" and hurt others experience evil. A person doesn't have to be "possessed" to be subjected to the evil in the world.

Check out what happened with the possessed man. Suddenly this poor, raging guy stood up in the middle of the synagogue (the Jewish church) and yelled out to Jesus, "Have you come to destroy us? I know who you are—the Holy One of God!" Even evil itself knows who God is and is afraid of him. All Jesus had to do was say, sternly, "Be quiet! Come out of him!" and the evil spirit left. The man who was possessed could go on and live happily.

What does that mean for you and the evil you face every day? Know what's evil and stay away from it if you can. Know, though, that God is bigger than evil, and you can call on God to destroy it. It's the first step in living a healed, healthy life. And it's a step you'll take again and again.

## Do That Little Thing: QUIZ

Check off the things below that you would like to see God destroy (the evil, not the people who do it!).

\_\_\_\_ kids being mean to each other
\_\_\_\_ anybody lying or gossiping or spreading rumors
\_\_\_\_ people offering kids drugs or alcohol
\_\_\_\_ folks being cruel to animals

Knowing that God is more powerful than any of the ones you've checked off, pray that he will say, "Come out of him/her." It may not change things overnight, but it's a start.

# Monday

Filled with compassion, Jesus reached out his hand and
touched the man. "I am willing," he said. "Be clean!"

Mark 1:41

The man that Jesus touched in the verse above had leprosy, an
incurable disease that attacks the skin and the nerves. The leper
develops sores and white scaly scabs. Eventually he or she will be
deformed and maybe even lose arms or legs. It is so contagious that
people wth leprosy in Bible days were made to live far outside the
city. According to the Law of Moses, if anybody touched a leper,
that person was also considered unclean before God.

No wonder the man begged Jesus to make him clean again. Now
here's the thing about Jesus — about our God — that is the *best*. He
didn't stand across the road from him and holler, "Be clean!" He
*touched* him. He could have gotten leprosy himself and been considered unclean. He could have been run out of town because he broke
the law. But he touched the man, and he was cured.

Jesus told the man not to spread it all over town but instead to go
to the priests and offer a thanksgiving. That was part of the law that
Jesus knew was good. It was a way to show that the cure was real.

But the guy was way too excited and told everyone he met. Then
everybody who had a hangnail wanted Jesus to heal them. That
wasn't all he was there for, but he just couldn't help healing the
people who came to him. God loves us and wants us to be clean.
Makes you want to reach out your hand to him, doesn't it?

## Do That Little Thing: FIND OUT

Ask some God-loving grown-ups if they have ever been healed by
God. Be sure they know you don't mean just in big ways — it doesn't
have to be from cancer or a coma. As we know from the Bible,
there's nothing like a story to convince us that God is there, healing,
all the time.

# Tuesday

> When Jesus saw their faith, he said to the paralytic, "Son, your sins are forgiven."
>
> Mark 2:5

You might remember this story from last week. A man couldn't walk—he might even have been more paralyzed than that, we don't know for sure—and his friends lowered him through Peter's roof so he could be healed by Jesus. By forgiving the man's sins first, Jesus showed that it's more important for our spirits to be healed than our bodies.

That sounds like something we SHOULD say. But if you've just closed your thumb in the car door, do you call out, "God, please forgive me!"?

It's very much okay to want to be relieved of pain and scary doctors. Go ahead and pray for that kind of healing, because God wants to hear that from you. Just don't forget to ask for forgiveness too. Carrying around guilt can make you sick in another way that makes you feel just as bad. Would you rather be in bed with a sore throat, a popsicle, and a mom waiting on you hand and foot, or walk around knowing you've done something wrong and any minute now someone is going to find out? Just something to think about.

## Do That Little Thing: JUST THINK

Imagine these two situations. Think about how you felt. Those feelings will tell you a lot about our healing God.

- What was it like the last time you recovered from being sick or hurt? Remember the day you got your cast off that broken arm or the morning you woke up and didn't have that earache any more? How was it to feel good again? That was God at work.
- What was it like the last time you got something off your chest and were forgiven? Remember the moment you confessed to your mom that you lied to her or the night you cried to God because you felt so bad about what you said to your sister? How did it feel to be forgiven? That was God at work.

# Wednesday

Which is lawful on the Sabbath: to do good or to do evil?

Mark 3:4

You probably know the commandment: "Remember the Sabbath day and keep it holy." To you that could mean "go to church on Sunday." In Jesus' day, the Pharisees made a much bigger deal out of it. You could only walk a certain distance on the Sabbath, and you couldn't carry anything bigger than a certain size. You couldn't do work of any kind. Healing somebody was definitely out.

That's what came up the day Jesus was in the synagogue and a man with a shriveled hand was there. Wouldn't that be a bummer, to have fingers you couldn't use and just have your hand hanging there like a bunch of raisins? And yet, it was the Sabbath, so the Pharisees were watching to see if Jesus would break the law so they could trap him.

Jesus used it as an opportunity to teach about God. He made Mr. Shriveled Hand stand up in front of everyone and said, "Which is lawful on the Sabbath: to do good or to do evil?"

Now who was in a trap? The Pharisees knew it would be evil to let this man continue to suffer when all Jesus had to do was say the word and he'd be healed. Being the cowards they were, they just didn't answer. And Jesus told the man to stretch out his hand, and just like that he was healed.

God set up the Sabbath as a day to rest and be filled in body and mind and spirit—not to be afraid we are going to break some itty-bitty law. Every day is a day for being made whole with God. So take that, Pharisees!

## Do That Little Thing: GOD? CAN WE TALK?

Ask God if you have any shriveled-up places he wants to work on in you. Maybe you spend more hours playing computer games than you do hanging out with other people. Could you need a little plumping up in the love department? Or perhaps you're upset with your mom, and you're not talking to her. Might it be that your willingness to communicate what you're feeling could use a boost? Talk it over with God. Then stretch that place out to him. You'll be restored, and you can go to work on it.

# Thursday

She thought, "If I just touch his clothes, I will be healed."

Mark 5:28

I don't want to bother God with that. He has all those really sick, hurting people to take care of."

Has that thought ever flickered through your mind? When you were nervous about a test you'd really studied for, or you wanted to heal fast from bronchitis so you could compete in the gymnastic tournament? Did you decide not to pray about it because it wasn't as bad as what your friend was going through, with her parents getting a divorce?

That may be how the lady felt in this story in Mark 5:25-34. She'd been bleeding for twelve years, which is probably longer than you've even been alive. She went to one doctor after another but none of them could help. Since she was bleeding, she was considered unclean, so nobody wanted to hang out with her, much less take care of her.

But she didn't think she was as bad off as the guy who got to Jesus before she did. His little daughter was dying. She had so much faith, though, that she figured if she could just touch a corner of Jesus' robe she'd be healed, which turned out to be true. Her bleeding stopped immediately.

The cool thing about God is that Jesus stopped and told her that her healing was going to last forever. We not only get better when we turn to God; we also know it's for real. Like the bleeding lady, we can go in peace.

## Do That Little Thing: LISTEN UP!

When you get quiet with God today, listen for things in your life that are healed for good. Think back to past issues you used to pray about all the time that you don't worry about any more. Are you way more brave about the lights being out than you used to be? Do you pitch fewer fits when you don't get your way? Sounds like you believed. God has been at work.

This kind can come out only by prayer.

Mark 9:29

Jesus didn't come just to heal, but to give the ability to be healers to others, which is why he taught his disciples and sent them out to cure the sick and cast out demons.

Can you even imagine being one of the people Jesus trusted to heal the way he did? What a rush, huh? You put your hands on people who were crippled or mentally confused and just like that, they can walk and think like everyone else. After you do that a few times, do you think you'd start to get pretty proud of your sweet self? That might be what happened with the disciples.

A man had brought his son to them because he was having foam-at-the-mouth seizures. The disciples couldn't drive out the spirit. Why couldn't they do it, even though Jesus had given them the power to heal? After Jesus drove out the spirit, he explained to the disciples that they had forgotten to pray, to call on God's power to do the healing. They didn't remember where their ability to heal came from.

Whenever we need healing or we want to help someone else get better, we need to call on God. If we have trouble believing that God's going to come through, we can do as the boy's father did and say, "Help me overcome my unbelief." God will do that. He alone can do anything.

## Do That Little Thing: YOU CAN *SO* DO THIS!

Think of someone you know who is suffering in some way. A sick relative? A friend who is going through a tough time? A classmate with a struggle that doesn't go away (maybe ADD or trouble learning to read)? Is there something you can do to relieve a little of the suffering? Send a card you've made? Give a hug or offer to do some chores? Help with a tough assignment? Before you take part in their healing, pray by calling on the power of God. If you have trouble accepting that he will be there, ask for some help with that unbelief too!

# Saturday

We also rejoice in our sufferings, because we know that suffering produces perseverance ... character ... and hope.

Romans 5:3–4

Everybody in the Gospels who went to Jesus to be healed was cured, on the spot. No wonder people followed him around and believed in him.

That still happens today. Someone with a terminal illness is prayed over and healed. A kid everybody thought would end up in jail gets turned around and becomes a missionary. We all praise God and know that he is good.

But then there are those other situations. The entire church prays that a beloved friend will be cured of cancer, and she dies. The pastor visits that kid in juvie hall every day, and he still robs a bank and goes to prison.

Why doesn't God heal everybody who turns to him?

Actually, he does. We just have to understand what the word "healing" means.

It's easy to confuse "healing" with "cured." When a person is cured, the physical problem goes away and doesn't come back. Healing means that a person is saved from suffering, even suffering of the soul. For example, there is no cure for a disease called diabetes. However, a diabetic person can experience healing when God helps him accept his condition and not be angry about it all the time. Anyone who goes to God with a sickness of body or spirit will be healed, will be able to live with some happiness. Not only that, but the suffering itself will make that person stronger and wiser. That's healing.

## Do That Little Thing: SHOUT-OUT

You know all those people you've been praying for this week? Who among them has been healed — either in body or spirit? Make a list. Then tell somebody — maybe even a lot of somebodies. Give God a shout-out for making things better, so his children can go in peace.

## God: The Savior Of The World

My soul finds rest in God alone; my salvation comes from him ... I will never be shaken.

Psalm 62:1−2

Have you ever been rescued?
Maybe you were in water that was too deep for you, and somebody had to haul you to the shallow end.

Or you got separated from your family at a theme park or mall, and somebody found them for you.

You've been "saved" plenty of times, and probably will be again and again for the rest of your life. Hopefully you'll never have to be pulled out of a burning building or given CPR, but if that happened, you'd definitely know the meaning of being saved.

Christians talk a lot about another kind of "saved"—when a person discovers that she believes that Jesus Christ is the Son of God, that what he came to teach is the way she wants to live, and that by believing that, her soul will never die. After this earthly life, she will spend the rest of time in heaven with God. That's called "salvation."

This week we'll look at God as the Savior, the only one who can give us that salvation. It might be like being reminded of that homework you forgot to do, or it could be like being swept up from that cliff you're about to fall from. Whatever it is, prepare to feel rescued.

# Sunday

I am bringing my righteousness near, it is not far away; and my salvation will not be delayed.

Isaiah 46:13

You remember Isaiah, don't you? The prophet God sent to talk to the people of Jerusalem when they were at their worst?

Seriously, those people were a mess. God said they were so stubborn that it was like the muscles in their necks were iron and their foreheads bronze. They absolutely refused to listen to God and obey him, which put them so far from him they were barely in the same universe.

And yet God still said, "I am going to save you. I'm going to bring peace and justice, and nobody can put you down any more."

"What's the deal?" you may ask. "They didn't deserve to be saved!"

That's just the point. God doesn't save us from our own bad behavior and stubborn thoughts and downright yuckiness because we deserve it. He saves us because he loves us and just wants us with him. All we have to do is trust him.

It's that simple.

The guy writing the psalm above was running from people who were seriously out to get him. He knew the only one who could save him, even if he died, was God. If he could trust that, surely we can too.

## Do That Little Thing: QUIZ

When you think of God saving you, what is the first thing that comes into your mind? You can check off one of these, or come up with your own.

\_\_\_\_ God doesn't let anything bad happen to me or my family.

\_\_\_\_ God rescues me when I get in trouble.

\_\_\_\_ God forgives me when I make a mistake — and he always will.

\_\_\_\_ No matter what happens in my life, I will spend all of time with God.

Hold onto your answer until tomorrow's "Do That Little Thing."

# Monday

The heavens will vanish like smoke, the earth will wear out like a garment and its inhabitants die like flies. But my salvation will last forever.

Isaiah 51:6

Something breaks — a favorite toy. Or something rips — your BEST jeans. Or something just falls apart — like a friendship that means everything to you.

You're heartbroken. And then some adult comes along and says, "Well, nothing lasts forever."

Don't you hate that? Maybe it's true. Maybe all toys and jeans and friends "vanish like smoke" sooner or later. But it sure doesn't help to hear it when you're missing those things! What you want is the assurance that there is *something* you can count on.

And there is. Even God says that the heavens will disappear and the earth will wear out and the people will drop like flies (not a happy thought!). But God will always be there, showing kindness, showing you the right way to go, forgiving you. You don't even have to worry about what happens after you die.

So how much does it really matter if your little brother colors in your Nancy Drew collection, or the popular clique decides you're not "in" this week? It hurts, and it's hard, but when the tears dry and the shouting stops, there's God saying, "Here I am. Let's move on together."

## Do That Little Thing: FIND OUT

Take your quiz from yesterday's "Do That Little Thing" to an adult God-lover and ask him or her to look at your answer. Does she think you understand what being saved by God means? Is there something she wants to add to your understanding? What you find out may bring you even closer to the God who wants so much to be your salvation.

# Tuesday

He has raised up a horn of salvation for us ... Salvation from our enemies and from the hand of all who hate us.

Luke 1:69, 71

Got any enemies? People who don't seem to want the best for you and wouldn't mind too much if the *worst* happened to you?

Most of us make an enemy or two along the way. We usually don't do it on purpose, but disagreements happen and people get their feelings hurt and get resentful or angry and before you know it, there's this hate thing going on. Half the time, the people involved can't even remember what started it—they only know they can't end it.

Having enemies can be scary. What's to keep that girl who despises you from spreading a rumor about you that isn't true, but could wreck your friendships? Who's to say that kid who has it in for you won't grab your poster—the one you worked so hard on for language arts—and ride his skateboard over it five or six times?

Actually, you can't be absolutely sure nothing like that is ever going to happen, but you can be sure that God will save you from being destroyed by it. The rumor may start, but God will work to make sure that it doesn't ruin your reputation. The poster may be a mess when you turn it in, but God can make certain that your teacher understands. You may have enemies, but they are never bigger than the God who saves.

## Do That Little Thing: JUST THINK

Take a few minutes to consider any enemies you may have. Think about these things:

- What happened to cause the bad feelings you have toward each other?
- What things have happened because you are enemies?
- How have those things made you feel?
- How did it change you?
- What might you be able to do to stop being enemies?
- How can you talk that over with God?

Just think about it. If it seems like a God-thing, take steps. God's there.

# Wednesday

Everyone who has left houses or brothers or sisters or father or mother or children or fields for my sake will receive a hundred times as much and will inherit eternal life.

Matthew 19:29

Yikes. Right now, the things listed in that verse are the most important parts of your life: your home, your family, your community (including, hello, your friends!!). And Jesus is asking you to give that up? Seriously?

This is one of the hardest things Jesus says, but one of the most important. Jesus is not asking you, a tween girl, to walk out on your family if they aren't Christians! He doesn't call tweens to pack their bags and leave home to go live with the homeless and work in soup kitchens. This time in your life is for growing in faith and becoming strong enough to do the work he will someday ask you to do. God wants you in the tender care of grown-ups who love you.

But understanding now that God comes first will help you make those choices in the future. Today, you may have some hard decisions to make. You might have to end a friendship over swearing or cheating or gossiping. If your family has to leave a church for spiritual reasons, you may have to develop a good attitude about leaving your friends behind. Things can happen that call for sacrifices from you, even now. But the good news is "you will receive a hundred times as much." Who knows what that will be? What we do know is that it will be worth it.

## Do That Little Thing: GOD? CAN WE TALK?

In your quiet time with God today, fill in this blank:

"God, I really, really hate it that I had to/have to give up _____ _____, because it isn't right and good."

Say it out loud to God. Pour it all out. See if you don't feel better about it. Don't be afraid to ask God to pour out whatever he has in mind to take its place. Open your arms and receive.

# Thursday

All mankind will see God's salvation.

Luke 3:6

Do you have a group of friends that you feel comfortable with? Maybe you girls all giggle over the same things and finish each other's sentences and never worry about who's going to be mad at whom. It can feel so cozy that when one of your friends brings an "outsider" to your lunch table you get a little anxious. What if things change?

Christians can get like that. We have our lovely churches where everybody knows everybody, and we all feel safe because we come from the same neighborhood. If a homeless person were to come in on a Sunday morning, the regulars would get all nervous and wonder what that smelly person thinks he's doing there.

Jesus made it clear that salvation is for absolutely everyone. We have to pray for everyone, especially people who don't seem to have a clue about God; treat everybody with respect, even the kids who don't do anything to earn it from you; show Christ to all people through your words and actions, most of all those who don't even know about him.

It's perfectly okay to have your special group of friends. It's totally God's will for churches to be like home and family. But he wants that for everybody, in this life and after. He expects us to help with that. Christianity is not a Private Club.

## Do That Little Thing: LISTEN UP!

When you get quiet with God today, listen for ideas for opening up the path to God to somebody who doesn't even seem to know there *is* a path. You might take a paper plate full of brownies (with your favorite Bible verse attached) to the grumpy old man across the street — you know, the one who always yells at you kids for riding your bikes on the sidewalk. Or maybe you could invite the lonely new girl to a Sunday school party with you. Just listen. The idea will come, and someone will see God's salvation.

> Because he himself suffered when he was tempted, he is able
> to help those who are being tempted.
>
> Hebrews 2:18

All this talk about God saving us now as well as later makes it sound like once you believe in Jesus Christ, your life is going to be Disney World. Have you noticed that it doesn't exactly work that way?

There you are, trying to be all good for God, and kids say you're a geek because you don't watch MTV, or your coach won't let you play because you can't come to a Sunday morning practice. That doesn't feel like salvation—that feels like suffering!

And then there's the temptation thing. You believe in our Lord and you vow to do the right thing—and then here comes the cool girl at the sleepover with her R-rated movie, wanting you to share her sleeping bag while you watch it. Up pops the opportunity to make an A+ on the test, if you'll just glance at the answer sheet the teacher left on her desk. *If I'm saved*, you may wonder, *why am I still tempted?*

Being tempted happens to all human beings, even to Jesus when he was in human form. He asked God not to make him die on the cross, but God helped him realize that dying was the only way to save us. That makes Jesus the perfect one to turn to when *you* get the urge to mess things up. That's how God saves you, by giving you Jesus to say, "Been there, but didn't do that. I can help you resist temptation just like I did." Now that's what you call a rescue.

## Do That Little Thing: YOU CAN *SO* DO THIS!

What is a temptation you're struggling to resist? Maybe you've given in to it, and you're trying to change, or you haven't quite gone there but, man, it's hard not to. Or perhaps there's just some temptation that you wish didn't exist so you didn't even have to deal with it. Write it here:

_____

_____

_____

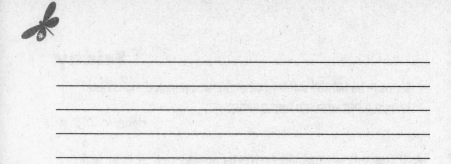

_____

_____

_____

_____

_____

_____

What is one thing you could do to make that un-God thing easier to say no to? Could you:

- avoid it?
- erase, delete, or destroy it?
- say no to it?
- hang up on it?
- put something good in its place?
- ask a grown-up to protect you from it?
- laugh at it?

Now take that step. It may be a little thing, but it's definitely a Jesus-thing.

# Saturday

Peace I leave with you; my peace I give you. I do not give to you as the world gives. Do not let your hearts be troubled and do not be afraid.

John 14:27

Okay, let's just admit that we've all thought about this: if salvation doesn't make life on earth perfect, or at least easy, and if you're still going to be faced with temptation, even though you're saved, and if people are going to give you a hard time about it ... uh, why, again, do you want it? There's the life-after-death thing, but you aren't really thinking about dying right now, when living is hard enough in this unpeaceful world where:

- kids fight on the playground.
- kids are mean to each other on the bus.
- people make rude remarks right in the classroom.
- boys make fun of girls.
- girls say boys are gross.
- teachers get sick of it and tell everybody to shut up.

And that's just in school. We haven't even started on what goes on at home, on the playing fields, even in church. But Jesus said to his disciples, who were asking the same question, "I give you peace as a gift to carry inside and the knowledge that nothing can separate you from me." Don't be afraid. It's always here, no matter what the world may throw at you.

## Do That Little Thing: SHOUT-OUT

Celebrate peace today! First, know that God's peace is in you, because Jesus put it there under all the troubles that make you frown and pout and stomp your feet. Then spread it around. Bring peace to as many people as you can today. Stop an argument before it starts. Break one up with a hug or a cookie or a simple, "Listen to each other!" Ease somebody's worry. Promise your mom she doesn't have to worry about you messing up whatever today because you're not going to. Wherever you bring peace, give God the credit. After all, we wouldn't have a moment of it without his promise. Not in this worry-wart world!

# PART II

# So Who Does God Say I Am?

Both the one who makes [people] holy and those who are made holy are of the same family. So Jesus is not ashamed to call them brothers [and sisters].

Hebrews 2:11

If you and the other kids living in your house have the same father, you are sisters and brothers, right? That's one of the closest relationships you can have — even though it might not seem like it right now when you're fighting over the front seat, the remote control, and the last Oreo. If one of you were in trouble, the other would be there in a heartbeat. Even if you're an only child, you've seen it happen in families. There's just a bond there.

As you've learned in Part I, all of us share another Father, our Father God. Has it occurred to you that since Jesus was and is the Son of God, he's our brother?

Brothers and sisters are not exactly alike (thank goodness, huh?), but they do share certain traits because they have the same parents. It's the same in God's family. He showed us Jesus and said, "This is who you are, too, in my eyes."

In the next thirteen weeks, you'll get to know Jesus so you can see who you truly are. Get ready for a look in the mirror like you've never had before!

# You Were Worth Creating

*You knit me together in my mother's womb.*

Psalm 139:13

What do you *have* to do?

There probably isn't enough room on a piece of paper to write down all the things you are required to do, right? (Not unless it's the size of a football field!) The have-to's of school alone are enough to give you writer's cramp, not to mention your home life, your activities, and the job of just plain being a kid.

If you asked your parents what they *have* to do, they'd probably groan and tell you they don't have time to list them all because they're too busy doing them.

While we're on the subject—what does God *have* to do?

Hello! Nothing—he's God! He doesn't *have* to keep the world going. He doesn't *have* to answer prayers. He doesn't have to do anything he doesn't want to because he's in charge.

Which means God doesn't *have* to keep making people. Nobody told him he had to create you. He did it because it was worth it to him. *You* were worth it to him—so worth it that he attended to every little fingernail and nose hair and piece of navel fuzz that grew on you before you were even born.

Look at that in the week to come. You're going to see that you are worth a whole lot more than you ever dreamed.

# Sunday

I praise you because I am fearfully and wonderfully made;
your works are wonderful, I know that full well.

Psalm 139:14

Does God make junk?
Seriously. Is there anything tacky about a box turtle? Anything fake about a velvety red rose? Anything boring in a sunset over the water after a great day of swimming?

Since God created you, obviously you aren't junk either. In fact, you are, as David puts it in the Psalm for today, "fearfully and wonderfully made." Fearfully, by the way, doesn't mean Godzilla. It means "awesome"—you were made to be awesome. God knit you together that way, with love in every stitch. He thought of you, and you *became*.

You are the result of God's precious thought, which means several things for you:

- You are beautiful. Maybe not modeling agency beautiful, but gorgeous in your own way. Believe it.
- You have a responsibility to find your true beauty. That doesn't mean plastering on what everybody else says is "beauty." It's about discovering your best qualities.
- God wants you to show that beauty in everything you do. Just let what is beautiful within you shine to every person you meet.

Doing that involves a journey. It's the one God wants you to take. It's the reason he made you—fearfully and wonderfully.

## Do That Little Thing: QUIZ

Start your journey by seeing where you are right now. Put a check next to EACH statement below that you believe about yourself.

\_\_\_\_ I'm fat

\_\_\_\_ I'm ugly

\_\_\_\_ I'm too tall (or short)

\_\_\_\_ I don't like this one thing about me

\_\_\_\_ I want to look like a movie star

\_\_\_\_ When people say I'm pretty, I don't believe them.

Count the number of checks you have and write the number here: \_\_\_\_. We'll look at that more this week.

# Monday

> You [God] created my inmost being... all the days ordained for me were written in your book before one of them came to be.
>
> Psalm 139:13, 16

Have you ever known identical twins? At first it was probably hard to tell which one was which, until you got to know them. Then it was like, duh, anybody could tell them apart. One was super-quiet, the other would talk your ear off. One could run like a track star, the other could always be found curled up with a copy of *Anne of Green Gables*. Two people might look exactly alike, but each one is totally different on the inside.

So not only were you worth creating on the outside in all your one-of-a-kindness — you were custom-designed, tailor-made, hand-crafted on the inside too. That's because you were set up for a purpose nobody else has. Doesn't it make sense that God gave you the right personality to carry it out? And that personality is different from anyone else you might want to copy. Why miss out on what God has in store for you while you're trying to get in on his plan for somebody else? Your plans are the best — for YOU — and so is your personality. You're so worth it.

## Do That Little Thing: FIND OUT

Do this "quiz" with some God-loving adult friends. It's just a crazy-fun way to see how different — and how worthwhile — every God-child is on the inside.

If I were a car, I'd be a

\_\_\_\_ cherry-red Camaro
\_\_\_\_ yellow pickup truck
\_\_\_\_ silver Lexus
\_\_\_\_ white SUV

# Tuesday

God is greater than our hearts, and he knows everything.

1 John 3:20

You are so sweet."

"Isn't it wonderful that you come to church every Sunday with your mama and daddy?"

"I'd just like to bundle you up and take you home!"

Have you ever received comments like that from the lovely white-haired ladies at your church — and thought, "What is she, blind? That can't be me she's talking about."

You're the only one who knows what's really going on inside your head, so you're the only one who knows it isn't always sweet and wonderful. You're the only one, that is, except God.

That would be a scary thought, except that the God who created you knows you even better than you know you. He understands you don't always think "sweet" thoughts, because other people are not always sweet to you. He gets why it's hard for you to sit through church and be polite and part with a tenth of your allowance. And yet to him, you're still worth it.

Makes you believe that little white-haired lady, doesn't it?

## Do That Little Thing: JUST THINK

Imagine what it would be like if someone else could tell what you were thinking all the time. That would be so embarrassing! Now think about God actually knowing (because he does) and loving every thought you have — even the ugly ones, because they're there for a reason. Picture him nodding. Picture him reaching out to change those reasons. It's suitable for framing in your mind.

# Wednesday

Woe to you when all men speak well of you, for that is how their fathers treated the false prophets.

Luke 6:26

How about a round of "Have You Ever?" Have you ever:

- told a lie so you'd fit in or wouldn't feel like a weirdo?
- worn an outfit like everybody else had and felt totally self-conscious the entire time?
- been at a party where you felt like an alien?
- not been able to think of anything to say when somebody you really wanted to be friends with started talking to you?
- snubbed somebody you liked because you were with girls who probably wouldn't accept her?
- pretended to be fine when you weren't, so nobody would know what you were really feeling?
- not raised your hand in class, even when you knew the answer, because other kids might think you were a know-it-all or not cool?

We've all done things like that because we're not totally sure we're "worth it" when we're just being real. Here's the deal: you were worth creating, even if somebody else doesn't think so. So drive right through the roadblocks that keep you from being the real you, things like:

- thinking you have to be perfect.
- thinking your true self isn't good enough.
- thinking your true self is way too much.
- thinking you won't be able to keep up if you live honestly.

You are perfectly you — good enough, unique enough, you enough. God wouldn't have made you any other way.

## Do That Little Thing: GOD? CAN WE TALK?

Set up a book for each of your roadblocks so that they're standing like walls. Then ask God to knock them down. Just blow them out of the way so you can believe that you are worthy just as you were made. When you feel like that's happening, push them over yourself, until for now there's nothing standing between you and the freedom to be you.

# Thursday

*Everyone who exalts himself will be humbled.*

Luke 18:14

With all this "I was worth creating," going on, this is a good time to stop and look at what happens when we fall into the "I was more worth creating than *she* was" trap.

None of us is above it. It might come out something like, "Well, I may not be as pretty as she is, but I'm WAY smarter." It doesn't take a brain surgeon to figure out that's just a way to make yourself feel better when some drop-dead gorgeous girl walks in and everybody goes, "Ahh!" and you go, "I feel pretty ugly right now." But if it gets to be a habit, you actually start believing that where it really counts, you're a far better person.

Jesus called the Pharisees on that kind of thinking. He told a story about a Pharisee who prayed, "Thank you that I'm not a loser like other people. I do everything right," and a tax collector who prayed, "God, have mercy on me, a sinner." God, Jesus said, would look much more kindly on the second man, who was honest about himself.

You don't need to beat your chest like that guy did, but do look at yourself as you really are. Both the good stuff and the stuff that still needs work are worthy before God.

## Do That Little Thing: LISTEN UP!

It can be confusing, this who-am-I thing. Just get quiet and let God tell you. Every time one of your good qualities comes to mind, thank God that's you. When the guilt bubbles up, ask God to help you work on that. Most of all, just sit with him awhile, and simply be.

# Friday

It is not good for the man to be alone. I will make a helper suitable for him.

Genesis 2:18

Do you totally love being a girl?

Painting your toenails, buying an Easter outfit, giggling until you cry at a sleepover—that can all make girl-ness the best thing ever.

Of course, if you aren't into girly-girl stuff, taking care of your hair, picking out school clothes, making cutesy crafts in Sunday school can be such a waste of time when you'd rather be riding your bike, practicing your free throw, or writing a fabulous short story.

Maybe you love sports and there aren't as many opportunities for you to be on teams as there are for boys. Perhaps you'd like to do boy things with your dad, but you aren't included when he and your brother go off to fish or eat hot dogs at baseball games.

But God wanted you to be a girl. He actually made women special—because basically men couldn't make it without us. What happens when your mom isn't there at supper time? The average dad orders a pizza.

Now, that does NOT mean that ALL you were made to be is a helper for some guy. You were created with certain qualities only a woman has. For instance, scientific evidence shows that women can do more than one thing at a time better than men, and that we can make decisions faster. Whatever being a girl means to you, celebrate it. God needs you—and so do men!

## Do That Little Thing: YOU CAN SO DO THIS!

Today, do one thing only a girl like YOU can do. Some suggestions:

- paint your dad's toenails (he doesn't know how to do that himself)
- rock a baby (boys usually can't sit still long enough for this job)
- cheer up a friend by giggling with her (males do not have the giggle gift)
- make an old person smile by skipping around (most boys never quite master the art of good skipping)

Bring joy, just because you are a girl.

# Saturday

He created them male and female and blessed them.

Genesis 5:2

When somebody sneezes, you say, "God bless you." When you sit down to eat a meal, someone asks the blessing. If you live in the South, whenever anybody does anything nice, somebody else is sure to say, "Bless your heart."

We bless all over the place, most of the time without even thinking about it. But when someone is blessed by God, that means:

- she will grow to be fabulous.
- she can influence others in major ways.
- people will listen to her.
- she has a responsibility to care for the world and for the life she's been given.

From the beginning, God has blessed each newborn baby in that way. You, then, can grow and be even more awesome than you are now. You can show God to other people so their lives can be amazing too. You can do that because you know it's your job. You can, because you are blessed.

Not everybody takes that blessing seriously. Some people don't even know about it. But it's who you are in God's eyes.

So go, Blessed One. Grow and be fabulous. Change lives. Speak out. Care for the world. It's what you were made to do.

## Do That Little Thing: SHOUT-OUT

Go back to the quiz you took under "Do That Little Thing" on Sunday. This time, instead of putting a check, put a star next to each statement you think is true for you. If you have even one less star than you had checks, tell somebody about it. Share that God has helped you accept that you were worth creating, that you were made to be beautiful, that you already are a "star."

# You Are One of a Kind

From heaven the Lord looks down and sees all mankind;
from his dwelling place he watches all who live on earth —
he who forms the hearts of all, who considers everything
they do.

Psalm 33:13–15

Think about the biggest crowd you've been in lately. The line at the movies when the latest Pixar film opened. The mob at the mall right before Christmas. The halls at school when the last bell rings. You may have felt really small, squished in with all those bodies.

Now think about all the crowds in all the places of the world. It's too many people to imagine. In fact, it's like trying to picture how many grains of sand there are on just one beach. Boggles the mind, doesn't it?

Put this thought next to that one: every single one of those people is different.

Seriously. If you've ever watched a TV crime show, you know that each individual has his or her own unique fingerprints that are different from every other person's. Each man, woman, and child carries DNA that is like no one else's. There are even voice prints — because no two people speak exactly the same way.

You, then, are one of a kind. This week you'll have a chance to explore and love that fact. There is nothing more fun than discovering the You-nique person God created you to be. Get ready to grin!

# Sunday

Does the clay say to the potter, "What are you making?"

Isaiah 45:9

Imagine you're making a snake out of Play-Doh, and it suddenly looks up at you, opens its big clay mouth, and says, "What do you think you're doing? I don't want to be a snake. I want to be an elephant."

Obviously that isn't going to happen, which is exactly the point of this verse. God is like a Great Potter, creating each person just the way he wants him or her to be. As his creations, we don't get to say, "But I don't want to be who you're making me. I want to be something else!"

But we try it anyway. Have you ever heard yourself say ...

- I wish I were more _____
- I wish I weren't so _____
- If I were more like _____, things would be better.

The first step in discovering your one-of-a-kind-ness is accepting that you are made by God to be exactly who God wants you to be. You can be the best you, but you can't be somebody else. Try, and you'll only feel like you're not good enough.

Right now, you don't know everything that makes you uniquely you because it takes most of a lifetime to figure it out—which is why life is so interesting and fun. But one thing you can know: God decided who you are and will be, and God will reveal that plan to you—one wad of clay at a time.

## Do That Little Thing: QUIZ

Write one thing about each of these areas that makes you different from everybody you know.

My face _____

My body _____

My voice _____

My favorite thing _____

My pet peeve _____

Add anything else you think of as the week goes on. We'll look at this list in the days ahead.

# Monday

Sixty queens there may be ... but my dove, my perfect one, is
unique.

Song of Songs 6:8–9

"Okay," you may be thinking. "Is that some kind of mushy love poem? EWWW."

Song of Songs in the Bible *is* a love song, but not like the kind you hear on the radio about a guy and a girl who slobber all over each other. This one is about God and the ones he loves—all his children. When it goes on about, "How beautiful you are, my darling! Oh, how beautiful! Your eyes are doves" (Song of Songs 1:15), God is talking about YOU.

To him you are beautiful. And not just beauty-pageant pretty, but unique. Perfect.

Before you go off with, "But I have this funky nose, this wart on my thumb, this hyena laugh ..." remember that "perfect" is not how you measure up to what the world says is beautiful. Even the girls you see in teen magazines with no-pimple skin and no-split-ends hair don't really look like their pictures; their photos are perfected by computers.

God's "perfect" means being exactly who you were made to be. You can't compare yourself to other people to decide if you are perfect, because God has a different plan, a different perfect, for them. If you go to see a movie that's meant to be sad, do you complain because it didn't make you laugh? If you get a kitten, do you whine because it doesn't bark? The second step in your search for your one-of-a-kind-ness is to take it easy on yourself. You, Perfect One, are unique.

## Do That Little Thing: FIND OUT

Ask three adults you trust what they think makes you unique. Write down their answers on that list you're keeping. Savor them, the way you would a double ice-cream cone. While you're at it, you might tell those grown-up people what makes THEM special. We all need to hear that now and then.

# Tuesday

If I want him to remain alive until I return, what is that to you?
You must follow me.

John 21:22

Have you noticed some girls are considered "cooler" than others? Because the cool girls get a lot of attention, almost everybody wants to be like them. Then the comparing starts:

- "Her hair is blonder (or darker) than mine."
- "My clothes aren't as cute as hers."
- "She doesn't have to wear stupid braces (or glasses) like I do."

You might try to change yourself to be more like the cool girls. Or you may get an attitude about a cool girl because she makes you feel so bad about yourself. Or — if you happen to *be* a cool girl — you may work overtime trying to *stay* cool. None of that helps you find out what makes *you* cool. It just makes you unhappy or resentful, and that isn't who anybody really is.

There is to be no comparing in God's kingdom. Just before Jesus left the disciples to go back up to heaven, he told Peter his job was going to be to take care of the "lost sheep," those people who need to hear the message of Jesus and be saved. Peter at once pointed to John, another disciple, and said, "What about him?" Jesus gave him the answer he wants us to remember: "What is that to you? You must follow me." Step three: enough with the comparing. Follow, and find out what *your* job is.

## Do That Little Thing: JUST THINK

Put a check next to the statement you think God would make:

____ a. "Oops. I didn't make little Megan as precious as baby Brittany. I hate it when that happens."

____ b. "Some of my children are more perfect than others, but I love them all the same."

____ c. "Every child I make is perfect in my eyes. I love that."

If you didn't answer *c*, girl — go back and read today's entry again!

Love your neighbor as yourself.

Matthew 22:39

Does that say you're supposed to love yourself?
Isn't that conceited?
Selfish?
Stuck up?

Sure, if you go around saying, "I am so in love with myself I can't think about anything else." Obviously, God's saying "Love other people in the same way you love yourself. Take care of them. Make them happy."

See, God loves what God has made: palm trees, snow leopards, mosquitoes (yeah, even those pesky little critters), and you. God loves you, so how can you do any less than love you too? It's hard, though, with the world telling you to pick yourself apart all the time. Are your clothes hip? Is your slang up-to-date? Are you friendly enough, funny enough, smart enough? It has to be done, though, because basically, if you don't love yourself, you're not going to be very good at loving other people.

Loving yourself doesn't mean you're conceited. It's a requirement! In fact, Jesus goes on to say that all the other commandments are based on this one and the one before it (Love God with everything you have). If you can't love God like that—and love yourself and other people the same way—you don't have a chance of obeying "honor your father and your mother" (Exodus 20:12) or "do not envy" or any of the rest of them. That could get to be a mess.

And if you hate who you are, you'll try to be something or someone else and grow false. You'll move away from your true, beautiful self. So go ahead and love you. You are, after all, one of a kind.

## Do That Little Thing: GOD? CAN WE TALK?

Get in there with God and hash out anything you don't like about yourself. Take him a list or just spew it all out. Then sit back and feel him loving you because of all that stuff. You do that too. Love it. Love you. It's required.

# Thursday

All these [gifts] are the work of one and the same Spirit, and he gives them to each one, just as he determines.

1 Corinthians 12:11

Do you know anybody who's considered "gifted?" You know—she sings like a rock star or whizzes through math problems like a genius. People say she has a "gift," and you wish you had one too.

But you do have a gift. Okay, so people notice when a three-year-old can play a Mozart piece on the piano, but they might not pick up on the fact that you can always make even the grumpiest person smile. But anything that you do naturally well is a gift God has given you because he wants you to use it.

In the early church, people argued about which spiritual gifts were the most valuable—wisdom, knowledge, faith, miraculous powers, prophecy, speaking in tongues. It would be like people in today's church bickering about whether it was worth more to God to teach Sunday school or sing in the choir.

Paul explained to them that (a) God gives each one of us a gift and (b) every gift comes from his Holy Spirit, so they're all equally important. Seriously, he asked them, are you going to look at God and say, "The job you gave me isn't as important as Susie Schmo's job so YOU, God, must have made a mistake?"

Whatever your gifts, they're from God and are therefore valuable. Even if no one else pays much attention to them, God does. He wants to see how you're going to use them. So hug your gifts and say, "Thanks, God."

## Do That Little Thing: LISTEN UP!

Listen to your memory voice. What are the nice things people have said about you, especially those you've heard over and over? Do they say you're funny? Thoughtful? Practically a pro at miniature golf? The best peanut-butter-and-jelly-sandwich maker in the family? They are your gifts, whispering to you, telling you just a little more about who you are. Add them to your list.

# **Friday**

Let your light shine before men, that they may see your good
deeds and praise your Father in heaven.

Matthew 5:16

On Christmas Day or your birthday, when you get a gift you
totally love, you:

> (a) use and admire it and tell people about it.
> (b) hide it under your bed.

Unless you're afraid somebody's going to steal it, you probably
answered (a). What is the point in having something very cool if you
don't keep it out where you can see it and play with it and share it?

When you say, "See what I got for Christmas!" people often ask,
"Who gave it to you?" You answer:

> (a) "My mom and dad (or whoever). Aren't they the best?"
> (b) "Oh, nobody. I gave it to myself."

Your answer is no doubt (a).

It's the same with the gifts God has given you that make you
uniquely yourself.

- No one can steal them from you. They are yours to keep.
- He wants you to use them and share them, not hide them.
- He hopes you will tell other people that he gave those gifts
  to you so they'll say, "Wow. Who is this God? I want to know
  him too."

Your gifts are the light the verse talks about. Let it shine, right
out there where everybody can see what makes you the special person you are. And when they notice, give God the credit. What a
cool way to show people who you are AND who God is.

## Do That Little Thing: YOU CAN *SO* DO THIS!

Look at that list you've been keeping since Sunday. Is there anything on there that you've been hiding? Maybe you're a really good singer but you've only been breaking into song in the bathtub instead of joining the kids' choir. Perhaps you're the only one in the family who can get Grandpa to talk about his boyhood mischief (which gets him out of his blues), but lately you've been playing video games when he comes over. Whatever gift you've "shoved under the bed," get it out today and use it in some small way. It will bring you another step closer to being totally you.

# Saturday

He calls his own sheep by name and leads them out.

John 10:3

For the first few days of school, you might wear a nametag until the teacher learns who everybody is. Don't you love it, though, the first time she calls you by your name, without having to look at your tag? She took the time to learn your name. It's cool.

The bigger the class, the longer it takes. And in middle school, when a teacher has more than one class, it could be a week or two. Think about God, with the billions of people on the earth he has to teach—not to mention all the ones who have lived before now. He knows every one of them by name. Not just "Shelby," "Meg," "Bethany." He knows middle names, last names, nicknames—without nametags or a seating chart.

Imagine God calling your name right out loud. If it feels so good when a human teacher knows who you are, how would it feel to hear your name coming out of that almighty mouth?

That's how important you are to God—enough for him to know your one-of-a-kind name and call you by it so he can lead you into the life he has planned for you—the life with your name on it.

Listen. He's calling.

## Do That Little Thing: SHOUT-OUT

God knows your name, and you know his. See how many times you can use it today — to praise him, to share him, to point to him — and most of all, to thank him for making you exactly who you are.

# WEEK 16

## You Come with a Plan

"I know the plans I have for you," declares the Lord, "plans to prosper you and not to harm you, plans to give you hope and a future."

Jeremiah 29:11

D o you think it would be way cool to be able to see into the future? To know whether you're going to go to college and where? To find out if you're going to get married and to what lucky guy? To get a glimpse of your kids, your career, your thirty-year-old face?

It might be kind of fun, if everything in your future were going to be happy, peaceful, and perfect. It wouldn't be a good deal to see the not-so-happy things that are bound to happen. Who wants to live in dread? God knows what he's doing by only letting us see what's happening in our lives right now, today, this moment. We couldn't handle more than that.

Still, the future can seem scary. What *are* you going to do when you grow up? Or for that matter, what are you going to do tomorrow if the teacher introduces a new concept you don't understand, or the other kids suddenly decide to make fun of you, or your nose starts running when you're giving your oral report? Yikes!

Not to worry. This week you're going to learn that whatever happens has already been taken care of, because God didn't just create you. He sent you here with a plan in place.

# Sunday

Before a word is on my tongue you know it completely, O Lord.
Psalm 139:4

What have you planned lately? Your birthday party? A sleepover with friends? A way to keep your little brother from reading your diary? To make sure it was going to work out, you had to have all the information beforehand. For a party, for instance, you needed to know how much money you had to spend, how many friends you could invite, and how much chaos your mom was willing to put up with.

God has a plan for your whole life, which means he has to know absolutely everything about you. Everything—like:

- what you can do without so much as a thought (your natural strengths).
- what you have to work at (your challenges).
- how you best express yourself.
- how you get along with people (and don't!).
- what scares you.
- what makes you totally jazzed.

There isn't anything about you that God doesn't know. Since God is the only one who knows you that well—even your parents don't know your inmost thoughts all the time, right?—only God can set up a life for you. In fact, it's already done: "All the days ordained for me were written in your book before one of them came to be" (Psalm 139:16).

Take a nice big breath and realize that Somebody knows you even better than you know yourself. That Somebody has a great life mapped out for you.

## Do That Little Thing: QUIZ

Write down or think of three things that nobody — or almost nobody — knows about you.

Examples:

- *I daydream about being an astronaut.*
- *I still like to watch "Sesame Street" when nobody's around.*
- *I have wondered if Adam and Eve had belly buttons.*

_____

_____

_____

_____

_____

_____

_____

_____

_____

_____

When you look at your list, remember that God already knows those things about you. And he loves you because of them.

# Monday

I know that you can do all things; no plan of yours can be thwarted.

Job 42:2

Have you ever made a plan, done all the work required to make it happen—and then it turned out to be a mess?

Who *hasn't* had that happen! There are so many things that can go wrong with any plan, and sometimes it seems like *all* of them do. That isn't always true, thankfully. And it's never true with God's plan.

"Wait a minute," you may be thinking. "A lot of bad stuff happens. Is that part of God's plan?"

That is a very tough question. When things that we consider to be bad happen, we only know that:

- people have the freedom to act as they will, so sometimes they'll try to mess up God's plan. That's when bad stuff happens.
- God's knows the WHOLE plan for the WHOLE world, and we don't. What we consider to be "bad" may be a necessary part of the BIG PLAN.
- God is always there to help us through the bad, hard things.
- If we listen to him and follow what we hear, nothing can thwart God's plan for US. Like it says in Isaiah 14:24: "The Lord Almighty has sworn, 'Surely, as I have planned, so it will be, and as I have purposed, so it will stand.'"

## Do That Little Thing: FIND OUT

Ask one of your God-loving grown-up friends when something happened to them that just didn't seem like it could be part of God's plan. Ask how they reacted, how they handled it, and what they learned. Best of all, see what's happened since then that might have changed their minds.

# Tuesday

The things you planned for us no one can recount to you; were
I to speak and tell of them, they would be too many to declare.

Psalm 40:5

Think about the last mystery movie you saw or book you read. Was there a place in it where you said, maybe even out loud, "Oh, I get it!" It was probably the moment when enough things had happened that you could look back and figure out what was going to come next.

Your life is kind of like a mystery—that at times you can look back at and see why certain things had to happen. Maybe:

- you didn't want to move from your old school, but in your new one you found a best friend you never would have met otherwise.
- you got sick and couldn't go to THE birthday party of the year, but you were home when your mom broke her ankle. What if you hadn't been? Who would have called 911?
- you didn't make the select soccer team, which meant you could go on vacation with your family to Mexico, where you got to play with some pro soccer players on the beach who let you score a goal. (We can dream, can't we?)

When it seems like none of your prayers are being answered and God couldn't possibly have a plan in the middle of the chaos of your life, take a few minutes to look back at what's happened so far. There might be tons of "Oh, I get it!" moments to declare.

## Do That Little Thing: JUST THINK

What are you struggling with right now? Maybe your best friend isn't treating you like a BFF, or your dad just doesn't get you any more. If you just stopped fighting it and asked God to let his Holy Spirit do some work in you, what do you think would happen? At the least, there might be one less disappointment, one less argument. With the Spirit involved, there will be a whole lot more that will surprise you — guaranteed.

# Wednesday

I am convinced that neither death nor life, neither angels nor demons... nor any powers... will be able to separate us from the love of God.

Romans 8:38-39

Everybody's different. You've noticed that, right? So each person's plan is obviously different from all others too. But there are some parts of God's vision that apply to all of us, and we already know what they are.

Part One is this: nothing will come between you and God. Once you've accepted that God IS your life, you can't take that away. It would be like trying to un-ring a bell. You can make bad choices, ignore your parents, pick the wrong friends, and God will still love you. Everybody else might give up on you, but God won't. You might even feel like God has forgotten your name, but he never will.

Can you do anything you want and get away with it? Uh, no. There are always consequences for breaking God's rules. He is a parent, after all. But those consequences do NOT include him telling you to get lost. He'll love you anyway and do everything possible to get you back on track.

So why not save yourself the trouble and do it God's way to begin with? It's a whole lot easier to get the plan and go with it if you follow what you know: God loves you and only wants good for you. Stick with him.

## Do That Little Thing: GOD? CAN WE TALK?

Go to God with a list of questions starting with "Why did THIS have to happen?" Read your list out loud. Even as you talk, you'll probably realize you already know some answers. If not, don't worry. In time, God will make sense out of everything, even if it's in the peace of just accepting.

# Thursday

It is God who has made us for this very purpose and has given us the Spirit as a deposit, guaranteeing what is to come.

2 Corinthians 5:5

Wouldn't it be the best if every time you took a test in school, you had a friend whispering the answers to you?

And how way cool would it be if whenever you had to confess something to your parents, that friend murmured the right words in your ear?

Oh—and would it not be totally awesome if the very minute you started to do something wrong, this friend froze you in place so you couldn't mess up?

The Holy Spirit is just such a friend. It's the Spirit that guides our thinking and gives us our words and influences our actions. Part Two of God's plan for everybody, including you, is that you don't have to figure out everything on your own.

The Spirit has already been working in you for some time. That day you almost laughed at the kid who stutters, and then you suddenly told everybody to leave him alone; that night you nearly lied to your mom about your report card, and then blurted out the truth; that morning you woke up deciding to get ready without being nagged and see what would happen are all evidence that God's Holy Spirit was working in you, showing you how great life can be if you just let him have his way with you.

Your part is to go with the Spirit when it moves you. You have two choices:

- struggle trying to figure out your own way.
- flow with a plan that's already laid out for you.

It's a no-brainer, don't you think?

## Do That Little Thing: **LISTEN UP!**

If you get really quiet, you will be able to hear God's love. Try it. Close your eyes and get still. What do you hear? Your little sister giggling somewhere? Your mom humming in the laundry room? A squirrel freaking out in a tree (as only a squirrel can)? The sounds of life are God speaking his love for us. See how many you can gather in your ears, in your heart.

# Friday

*Then make my joy complete by being like-minded, having the same love, being one in spirit and purpose.*

Philippians 2:2

Before you have a sleepover or a birthday party, do you daydream about what it'll be like? All your friends arriving with big ol' grins on their faces. Everybody loving the pizza-making and the oatmeal facials you've planned. The whole crew piled up like a litter of puppies in front of a movie. Every last person hugging you as she leaves and saying it was the best ever.

You probably do NOT envision half your guests arriving all grumpy and ready for a fight. Or girls whining that they're bored and going off into little groups to whisper about each other. Or friends telling you the party would have been a whole lot better if SHE hadn't been invited. Who would ever plan for that?

Certainly not God. When he planned out this party known as life, he did not arrange for his children to fuss and fight and get jealous and dis each other in the girls' bathroom. HIS plan is for us to get along.

That's impossible unless the people we're with are all focusing on God. Then you can't really fight about who God loves more, because he loves us all the same. You can't argue over what's right and wrong, because he's already told us. You can't get all jealous of each other because you're all going to get the prize — him. Doesn't that sound like a party you want to go to?

## Do That Little Thing: YOU CAN *SO* DO THIS!

Give a party for God. It can be just you and your best friend or even you and your mom, doing everything in honor of God. Bless the food. Dance to praise music. Drink milkshake toasts to all the great things God's done for you until you can't take another sip or you'll explode. There probably won't be one tiff or scowl. That will make God's joy complete.

# Saturday

He made known to us the mystery of his will ... to bring all things in heaven and on earth together under one head, even Christ.

Ephesians 1:9–10

You've probably been asked this question — probably by some grown-up who was trying to have a conversation with you and couldn't think of anything else to ask: What do you want to be when you grow up?

If you were five or six at the time, you probably had an answer all ready — firefighter, doctor, astronaut, rock star. And if asked the following week, you had a different answer — ballet dancer, zoo keeper, ice skater, depending on what you saw on TV in between.

These days it might be a little harder to discuss that. Who has time to think about what you'll be doing a bajillion years from now?

There's one specific thing you CAN know now, because it's what God has planned for each one of us. He wants every single one of us to belong to Jesus Christ. That's why he sent Jesus, and why Jesus appointed apostles to spread his message, and why Jesus will return when God has everybody gathered together. That's the way he wants it, and that's the way it will be.

So next time a grown-up asks what you're going to do with the rest of your life, you can tell her: I've already started. I'm a Christ-follower.

There's no mystery about that.

## Do That Little Thing: SHOUT-OUT

As a matter of fact, don't wait for someone to ask you about your future plans. Tell a person you trust what you've learned about GOD'S plan for you. Go ahead and say it: you are and always will be a Christ-follower. Whether you follow as a judge or a firefighter or a costume designer, that part will be a surprise. But this part you know for sure. Amen!

## You Are Worthy of Love, No Matter What!

> I have not come to call the righteous, but sinners.
>
> Matthew 9:13

I bet people would like me better if I ..."
How would you fill in that blank? If I:

- were funnier?
- had blonde hair?
- wore cooler clothes?

Whatever you might put in that space, the point is that you would put *something* there, because most of us think if we could just be a little more this or less that, we would be worthy of love. We get that crazy-wrong idea from things like TV commercials that tell us we'd be popular if we'd eat the right chips or use the correct mouthwash. We also get it from other kids who form "rules" for belonging to their group of friends. Like you're only accepted if you own a pink cell phone and have more clothes than the Gap. You sometimes even *think* that's what's going on when your parents say you're driving them nuts with your whining and your arguing and your picky eating.

Here's the deal: Love should never be something you have to earn. Love is a gift that you are already worthy of — just because God made you. The fact that he made you and cares for you is proof that you are worth loving. That's what this week is about, Loved One.

I praise you, Father, Lord of heaven and earth, because you have hidden these things from the wise and learned, and revealed them to little children.

Luke 10:21

One of the clearest ways God shows us that we are worthy of love without having to DO or BE anything is through Jesus. When our Lord picked his disciples, he wasn't like a team captain on the playground, calling out the names of the best players to be on his side. You know how that goes, especially if you're always the last one to be picked.

Jesus selected the most motley crew you could dream up — a big ol' fisherman, who was always losing his temper; a tax collector people couldn't stand (ask your parents about the IRS and you'll understand); a whole bunch of guys who had to have everything explained to them, like, twenty times.

In this verse, Jesus even says they're "little children," not all smart and educated, just open to learning, willing to obey, eager to please. Little kids don't try to be that way — they simply are. Jesus praised God for them. He praises God for you. And he reveals himself to you.

So don't worry. You've already been picked for the team. You don't have to stand there pretending you don't care while everybody else lines up behind the captains. You're in, and you always have been.

## Do That Little Thing: QUIZ

Write down three times when you haven't felt very loved:

When _____.

When _____.

When _____.

It was probably a bummer, but remember this — God was right there loving you through it all. And he still is.

# Monday

> Go out quickly into the streets and alleys of the town and bring in the poor, the crippled, the blind and the lame.
>
> Luke 14:21

Talk about not getting picked for the team—much less the birthday party, the sleepover, or the popular girls' table—the poor, the crippled, the blind, and the lame almost never get chosen. And not just them, but anybody who is "different" in any way.

Why do some people—usually the ones doing the "picking"—shun anybody who isn't like them? Why does that girl who decides who's in and who's out curl her lip at the girl with the scar from a cleft palate? Or laugh right in the face of the girl who can recite twenty of Emily Dickinson's poems from memory?

Sometimes it's because she's afraid. What if a cleft palate is contagious? What if kids start liking the poetry-spouting girl instead of her? What if her position as Queen is taken away from her? She thinks what you have and how many people follow you around like a litter of puppies make you who you are.

God doesn't operate that way. He shows us through Jesus that each of us is worthy of sitting down at a banquet with him, no matter what condition we're in. And this life we've been given *is* a banquet, with everything we need, including him sitting at the head of the table.

If you feel "different"—and everybody does from time to time, including the Queens—remember that you're loved not in spite of your differences, but because of them. God made you to be you, and he loves you that way. Doesn't it feel great?

## Do That Little Thing: FIND OUT

Ask some of your God-loving adult friends whether they ever felt "different" when they were your age. Can they remember being teased or left out? How did they handle it? Most important, how did they find love in the midst of it? (If you have to, assure them that God's love was always there. Sometimes even grown-ups forget that.)

# Tuesday

Let's have a feast and celebrate. For this son of mine was dead and is alive again; he was lost and is found.

Luke 15:23–24

The son in this Jesus-story really, really messed up. He got rebellious and asked for his share of his dad's money and took off, leaving his brother to do all his chores. He blew it partying and ended up in a pig sty wishing he had as much to eat as the hogs did. Then it occurred to him—duh—that the hired hands at his dad's house ate better than this, so he decided to go home and offer to work as a servant, even though that meant he basically couldn't look anybody in the eye ever again. You get the idea that this dude had really hit rock bottom.

But when he came home, it didn't matter to his father that he'd made the whole family look ridiculous. He was back, safe and sound. The father did what God does every time we realize we've made a mess of things and go to him. He threw a party, and assured the son that he had never stopped loving him.

As the father explained to the other brother—who was NOT pleased—when you feel like you've botched things up so badly you couldn't possibly be loved, that's when you most need to know that you're loved, that what matters is where you are right now, with your Father.

Nice, huh?

## Do That Little Thing: JUST THINK

Think about the last time you made a mistake that made you feel like you weren't so loveable. Maybe you were mean to your little brother, or you said something ugly about your best friend because you were jealous of her. Now think about the moment when you knew you were still loved. The instant your little brother climbed into your lap, or your best friend passed you a note that said, "I forgive you, moron." Stay with that feeling. That's the God-feeling.

# Wednesday

Let the little children come to me, and do not hinder them, for the kingdom of God belongs to such as these.

Luke 18:16

These days a kid basically has it made. You have a personal chauffeur (also known as Mom), chef (*also* known as Mom), maid (Mom again), and entertainer (Mom, Dad, and everybody else who doesn't want to hear you cry or whine). You have a ready-made audience for everything precious that you do, not to mention bodyguards who watch your every move and wouldn't let so much as a mosquito bite you if they could help it.

Back in Jesus' day, kids didn't get that much attention. They were taken care of, of course, but when adults were hanging out, kids better just stay quiet and out of the way. So when people brought their babies and toddlers to Jesus, the disciples got all freaked out and told them to back off. Jesus had more important things to do than hold their kids, right?

People were probably way shocked that Jesus said, "Bring those little ones to me. I want them here on my lap." He even said, "You need to be more like them when it comes to believing. Enough with being so adult. Be innocent. Believe. Obey—like the children do."

You, too, are innocent. And that gives you a place of honor on Jesus' lap. The whole kingdom of God belongs to you. You don't get much more worthy than that.

## Do That Little Thing: GOD? CAN WE TALK?

Imagine yourself in the lap of God, whatever that looks, feels, and smells like to you. Close your eyes and snuggle in. Then talk to your Daddy-God about anything that's on your mind. You are safe, so don't be afraid you'll be "wrong." You are loved, so don't worry that you'll be dumped off for being "bad." Just be there, in the kingdom, where you belong.

# Thursday

Those who led the way rebuked him and told him to be quiet
... [but] Jesus stopped and ordered the man to be brought to
him.

Luke 18:39-40

Why is it that sometimes—a lot of times!—when you speak up about something that's bugging you, people shush you?

Seriously, you're on a car trip and you say, "I'm hungry," or "I have to go to the bathroom," or you just want to know, "Are we there yet?" and your parents jump all over you like you're asking them to stop the world instead of just the minivan.

The blind man in the Bible story must have felt that way. He was sitting by the roadside when Jesus passed by, and he realized he might actually have a chance to see again and not have to beg for food and money. So he called out, "Jesus, Son of David, have mercy on me!" And what did the people in the crowd with Jesus do? They "rebuked" him. They told him, sharply, to back off. Jesus, they said, didn't have time to listen to him.

Hello! Healing people was what Jesus *did!* He ordered the man to be brought to him and healed him on the spot. People praised God.

If you have something important to say, especially if you want to be "healed" of something—whether it's cluelessness in math or loneliness for your always-working dad—speak up to God, and don't shrink if people tell you to hush up. God wants to hear you. You are worthy of his attention.

## Do That Little Thing: LISTEN UP!

For one whole day, listen carefully when people speak up, whether it's to complain, express an opinion, ask for help, whatever. Notice how they do it, and see if you can figure out what approaches get the best results. For instance, you may discover that when people whine they get squashed, but when they ask with a grin, they are at least heard. (Or you may find that the whiners get the most attention!) It may help you in your quest to get somebody to listen to you. Just remember that God always does. You're worth it.

# Friday

> "Zacchaeus, come down immediately. I must stay at your house today... For the Son of Man came to seek and to save what was lost."
>
> Luke 19:5, 10

What's with all the tax collectors in the Bible? Zacchaeus was one of them, and in fact, he was a *chief* tax collector, which meant he was in charge of a whole bunch of those little weasels that nobody liked. What was that about? Weren't they just doing their jobs?

The Roman government had taken over Israel, so the Jewish people were totally at the mercy of those who couldn't have cared less about their God or their ways of living for him. They even had to pay money (taxes) to the Roman government, and they didn't get much in return for the money they were paying.

Worse still, the Roman government hired Jewish people to collect the taxes from the Jews. It was way insulting to have one of your own people demand money at your door. And even *worse*, sometimes those tax collectors asked for more than they had to and kept the extra for themselves. No wonder people hated them and wondered why Jesus would want to hang out with them.

Jesus knew that even cheating little tax collectors were worthy of God's love, and he showed them that love. That's why Zacchaeus thought, "Man, I've got to see this guy," and climbed a tree to get a better look. So no matter what kind of "tax collector" you are, God loves you and wants to come to your house. You're worth it.

## Do That Little Thing: YOU CAN *SO* DO THIS!

Since you're worthy of God's love no matter how small or greedy or dishonest you are at times, why not do what you have to do to "see" God, like Zacchaeus did? Try doing one of these:

- Spend five minutes more talking to him today than you usually do.
- Write a story or draw a picture of Jesus coming to your house.
- Climb a tree or a set of monkey bars or some other sort-of-high thing and imagine listening to a Jesus story from there.
- Stop one "tax collecting" activity (like gossiping or teasing or telling a fib), just because you're better than that.

# Saturday

Go and make disciples of all nations.

Matthew 28:19

What would it be like if everyone were considered special? What if the girl who takes your tickets at the movie theater were as important as the one who wins the gold medal for figure skating at the Olympic Games? Or the girl in your class with yellow teeth who snorts when she laughs were as popular as the one decked out head to toe in Abercrombie and Fitch?

It's hard to imagine, because in our world some people do seem to be more important than others. It was the same in Jesus' time. His people were used to being told they were God's chosen ones. Then along came Jesus, informing them that God loved everybody, from every nation, and he wanted them all to be saved from their own badness by him. It was huge.

Some people still find it hard to believe that God loves us all the same. That he wants all of us to come to him and live his way—and because of that each of us is special. The world probably isn't going to see it that way, but you can. You can know that God adores you. That you are as special to him as his figure skaters and presidents and class queens. That he just wants you to follow him.

## Do That Little Thing: SHOUT-OUT

If you go around telling everybody how special you are to God, you're likely to get some pretty weird looks. So why not tell somebody who needs to hear it how special SHE is to the Father? Pick out three (or more!) people who obviously don't feel very important and tell each one how much he or she matters to God, just because she *is*. It'll be just like going to "all nations," because that's what disciples do.

## You're Worth Taking Care Of

When I consider your heavens, the work of your fingers, the moon and the stars, which you have set in place, what is man that you are mindful of him . . . ?

Psalm 8:3–4

Do you ever get stressed out? Feel like you have SO much to do or SO many things to worry about? There's school. Homework. Church stuff. Sports and lessons. Friends and their drama. Family and theirs. No wonder sometimes you just want to veg in front of a computer game or a rerun of *Hannah Montana*.

If you aren't stressed, your parents probably are sometimes. Just thinking about all the stuff they have to be responsible for boggles the mind. Your brother alone is enough to keep a person awake at night, right?

Can you even imagine what it's like to be God, with the entire world to take care of? He has to keep the sun coming up and the planets rotating around it and the seasons up to date and the animals fed . . . As lovely as it would be to have all that power, the stress is so not worth it!

So if God has all that on his almighty shoulders, how is it that he has time to think about each of us? Does he really keep track of everything we need and provide it? How can that be?

That's what we're going to explore this week. It's as important to know that you're going to be taken care of as it is to feel that you are loved, and God knows that. So wouldn't you know there'd be proof of it in the Bible? Let's see!

# Sunday

*Are not two sparrows sold for a penny? Yet not one of them will fall to the ground apart from the will of your Father. And even the very hairs of your head are all numbered. So don't be afraid; you are worth more than many sparrows.*

Matthew 10:29–31

Ever wished you could be a bird? Longed to spread your wings and dart all around above everybody's heads—maybe poop on that one boy who's always unzipping your backpack? Wouldn't you feel free, not having to worry about school or bullies or cheerleading tryouts?

Jesus says *don't* worry about school or bullies or cheerleading tryouts. Don't worry about anything, because if God takes care of a bunch of sparrows, which frankly nobody pays much attention to, he's sure going to take care of you. Why would he create you so carefully that he even knows exactly how many hairs you have on your head, and then leave you to fend for yourself?

Think about something that you've spent time making, maybe a glitter-covered card for your mom for Mother's Day. Did you leave the card out on the front porch so it could get rained on or some squirrel could grab it? You probably guarded it with your life until it got into your mom's hands.

That's SO God. He made you to be one-of-a-kind. He's not going to be careless with you. Listen to that sparrow singing her heart out at seven a.m. and you know it for sure.

## Do That Little Thing: QUIZ

Put a star next to each item below that you think God cares about:

\_\_\_\_ whether I use sunscreen when I go out in the sun
\_\_\_\_ how I decide to spend my birthday money
\_\_\_\_ what I wear to school tomorrow
\_\_\_\_ who I invite to my sleepover
\_\_\_\_ why I get sad

If you didn't put a star by every single one, go back and do that—because God cares about all of it. And more.

# Monday

If that is how God clothes the grass of the field … how much more will he clothe you…!

Luke 12:28

W hat's for breakfast?" "What's for lunch?" "How about a snack?" "What are we having for dinner?"

Those questions you ask about food don't even include the times when you just stare into the full-to-bulging pantry and wail, "There's never anything to eat around here!" (That translates as, "You didn't buy any junk food, Mom!") We Americans think about eating all the time.

And then there are the clothes questions. "What am I going to wear?" "Can we go to the mall Saturday?" "Can I have a new pair of jeans?" Even if you aren't obsessed with fashion, you probably have a favorite t-shirt or a pair of flip-flops you can't part with. Clothes are huge with us. And why not? We can't go around naked, can we?

Jesus doesn't say we don't need sandwiches in our lunch boxes and new outfits in our closets. He says don't get all hung up on how you're going to get them and whether you're going to have enough and whether it's going to be as good as everybody else's. There are more important things to think about, like how you treat the other kids and how you act with your parents. Who really has time to stress over what color Crocs to put on? God has the footwear, and everything else you need, handled.

## Do That Little Thing: FIND OUT

Ask your God-loving adult friends what articles of clothing they just HAD to have when they were your age or in middle school. Get the details — and try not to laugh, especially if they show you pictures. Then ask what kind of difference having, or not having, those pieces of apparel made in their lives. It might help you think clearly about your own yearning for a spending spree at Limited Too.

# Tuesday

Your beauty should... be that of your inner self, the unfading beauty of a gentle and quiet spirit, which is of great worth in God's sight.

1 Peter 3:3–4

You've heard it so many times: "It's not what you look like on the outside that counts. It's who you are inside."

Do the people who say things like that ever watch TV? Pick up a magazine now and then? Where in our world is the proof that people don't look at each other and think, "She's a nice girl and all, but what is up with that funky haircut—those buck teeth—that baby fat she's hauling around?"

The world mostly looks at our outside appearance and judges us from there. It stinks, but there it is. What are you supposed to do with that?

That's where God's love comes in again. He cares what you believe about yourself, enough to make it possible for you to concentrate on your inner beauty, the amazing spirit he created in you. He will help you laugh at those people who think your nail polish and your nose shape are what you're all about. The world won't change, but you can depend on God to allow you to feel sorry for that shallow society and be the drop-dead gorgeous person you are inside.

And as soon as you let yourself focus on the loveliness of your laugh and your compassion for other people, the world will say, "You are so pretty. What's your secret?" Then you can tell them it's just God taking care of you.

## Do That Little Thing: JUST THINK

Think about a commercial or advertisement you've seen that focuses on outer looks — maybe a shampoo ad or one for a diet plan. How would you rewrite it as an ad for inner beauty? If you come up with a good one, perform it for your friends. Who knows? It could become your new slogan.

# Wednesday

Suppose one of you has a hundred sheep and loses one of them. Does he not leave the ninety-nine in the open country and go after the lost sheep until he finds it?

Luke 15:4

Have you ever been lost? Maybe as a little girl you got separated from your mom in Wal-Mart and the store manager tied a balloon to your wrist and let you have a sucker while she paged your mother over the intercom. When Mom barreled up to the counter, she probably picked you up and squeezed you, balloon, sucker, sticky face and all.

Maybe later she scolded you for wandering off, but for the most part she kept gazing at you, looking like she'd just won the lottery. And forget about the shopping cart she left parked in Aisle 8, loaded with that great buy on paper towels — you were lost and she left everything to find you. And when she did, she rejoiced.

You've been lost many times since then. What about when you went through that phase of pouting every time somebody crossed you? Or when you decided you didn't have to cooperate with that substitute who came in when your teacher was gone, because you just plain didn't like her? Or when you ditched your BFF-since-kindergarten when that new girl moved in who was massively interesting and wanted only you for a friend?

Who came after you then? God. He doesn't let you wander around in behavior like that for very long before he makes you realize you're hurting yourself as well as somebody else. He cares enough to find you and bring you back. You can rejoice in that.

## Do That Little Thing: GOD? CAN WE TALK?

Who knows, you could be lost right now! Talk to God about that. Ask him if you're wandering around in some kind of foreign territory. Tell him you'd like to be found and brought back to your senses. God cares. He'll do that for you. All you have to do is pay attention and follow.

# **Thursday**

I no longer call you servants, because a servant does not know his master's business. Instead, I have called you friends, for everything that I learned from my Father I have made known to you.

John 15:15

Think about the people in your class at school or church, or some other group of kids your age. You probably know all of them, but only some of them are actually your friends. How do you know the difference?

The mere acquaintances will say "Hi" to you and smile at you and maybe give you a piece of gum if you look longingly enough when they open the pack. But if you were crying, they wouldn't come over and ask what was wrong, and if you came in ready to burst with news they wouldn't be at your elbow saying, "So, come on—tell me already!"

Your friends, on the other hand, would probably know you were going to cry before you even puckered up and would be there with the Kleenex. They'd see that "Have I got something to tell YOU" look on your face and be all over you. They would also give up their place at the head of the line to be with you at the end of it and give you that stick of gum before you started with the puppy dog eyes and a bajillion other things that only real BFFs do.

Now, consider God, who has no mere acquaintances. We are all treated with the same kind of friendship love. Whatever a friend gives you, God gives you, multiplied by thousands. That includes the secrets, the things you need to know so that you can live freely in this world. There is no other friend who cares that much.

## Do That Little Thing: LISTEN UP!

Next time you're with your closest friend, listen, really listen to her. You don't have to get her to talk for a straight hour (although she might be willing to do that!). Just pay attention to the things she says. Look for:

- how interested she is in you.
- how much she encourages you.
- how much she helps you with the things that challenge you.
- whether she laughs with you.
- whether she cares what you think.

Then think about God caring that much and more. After all, where do you think she learned that?

# Friday

My prayer is not that you take them out of the world but that you protect them from the evil one.

John 17:15

So far this week, you've seen that you are SO worth caring for by God. Although with all of that caring it seems you wouldn't have to be concerned with evil getting its teeth into you, you can't underestimate its power. Some people call that the Devil, others Satan, still others just a dark force. Whatever you call it, it's there. Otherwise, why would people lie, cheat, steal, and treat each other like dirt?

But you don't have to slink around looking over your shoulder in fear that evil is going to get you and make you do something horrible. God thinks you're worth protecting. He's always there to warn you, nudge you, poke you when the temptation to make the wrong choice lurks behind you like a shadow.

He doesn't take evil away, or put you in a lovely little bubble where evil can't touch you. He simply protects you from the harm it can do to you, by showing you what is good and making you strong enough to choose good over evil. It's like having a full-time bodyguard. How cool is that?

## Do That Little Thing: YOU CAN *SO* DO THIS!

What evil is teasing you right now, dancing around trying to look like good, tempting you to make a bad choice? Could it be the urge that's overtaken you lately to be a smart mouth to your mom? The nagging thought that if you weren't a straight-A student the popular girls might not be jealous of you, so why not settle for a B or two? Ask God for his protection. Beg him, in fact. And then let him help you turn your back on that temptation. That's what he's there for.

# Saturday

> God demonstrates his own love for us in this: While we were
> still sinners, Christ died for us.
>
> Romans 5:8

Has anybody made a sacrifice for you lately? Maybe your sister took your turn emptying the dishwasher so you could finish your science project, or your mom gave up going to her high school reunion because you had strep throat.

It could be that person made that sacrifice for you because you deserved it, being the sweetheart that you are. But would your sister be so willing to take dishwasher duty if you were a brat to her? Would you do it for her if she treated you like roadkill? It's just about impossible to make a sacrifice for someone who has acting ugly down to a science.

And then there's your mom. You might have had her wishing she'd never heard of motherhood the evening before, but if you wake up at two a.m. with a fever, she's going to give up her whole night's sleep to provide you with Tylenol and a tepid bath. In fact, if you walked out in front of a bus, she AND your dad would probably throw themselves in its path to get you out of the way—even though it was pretty stupid of you to cross the street without looking.

God cares that much, too, which is why he made the biggest sacrifice anyone could make. He sent his Son to die so that we could understand that we are saved from our own stupidness and moron-itis. What else could he possibly do to prove what we are worth to him?

## Do That Little Thing: SHOUT-OUT

Think about the last sacrifice one of your parents made for you, even if it was just a little thing (like giving you the last Thin Mint Girl Scout cookie). Go to Mom or Dad and say thank you — with a hug, or a card, but definitely a big old smile. Then go one step further and say that it reminds you of how God sacrificed himself for you. Expect a hug in return.

# You Are Strong!

He set my feet on a rock and gave me a firm place to stand.

Psalm 40:2

Have you ever had one of those days?

You know the kind, where from the time you crawl out of bed in the morning until you fall back in at night everything that can go wrong does?

Somebody ate the last of your favorite cereal. You drop your social studies homework in a puddle. Some kid takes your seat on the bus and you have to sit next to The Pincher. You flunk the vocabulary test you forgot to study for. You have carrot sticks in your lunch and your mom KNOWS you hate carrot sticks. Your team loses the soccer game. You leave your vocabulary list at school so you can't study for the next test either.

On those days, you feel like the guy who wrote the psalm: "I am bowed down and brought very low; all day long I go about mourning" (Psalm 38:6). You're convinced that you are a loser.

And then, two psalms later, the same guy writes, "He lifted me out of the slimy pit, out of the mud and mire" (Psalm 40:2). Not, "I pulled myself up and went on," but, basically, "God made me strong."

That's how God sees you: strong, capable, like you're standing on a rock — which is him. It's time to see yourself that way, so get ready to flex those muscles this week, girl.

# Sunday

My enemies will turn back when I call for help. By this I will know that God is for me.

Psalm 56:9

The first "muscle" God gives you is strength when you're in trouble. And who can get in more trouble than you? It might not be the principal's-office kind, but if you are a girl between eight and twelve, there are dilemmas in your life. This psalmist has nothing on you.

*"My slanderers pursue me all day long"* (verse 2). Heard any gossip this week? Any rumors?

*"Many are attacking me in their pride"* (verse 2). Anybody jealous right now? Seen any fights over who said what to whom?

*"All day long they twist my words"* (verse 5). Have there been any meetings in the girls' restroom about what she said, how she said it, and what she meant?

*"They conspire, they lurk, they watch my steps"* (verse 6). Has anybody criticized anybody this week? Told on anybody? Jumped at the chance to tease?

Ya think? A girl has to be strong to get through all that. You are. You just have to go where that strength comes from. "In God I trust," you have to say. "I will not be afraid. What can man (or girl!) do to me?" (verse 11).

Pray. Be the mighty mini-woman you are. You can put down rumors and gossip. You can stomp out jealousy and break up arguments and refuse to get pulled into the drama. You can do it, because God made you that way.

## Do That Little Thing: QUIZ

Test your Trust Muscle by circling the answer that is the most true for you. And don't worry if that muscle is still a little puny. We'll give it a workout this week.

When someone puts me down (gossips or spreads a rumor about me, makes fun of me, or gets me in trouble):

- I do the same thing to them.
- I run to the bathroom and cry.
- I yell at whoever hurt me.
- I try to forget about it.
- I go to God and ask him to help me be strong enough to stand up for myself.

The strongest Trust Muscle is #5. Keep flexing 'til you get there!

# Monday

You are my refuge and my shield; I have put my hope in your word. Away from me, you evildoers, that I may keep the commands of my God!

Psalm 119:114–115

We've talked about the strength you need when other people do bad stuff to YOU. Uh, but what about the times when you're tempted to put the hurt on someone else? It happens to the best of us. When you have the perfect insult for Miss Thing who is never without one for you, or you beat out the Class Queen for the lead in the play and you REALLY want to gloat—it's so hard to resist.

Actually, you can't resist—not on your own. But God has made you strong in him. He acts like a shield between you and that funny-but-nasty comment that wants to come out of your mouth. He's a place to hide from your jealousy so you don't take it out on somebody else. He keeps you away from whatever whispers, "Go ahead. She deserves it. She'd do the same to you in a heartbeat."

So think of yourself the way God does, as a strong mini-woman who doesn't have to prove she's all that. Who doesn't need to make other people feel bad so she can feel good. Who doesn't get all defensive and lash out at other people before they can hurt her. You have God-strength. Don't hesitate to use it.

## Do That Little Thing: FIND OUT

Ask your God-loving adult friends when they have the hardest time holding their tongues, not saying what they really want to say because they know it will wound someone. Talk about how they manage to resist the temptation. You'll find out that everybody needs God's strength when it comes to matters of the mouth.

I was overcome by trouble and sorrow. Then I called on the name of the Lord.

Psalm 116:3–4

When was the last time you cried? Last month? Last week? This morning? The world can be a sad place with plenty of room for tears. Sometimes it can be so sad, you feel "overcome." What's that like?

- Your sobs are so big you can hardly talk.
- You want to hide in your room.
- You want to curl up in your mom's lap like you were four years old.
- You think you might never smile about anything ever again.

Nobody feels strong in that kind of sorrow, not even big hulky men. But God sees us as strong when we go to him and say, "Help!— I can't stand this." That's when our Trust Muscle starts to flex—the tears slow down, and we come out from under the covers. We decide maybe we might like an order of fries after all. That's God at work, making us strong.

That doesn't mean it's wrong to get upset and grieve. We need to do that in order to work through our feelings. You just don't have to stay that way. Yes, cry. No, don't be hopeless. Yes, curl up with your teddy bear for a while. No, don't turn down an offer for a hug. Crying, hugging, thinking it over—all those things are God coming to the rescue, pumping up your Trust Muscle, making you stronger for next time sorrow hits. It will, but don't be afraid of it. There's nothing you and God can't handle together.

## Do That Little Thing: JUST THINK

Think about the last time you were really sad. You know, half-a-box-of-tissue kind of sad. What made you feel stronger once you got past the tears you had to cry? See if you can find God in that. He's in there.

# Wednesday

My grace is sufficient for you, for my power is made perfect in weakness.

2 Corinthians 12:9

Weak" is the opposite of "strong," right? Just like "hot" is the opposite of "cold," and "adults talking about insurance" is the opposite of "interesting."

That's usually true. But when it comes to God, sometimes he sees us the strongest when we admit we're the weakest. Here's what that looks like.

Let's say you don't have much trouble resisting temptation. Nobody can talk you into lying or cheating or talking about Susie behind her back. It's so easy for you, you hardly even consider where your strength comes from. You might even think it's just because you're naturally better than most people.

And then a new girl moves to your school, a girl who can play soccer like Mia Hamm. She scores more goals in the first game than you have all season—and suddenly it isn't so easy to keep from pointing out that her dribbling is sloppy or she commits fouls nobody else sees. You've found your weakness.

What do you have to do to avoid becoming what you always thought you were too good to be? You have no choice. You have to turn to God, who—hello!—gave you that strength in the first place. Now you can really be strong because you know you can't do it without God's help. God loves that. He says, "Now my power is made perfect in weakness." YOUR weakness.

It's almost worth being a little flabby in some areas, just to keep God in mind!

### Do That Little Thing: GOD? CAN WE TALK?

There's only one thing to do now, and that's go to God and talk about those places where you're a little out of shape. If you can't think of your weaknesses on your own, ask God to help you figure them out. Maybe ask a grown-up who knows and loves you — God speaks through them too. Simply ask God to turn them into your strong points. You're already halfway there!

I pray that you, being rooted and established in love, may have power ... to grasp how wide and long and high and deep is the love of Christ.

Ephesians 3:17–18

Wouldn't it be cool if somebody gave you a computer of your very own? What would you do first?

Find out what games it had on it?

Go straight to email?

Create your own webpage?

You might have fun right there for a while, but wouldn't it be a total waste if you didn't find out what else your computer could do? After all, the person who gave it to you said it could do everything but the supper dishes. Maybe you couldn't even imagine what all was in there, but you'd sure like somebody to show you.

It's that way with the love God showed us through our Lord Jesus Christ. The Bible tells us that love is bigger than anything we could ever dream up, so wouldn't it be a shame if we didn't explore everything that meant? Just how do we do that?

We ask God, of course, because he sees that we CAN understand it and we CAN find out how great that can make our lives and we CAN feel it in our souls. And just like all our other strengths, this one comes straight from God. He made us to be able to know he loves us, to listen to his love, to follow what he teaches, to dream with him, to let those dreams come true. Don't miss out on any of that.

## Do That Little Thing: LISTEN UP!

Sometimes your idea of God can be too small. Maybe you only think of him as the one to go to when you're in big trouble. Or just as the one who comforts you when nobody understands. Or merely as the Creator who makes the sun shine every day. Listen today for ALL the ways God shows his love. You'll hear it in every good sound, from the laughter of your baby sister to the engine of the car that brings your dad home safely from his business trip. Make a list. You'll be amazed at all God is.

# Friday

He will keep you strong to the end, so that you will be blameless on the day of our Lord Jesus Christ.

1 Corinthians 1:8

It seems like there are time limits on everything. That gift card you got for Christmas is only good for six months. The milk will go sour if you don't use it by the date on the carton. The coupon for a free ice-cream cone at Baskin Robbins has already expired.

Fortunately, God doesn't work that way. The strength he gives you lasts forever. It doesn't run out, expire, or need to be renewed. It's as much a part of you as the color of your eyes and the shape of your ears and the sound of your voice. It's something you can count on in a way you can't depend on anything else.

So let's review. God has made you strong enough to stand up for yourself in trouble. Strong enough to resist temptation. Strong enough to bear sorrow. Even strong enough to be weak, so you can depend on him. Maybe best of all, God has made you strong enough to really understand how much he loves you and what that can mean in your life. You have all that strength, and you get to keep it forever and ever, until the day you are with God himself.

How, then, can you ever think that what some mean girl says makes any difference at all? That having THE latest iPod says anything about who you are? That you aren't worthy of being loved? You can't — not a strong, empowered mini-woman like you.

## Do That Little Thing: YOU CAN *SO* DO THIS!

What good thing would you do if you didn't care what anybody thought? Would you invite the girl no one EVER invites to your birthday party — if you didn't think some of your friends would ditch you? Would you bow your head and pray before a spelling test — if you weren't sure the boy next to you would call you a Jesus Freak? Whatever that good thing is, can you forget how other people might react and just do it? Remember, God's strength goes on forever. Their opinions are gone the minute they hit the air.

# Saturday

Let him who boasts boast in the Lord.

1 Corinthians 1:31

Of course you wouldn't brag on PURPOSE. But isn't it hard not to tell at least your fifteen closest friends when you get the part, make the team, score the goal, or win the award? People might call it bragging, but it's so much fun to share and see the admiration in your loved ones' eyes. There's really nothing wrong with that.

But the eyes begin to glaze over when you go on for hours about your wonderful-ness. People start glancing at their watches, examining their fingernails, changing the subject to anything but how amazing you are.

Why is it that we all roll our eyes when somebody brags? Whether we realize it or not, it's because we know talents and successes aren't really that person's doing. Something inside tells us it's bigger than the bragger. Now you know it all comes from God.

So why not give God the credit? Why not brag on God, instead of yourself? When you win that award, put God first on your list of those to thank. When you solve the problem, let people know God helped you. When someone compliments you for being mature, be quick to say it's just God doing his thing in you. Go ahead and boast about your strength, as long as God gets all the credit.

## Do That Little Thing: SHOUT-OUT

For the next week, every time someone pays you a compliment, answer it with, "Thank you, but it's all God." Keep track of how many times those words cross your lips. God's about to get some big-time kudos!

## You Are a Precious Body

> Do you not know that your body is a temple of the Holy Spirit, who is in you...?
>
> 1 Corinthians 6:19

By now you probably get that it's what's inside of you—your spirit—that is the most important thing about you. But inside of what?

Well, duh, your body, of course. It's the place where all that important stuff about you happens. And it isn't just a shack. It's a temple.

The closest thing to a temple that you probably know about is a church. If you've spent time in one, you know it's a special place, set aside for people to worship in. There are probably flowers, maybe some art created in God's honor, and the building itself may represent faith in some way, with stained glass windows or high ceilings that reach toward heaven. Even if the church is very plain, it's probably kept perfectly clean and in order.

In Paul's day (the writer of the verse above), a temple was treated with even MORE reverence. Priests spent their whole lives making sure every detail was taken care of the way God wanted it, and there were some parts of it where non-priests weren't even allowed to go because they believed the temple was where God lived.

Paul said your body is like that. It's the house where the Holy Spirit—the part of God that lives in you—lives. This week you'll focus on how God sees his dwelling place within you, so get ready for some housecleaning!

# Sunday

Arise, come, my darling; my beautiful one, come with me.

Song of Songs 2:13

Just in case you still close your eyes and say EWWW during the kissing parts in movies, don't skip today's reading! The verse above isn't really about a guy taking his "darling" on a date. It's from the Song of Songs, which is a love poem about how much God loves you, just the way a groom loves his bride. Since it's sometimes hard to imagine that God would love your pudgy, funky pre-teen body, the poem uses word pictures to help you understand.

The Song of Songs was written a long time ago, so the idea of beauty back then is a little different from ours. Okay, a lot different. The guy in this poem talks about how his lover's hair reminds him of a flock of goats coming down a mountain. That wouldn't work in a shampoo commercial.

But you can get the point that God loves your body. It is as beautiful to him as the world of nature he's created. It's as drop-dead gorgeous as anything valuable — just as goats were to people back then. Just know that your physical being matters to God. He loves it just as he made it. He uses it to house your beautiful spirit, your soul that will last forever. So arise, Little Darlin', and go with God. He loves you.

## Do That Little Thing: QUIZ

Take a good long look at your whole self in a mirror. Then put a star next to the statement that's most true for you. It will help you check out your attitude about your body before we start our week taking better care of it.

_____ I guess my body's okay. Can I go play now?
_____ I kind of like what I see. Nice job, God.
_____ Ewww!

# Monday

> I give you every seed-bearing plant on the face of the whole earth and every tree that has fruit with seed in it. They will be yours for food.
>
> Genesis 1:29

If you're going to take care of the body God made for you, start with what you feed it. You come with feeding instructions; there are hundreds of verses about food in the Bible.

The one above sounds like fruits and veggies and grains. You don't hear anything about Twinkies and Pop-Tarts in there. Sugar does come from sugar cane, so chew on that to your heart's content. When sugar is refined, that's when it becomes bad for you; the same for white flour. God wants us to keep our fruits, veggies, and grains as close to their natural state as we can.

God then goes on to give forty-six verses worth of instructions about what animals to eat and how to cook them. We don't have to follow all of that exactly (although how hard would it be not to eat camel or vulture meat?), but we can pay attention to how natural and well-cooked our meat is. God did not have in mind a burger that's made with icky fillers that clog up your body.

And check out this one: "When you sit to dine with a ruler... put a knife to your throat if you are given to gluttony" (Proverbs 23:1–2). That doesn't mean you should literally put a blade to your neck! If you catch yourself eating junk when you're nervous or unhappy, cut off that habit (not your throat!) and do something healthy for yourself, like talk to a grown-up about what's bothering you.

## Do That Little Thing: FIND OUT

For one whole day, write down everything you eat, even the handful of chips you devour on your way out the door. At the end of the day, look at your list and, maybe with a grown-up's help, decide if you're feeding the body God gave you the way he wants you to.

# Tuesday

You are not your own; you were bought at a price. Therefore honor God with your body.

1 Corinthians 6:19–20

Has anyone ever asked you to take care of something of theirs for a while? Maybe your best friend trusted you to take care of her pet turtle while she was on vacation.

It's a big responsibility. You probably took better care of that thing than you would something of your own. That turtle ate gourmet meals! When something doesn't belong to you, you don't want to return it in bad shape.

Your body isn't actually yours either. It's on loan to you from God. He has given it to you to keep for a while, as long as you need it to hold your spirit. Do you want to come to the end of your life and give God back a body you haven't taken care of?

It also needs to be in shape now for the work God is giving you to do every day. You can't be ready if you're a couch potato, or if you don't work your muscles by playing games, or if you don't develop endurance by running around. Computer games and movies and girl talk around a pizza are fun, but they shouldn't be your only activities. Get up and get moving—for God.

## Do That Little Thing: JUST THINK

Think about all the ACTIVE things you did yesterday (or any other normal, routine day). Make a list or just line them up in your head as you review your day, from wake-up to lights-out. If you didn't do at least a few that required you to move around for twenty minutes at a time, sit down with a grown-up and together figure out how you can get more exercise into your life. God will be cheering you on.

# Wednesday

He who has clean hands and a pure heart ... will receive
blessing from the Lord.

Psalm 24:4–5

Have you noticed a change in your body—like maybe you sweat more than you used to? Maybe you've had to start using deodorant or you aren't as allergic to taking a bath as you used to be. It's part of that whole girl-growing-up thing, because God made our bodies full of sweat glands and hormones and pits and cavities for bacteria to set up house in.

Advertisers try to tell us we need to get rid of every human smell so we'll be liked by everyone. From the way those women freak out on the commercials, you would think it was a matter of life and death. God doesn't want us to stress out about our odors. He just wants us to be clean.

In the book of Leviticus (the handbook of rules for the Israelites when they were traveling through the wilderness to the Promised Land) there are six chapters about "the clean" and "the unclean." God provided that because he wanted his people to live long and healthy lives, and because he wanted them to think about him in absolutely everything they did.

God still wants us disease-free, without a bunch of bacteria taking over our bodies. If we're sick, we can't do what he's put us here to do. And God still wants us to live lives that are all about him and his love. One of the loveliest ways to do that is to cleanse our bodies and present our best selves for him, just as the Israelites did.

## Do That Little Thing: GOD? CAN WE TALK?

Next time you take a bath or shower, talk to God while you're soaping up and rinsing off. Ask him to guide you in using all those clean body parts for him. What can you do with your hands to serve him? Where can you go with your feet? What light can you bring to someone else with your face? When you step out, all scrubbed and fresh, you'll be ready.

# Thursday

We have a young sister, and her breasts are not yet grown.
What shall we do for our sister?

Song of Songs 8:8

Now smells may not be the only changes you've noticed in your body, and if you haven't yet, you will. Every girl wakes up some morning and realizes she has two bumps on her chest, or hair growing in strange places, or curves where she used to be straight.

It can be confusing, weird, and downright scary! It's a good thing you don't have to go it alone. You've got God, who designed the whole process in the first place. Even if you don't particularly feel like thanking God for that right now, take a look at the help God offers:

- God wants you to become a woman. He sculpted Eve (and all women) to be attractive to men so the guys would want to marry them and live their lives together.
- He's getting you ready to have kids, if that's what's in your future. You're still a kid yourself, but the preparations start now because it takes awhile for it all to come together.
- God knows how strange and frustrating and often embarrassing the process of becoming a woman can be, and he's there to help. You can go to him with body-change issues just like you can with everything else.

## Do That Little Thing: LISTEN UP!

This week, listen for the signs that your body is changing. Tune your ears to:

- things your mom says, like "Those jeans are getting too short. We need to go shopping."
- things your dad says, like "You're getting too big for my lap, aren't you?"
- things your friends say, like "I want a two-piece bathing suit this year, don't you?"

NOTE: Pay no attention to what boys your age say. They are even more confused than you are!

The list will help you see that the changes you're experiencing aren't just your imagination — they're a natural part of this thing called growing up. God wants you to feel comfortable with it.

# Friday

A man will leave his father and mother and be united to his wife, and they will become one flesh.

Genesis 2:24

Have you noticed lately that boys are changing too? That all of them aren't as absurd and creepy as they used to be? Maybe you used to be a Cootie Counter, and suddenly you find yourself smiling because a boy—okay, a cute boy—didn't move to another seat when you sat next to him on the bus.

That's part of God's growing-up plan too. The same hormones God puts into action so you can have babies cause you to be attracted to guys so you'll *want* to have their kids. That wasn't such a big deal back in biblical times (and even up to a hundred years ago) when girls didn't experience body changes until they were about fourteen and then got married not long after. In today's world, you're more likely to notice those changes at age nine or ten and not get married until you're in your twenties. That's more than a decade!

So it's important for you to know what God wants when it comes to you and boys and those confusing feelings. This is a good time to start talking to your mom and dad or some other adult you trust about what's okay with boys. It'll be a special conversation that will tell you a whole bunch about what God wants for you, and how he sees your body. Meanwhile, enjoy getting to know boys as friends. And thank God that he made them so cute!

## Do That Little Thing: YOU CAN *SO* DO THIS

This is also a good time to teach boys how girls need to be treated, before they learn any bad habits. Next time a boy does or says something nice to you, thank him. And next time a boy acts like an absurd little creep to you, tell him politely that you're better than that. He might just stare at you, but just let God do the rest. He loves them too!

# Saturday

Do not ... put tattoo marks on yourselves. I am the Lord.

Leviticus 19:28

If we still followed every rule set forth by God in Leviticus, your pastor would be sacrificing bulls in the sanctuary and your dad would have a beard down to his navel. Again, the rules were set up by God so the people would think of him in every detail of their lives.

The verse about not putting tattoo marks on your body is right in there with men not clipping the hair at the sides of their heads and nobody eating a rare steak. Nobody is going to say you don't love God if you do those things. However, when it comes to tattoos and piercings, we're getting into marking the body in ways that can't be easily turned around. And there are dangers involved. Those procedures can be painful and cause infection.

Perhaps the greatest danger is in the way people look at you when you pierce and tattoo and generally get that Bad-Girl look. No, people shouldn't judge you by your appearance, but if you're sending the message that you're angry and tough and disrespectful, that's the message they're going to get. Besides, if you make people work that hard to see who you are inside, you waste a lot of time that could be spent sharing great friendships.

If you think piercing your belly button or tattooing sleeves up your arm might be a good way to express your defiance or your unique-ness someday, go to a grown-up and talk about that. There are some God-ways to say "This is me!" that don't involve pain!

## Do That Little Thing: SHOUT-OUT

Today, tell someone how grateful you are for the body God has given you. Have a celebration together, treating your bodies to something wonderful and healthy. (And by the way, one small piece of dark chocolate is VERY good for a woman's body!)

# You Are in God's Group!

Be fruitful and increase in number; multiply on the earth and increase upon it.

Genesis 9:7

Imagine one day without your friends. Who would you talk to on the bus? Who would you hang out with before the teacher opened the classroom? Who would you run to the playground with? Eat lunch with? Argue with? Sing with? Giggle with? Dress like?

Before this gets any more depressing, let's just agree that life without friends would be empty and lonely and sad. That's because God never meant for us to be alone. The minute he created Adam he knew it was not good for him to be by himself and so he made, of course, a girl to keep him company. He told them he wanted them to get to work and fill his whole earth with people, who would live in community. All through the Old Testament we read about those people, traveling together, making homes side by side, building a society for God.

But when you look at the world today, you see a lot of people living by themselves. You see neighbors who don't know the names of the family next door. Life is lonely for a lot of people.

It might even be that way for you. You might feel very much alone sometimes, even when there are plenty of other people around. Perhaps you don't have as many friends as you'd like to. It might be that you don't feel like you really belong.

This week is about the community you do belong to—God's community. You'll read about some people who will model that for you, and show you that you, too, are a member.

# Sunday

He recovered all the goods and brought back his relative Lot and his possessions, together with the women and the other people.

Genesis 14:16

Do you live in the same town as your grandparents and aunts and uncles and cousins? If you do, you're very fortunate. In America, most extended families are spread out over hundreds, sometimes even thousands, of miles.

It wasn't that way in biblical times. Take Abram, for example. He and his wife Sarai didn't have any children, but they kept Abram's nephew, Lot, with them, because his father had died. No questions asked. No, "Aw, man, this kid is gonna slow us down." Taking care of family was just what you did. That had to be a safe, secure feeling. It's what God wants for us.

As Abram and his family traveled toward the land God had for them, quarrels broke out—as so often happens in families. The land couldn't support all of Abram's *and* Lot's herds and flocks. So they split up, but not on bad terms.

Which was a good thing, because when the town where Lot lived—Sodom—turned way wicked, a war broke out. The winners of the war carried off Lot and his possessions. When Abram heard about it, he got all his men together and rescued Lot.

Now, *that's* family. That's the family you belong to—God's family—where if evil tries to carry you off, your brothers and sisters in God will come after you. You will not be left alone.

## Do That Little Thing: QUIZ

On the next page, draw a circle big enough to write inside it the names of your family members who live near you. Draw a bigger circle around that and write in it the names of family members who live far away. It might help you see why sometimes you feel a little disconnected, or it may show you just how blessed you are to have so many loved ones close by.

# Monday

Where you go I will go, and where you stay I will stay. Your people will be my people and your God my God.

Ruth 1:16

Have you ever heard your mom—or any other married lady—talk about her mother-in-law? If not, you've probably heard jokes about how hard it can be to get along with the mother of your husband. After all, SHE had him first—and what woman is going to be good enough for her little boy?

Ruth didn't have that attitude toward her mother-in-law. Naomi was a widow, and when her son (Ruth's husband) died, she was left with nothing. In those days, a woman with no man to take care of her had to go back to her original family and hope they would take her in. In Naomi's case that meant traveling a long way across the desert to get back to people who might not even remember who she was. She was pretty old, after all.

It would have been easy for Ruth to go back to *her* own people. At least she was still living in the country where she'd grown up. Naomi was a foreigner. But even though Naomi told Ruth to go home to her people, Ruth said no way. She loved Naomi and she said wherever Naomi went, that's where she was going to go. Naomi's family was her family now. When you think about how far she would have to travel with the old lady, across dangerous territory where there were thieves and wild animals, that was huge. God puts that kind of loyalty into us. It's what holds his family together.

## Do That Little Thing: FIND OUT

Talk to as many grown-up family members as you can and ask them: What would you be willing to give up for the family? Give examples such as — Would you move? Take in someone else's kid? Give money if someone needed it? Then be ready to hear love that will show you how very much you belong.

# **Tuesday**

Jonathan said to David, "Whatever you want me to do, I'll do for you."

1 Samuel 20:4

Have you ever been friends with somebody that it didn't make sense for you to be friends with—but you just loved each other? You were pizza and she was shrimp scampi, and yet you got along. Your mother and hers did NOT care for each other but you two really hit it off.

That's the way it was with Jonathan and David. Jonathan's father was King Saul. God had already said David was going to replace Saul, and Saul wasn't having it. He was out to get David, and David was running scared.

But David and Jonathan were best friends. It was Jonathan David went to and said, "What have I done? What is my crime? How have I wronged your father, that he is trying to take my life?" (1 Samuel 20:1).

You'd think Jonathan would have been torn between his best bud and his dad, but Jonathan immediately said, "Never! ... You are not going to die!" (verse 2). Then he offered to do anything to help David escape Saul's wrath.

Jonathan wasn't being loyal to his blood family. His loyalty was to God's family. How did he know which to choose? How do *we* know? God puts it in us to be able to decide on his side. As members of that family, the love is deep inside us. Like Jonathan, we only have to listen to it.

## Do That Little Thing: JUST THINK

Think about your closest friend. What would you risk to be there for her? Sometimes friendship is just about sharing a bowl of popcorn and talking about your day. But if it should come to it, it's good to know just how far you would go for another member of God's community.

# Wednesday

> Blessed are you among women, and blessed is the child you will bear! But why am I so favored, that the mother of my Lord should come to me?
>
> Luke 1:42–43

What's the first thing you do when you get great news—like you get to go to Disney World over spring break, or your brother is coming home from Iraq?

You call your best friend.

Half the fun in having something good happen to you is sharing the joy with someone who's excited for you. God set it up that way. We see it in the Bible, when two women received fabulous news.

First there was Elizabeth, who was "well along in years" (Luke 1:7) and still didn't have any children. When an angel came to her husband, Zechariah (who was also no spring chicken), and told him Elizabeth was going to have a son, John, who would prepare the way for the Messiah, Elizabeth was one happy lady.

Six months later, her relative Mary also had a visit from an angel, telling her that she too was going to have a baby. Mary wasn't as excited as Elizabeth at first. She wasn't even married yet. But the angel assured her that this was a good thing, that this baby was the Messiah himself, the Son of God.

Mary hurried to Elizabeth's house, but she didn't even have to tell Elizabeth what was going on. John leaped inside Elizabeth's belly, and she was filled with God's Spirit. Next to Mary and Joseph, she was the first one to believe that Jesus was God's Son, before he was even born. That must have been reassuring to Mary. That's the kind of friends God made us to be.

## Do That Little Thing: GOD? CAN WE TALK?

Have a talk with God the way you would with your best friend. Provide snacks and pillows and stuffed animals if that's what you do with your BFF. Fill God in on all the details of your day, even though he already knows them (he likes to hear about them). Ask if there is anything he'd like you to do differently with your best buds. The answers will come in your future times with God's girls. Have the snacks ready.

# Thursday

On the evening of that first day of the week, when the disciples were together ...

John 20:19

Can you even imagine how close the disciples must have been?

- They spent three years traveling around as a group.
- They saw amazing things together that other people might not even believe.
- They learned things together that not even the smartest people got to know.
- They even had to go into hiding together after their Lord was killed so they wouldn't be put to death themselves.

They had their issues as a group. Jesus was always breaking up arguments over who was his favorite and who was going to sit next to him in heaven. Not everyone was in agreement about who Jesus was.

But when Jesus was crucified and they were left alone, they stuck together, just like he told them to. It might have been safer for them to separate and run in different directions, but he'd said for them to love each other, lay down their lives for each other, and that's what they were doing when he returned and appeared to them.

As members of his community, God gives all of us the courage to stick together for him. You can keep your friends going when other kids tease them. You know you have a place to go when the world says you're a geek. God gives you that place among the other members of his community. Stick together.

## Do That Little Thing: LISTEN UP!

For one day, listen to the talk that goes on around you when you're not with your friends. Do you hear things you believe? Things you agree with? Things that make you happy? Or do they cause you to doubt, feel confused, anxious? Most important, are those the same kinds of things you and your friends talk about? Are you pleased with that? Do you think God is pleased?

# Friday

> They devoted themselves to the apostles' teaching and to the fellowship.
>
> Acts 2:42

In the days soon after Jesus went back up into heaven and the disciples began to gather followers for him, anybody who gave his or her life to Jesus REALLY did. They sold all their stuff and put all the money together to make sure everybody had enough. They met every day and ate together and celebrated God with every meal. These were not just-go-to-church-on-Sunday people. It worked, because "the Lord added to their number daily those who were being saved" (Acts 2:47).

God still wants us to have that kind of family feel with our fellow believers. We're made to come together in groups and eat and share and praise together—otherwise, why would there even be churches, and church camps, and youth groups? Yes, we all need time alone to pray and listen to God, the way Jesus did. But just as much, we're created to bow our heads together, to hold hands as we go to God, to sing in choirs and serve each other communion.

When you worship with a community, you can't help but have a sense that you belong there. That's because it's all about God—God bringing us into his family like one big reunion.

## Do That Little Thing: YOU CAN *SO* DO THIS!

If you don't have a place to go where people pray and sing and listen as one, and you would like to, talk to a grown-up, or even to one of your friends who has such a place. That desire didn't come from nowhere, you know.

If you do have a church you love, look around for other girls your age who don't. Invite one to come with you. Be her guide and introduce her to other kids there and to your pastor. Make her feel welcome. It's what you were made to do.

# Saturday

There is one body and one Spirit — just as you were called
to one hope when you were called — one Lord, one faith,
one baptism; one God and Father of all, who is over all and
through all and in all.

Ephesians 4:4–6

Y ou're so much alike!"
Ever heard that said about you and your best friend—or even
your whole group of best buds? It's neat, actually, to be identified as
a group by your special phrases and your same taste in clothes and
your unanimous love for double-cheese pizza. Even though you're
each unique, it gives you a close feeling to know you're connected
by what you have in common.

The whole community of God is like that. Each person is created
as a special individual, and yet we're all part of one thing:

- One Body—the body of Christ, which is the whole Christian church
- One Spirit—the Holy Spirit of God which fills us all and
  guides us along
- One Hope—that Jesus will return and set everything right,
  once and for all—no more pain and sorrow and disappointment
- One Lord—Jesus himself
- One Faith—our belief that Jesus died so that we can live
  forever with God
- One Baptism—that sacrament that says we've committed
  ourselves to living as Jesus taught us and that we'll someday
  be in heaven with God
- One God and Father of All—which requires no explanation!

That's what makes us a family. That's what we belong to.

## Do That Little Thing: SHOUT-OUT

Tell as many members of God's community as you can that you are
glad to be in the same family. Hugs are optional, but encouraged!

# WEEK 22

## You — Yes, You — Can Be Holy

> He chose us in him before the creation of the world to be holy and blameless in his sight.
>
> Ephesians 1:4

Nobody's perfect.

That's been obvious since Adam and Eve first chowed down on that no-no fruit in the Garden of Eden. The only sin-free person ever was Jesus, and even he got all over one guy for saying Jesus was "good." Only God is good, he told him.

So what is up with this verse that says God chose us to be "holy and blameless"? You may be thinking, "If that's the case, I'm definitely not one of the chosen ones. I've made enough mistakes since breakfast to disqualify me for holy and blameless. I give up!"

Not so fast. "Holy" doesn't mean "perfect." It means "set apart for God." That part has already been done, by God himself. He has created you for himself. He has made you perfectly capable of living your life for him, even if you make some mistakes along the way. In God's eyes you are, then, holy.

This week we'll explore what that looks like to God. Right now you don't know what goodness you are capable of. In just seven days, you're probably going to see yourself a little differently. Enjoy the discovery.

I am the Lord your God; consecrate yourselves and be holy,
because I am holy.

Leviticus 11:44

The word "holy" is used more times in Leviticus than in any other book of the Bible. It's also the book that has all the rules (hundreds of them!) God expected his people to follow. It wasn't that if they didn't do everything right down to the smallest detail they wouldn't be holy. He just wanted absolutely everything they did to be about him.

Everything.

Here are a few of the more interesting ones:

- "Do not curse the deaf or put a stumbling block in front of the blind" (Leviticus 19:14).
- "Do not wear clothing woven of two kinds of material" (Leviticus 19:19).
- "Rise in the presence of the aged" (Leviticus 19:32).
- "Keep all my decrees and laws and follow them, so that the land where I am bringing you to live may not vomit you out" (Leviticus 20:22).

Yes, it actually says, "vomit you out." We are talking about some serious stuff here! There can be no doubt that God wanted every part of the people's lives to be an offering to him. While Jesus came to free us from all those picky rules, God still expects us to live for him. That's what being holy means.

If it were impossible for us to do that, God wouldn't expect it of us. You can live a holy life. Let's find out how.

## Do That Little Thing: QUIZ

Put a star next to each area of your life below that you think you're keeping holy. Remember, that means letting it be about God, about goodness.

\_\_\_\_ how I look
\_\_\_\_ how I take care of my body
\_\_\_\_ how I treat my family
\_\_\_\_ how I treat my friends
\_\_\_\_ how I treat people who aren't my friends
\_\_\_\_ how I handle my schoolwork
\_\_\_\_ how I behave in activities
\_\_\_\_ how I talk to God
\_\_\_\_ how I treat myself

Don't think you're unholy if you don't have many stars. You're just beginning. Now you know what areas need holy work.

# Monday

These are improper for God's holy people.

Ephesians 5:3

Although there were probably too many rules in Leviticus for anybody to remember, much less follow, at least the people knew what God meant by "holy." What does holy look like now, in the 21st Century?

The New Testament doesn't have a list of rules, but it does talk about things that aren't holy. Here are some from Ephesians 5:3-4 that might come up at this time in your life:

- Greed (Do you really need 47 presents at Christmas?)
- Obscenity (Thank you for not swearing)
- Foolish talk (Just don't make a moron of yourself)
- Coarse joking (No dirty jokes and teasing that hurts people's feelings)

The lovely thing about the New Testament is that it doesn't just tell you what NOT to do. It tells you what IS holy, what TO do—and that's give thanks. If you want to be as holy as God knows you can be, give thanks instead of joining in with the cussing and the teasing and the "Gimmes." What does that sound like?

- "Thanks for the great birthday present, Mom." (Rather than, "That's all I get?")
- "Well, at least you guys care about me enough to ground me." (Instead of "$%&##!")
- "Thanks for coming to my dance recital, Grandma." (A good substitute for, "Did you see me up there, huh? Did you? Was I not incredible?")
- "I'm really glad you're my friend." (Leaving out, "Even if you are a complete klutz.")

## Do That Little Thing: FIND OUT

Ask your God-loving adult friends what they think "holy" means. Share what you now know about holiness. You might come away feeling a lot holier than you did before.

# Tuesday

*So you may know that I am the Lord, who makes you holy.*

Exodus 31:13

What did you do last Sunday? Maybe you went to church—maybe not. Did you have a special meal? Do something fun with your family? Rest and veg and get refueled for the week?

Or was it a day like any other except that you didn't go to school? In fact, did you use the day to catch up on homework or do that science project you've been putting off?

God gave us one of the easiest ways to be holy. He said, "You must observe my Sabbaths. This will be a sign between me and you for the generations to come, so you may know that I am the Lord, who makes you holy" (Exodus 31:13). Seriously, how hard is it to:

- set aside time to worship God? (even if your family doesn't go to church)
- forget about work for the day? (which means getting your homework finished on Saturday)
- rest? (play, kick back, hang out)

That doesn't sound like a tough rule to follow—that sounds like a gift! And there is nothing like enjoying a gift to make you think about the giver and be grateful. Next Sunday, worship God, put work out of your mind, and rest up for the week. In other words, be holy.

## Do That Little Thing: JUST THINK

Think out how you will spend this coming Sunday. If your family attends church, that part's taken care of. If not, ask a friend if you can go with her, or plan what you'll do by yourself to focus on God—even if it's just reading next Sunday's entry in this book. Plan what you'll do after worship too. (Don't forget to finish your homework before Sunday dawns.) Maybe you'll want to do something actively fun, like invite a friend over and go for a bike ride. Or perhaps you'll go for a day of rest, watching movies or curling up with your cat and a good book. Dream up the best day you can. Make it a holy thing for God.

# Wednesday

I urge you ... in view of God's mercy, to offer your bodies as living sacrifices, holy and pleasing to God — this is your spiritual act of worship.

Romans 12:1

Even after all we've said about holiness, it's hard NOT to think of being holy as sitting around looking angelic and praying 24/7. But no — being holy can be a messy business.

- While he was being holy, Daniel got thrown in a lion's den.
- Job, in his holiness, wound up covered in boils.
- And Paul? Being holy got him beaten up, thrown in jail, and tossed around in a shipwreck.

God gave us bodies and energy so we could get out there and DO holy things like:

- include kids who are being left out.
- tell people that gossiping and teasing and girl-drama are a waste of time.
- encourage students in your class who are struggling.
- share your stuff with kids who don't have much.
- lead the battle against bullying.
- forgive kids who just don't know any better.

Be a holy doer. It's what you were made for.

## Do That Little Thing: GOD? CAN WE TALK?

In your quiet time with God, ask him what he wants you to DO tomorrow that is within your holy power. Is it one of the things on the list above, or is it something else that's been niggling at you? If nothing comes to you right away, sleep on it. If you've really talked to God about it, he'll show you very soon what needs to be done. Then use your holiness, and just do it.

# Thursday

> In him the whole building is joined together and rises to become a holy temple in the Lord.
>
> Ephesians 2:21

If you're practicing your holiness, you might notice that not everybody totally appreciates it.

The bully you've told to back off the new girl doesn't like being called on her meanness. The kid who got all the attention for his teasing has a problem with you saying he really isn't funny. Even your friends get huffy when you announce that you're giving up dissing other girls behind their backs. Being true to your holiness doesn't necessarily make you popular.

Remember that you are not alone in Holy Land. All the "members of God's household" (Ephesians 2:19) are doing the same thing. Help each other and encourage each other when people make it tough to stay on the right track.

Let's say you're standing up for the kids who always get bullied on the bus. You've informed the bus driver that lunches are being grabbed and smashed and kids are being made to sit on the floor. You've put yourself between Mean Girl and her prey so there can be no pinching and threatening. You've even smothered that Queen Bee with kindness, smiling at her, telling her you like her shoes, giving her no reason to hate you.

Oh, but she does. She's started trying to bully *you* because you're interfering with her fun. Not to worry. You are "fellow citizens with God's people" (verse 19). You surround yourself with them in the lunchroom and on the playground so Mean Girl can't get to you. You all pray for her. As a group you truly hope she'll change.

That's how holiness works in the community of God.

## Do That Little Thing: LISTEN UP!

For the next week, listen for the work the other "members of God's household" are doing that is holy. Do you hear them defending the outcasts and calling people on their cussing and saying "good job" to kids who never get praised? If you do, join in. Holiness grows when God's people practice it together.

By the power of God, who has saved us and called us to a holy life — not because of anything we have done but because of his own purpose and grace.

2 Timothy 1:8–9

It's easy to start thinking your sweet self is pretty special when you're out there being all holy. No doubt you *are* being wonderful, and God is proud of you. But you're not holy because of all the good things you're doing. You're holy because God made you holy, and that's how you can do that great stuff.

If God hadn't put you together the way you are, it wouldn't occur to you to help a little kid or stop a girl-fight in the restroom.

So whenever someone compliments you on being a kind, giving, unselfish person, tell them it's just God working in you. Each time you do something nice for somebody, silently thank God for nudging you to do it. Ask God how he wants you to practice holiness in the next twenty-four hours, so that it's always a plan you come up with together.

It's not like it's a bummer to have to share the credit with God. It's actually nice not to have to think of holy stuff to do on your own. With all the other things you have to occupy your mind — school alone is enough to fill an entire brain — who could be responsible for all that? Only God. And that is a good thing.

## Do That Little Thing: YOU CAN *SO* DO THIS!

Make three columns on a piece of paper. In the left column, make a list of the last five things you did that were, uh, NOT holy, whether anyone else knew about them or not. In the center column, write down how you were punished or what the natural consequences were. For example:

| | |
|---|---|
| *I told Caroline's secret to Kim.* | *Caroline's not speaking to me.* |
| *I told my sister to shut up.* | *I got sent to my room.* |

In the right column, write the holy thing you'll do next time. And then close your eyes and know that you are God's holy princess, loved and forgiven, your sins forgotten.

# Saturday

[God] has reconciled you by Christ's physical body through death to present you holy in his sight, without blemish and free from accusation.

Colossians 1:22

What happens when you just can't be holy?

Let's say you're stressed out because you have to revise the rough draft of your essay and make it perfect. Your little brother comes into your room for like the thirteenth time, knocks your elbow, and your perfect paper has vanished from the screen. You grab your little brother by the arm and shove him out into the hall while screaming, "I hate you, you heinous little slime ball!"

You are automatically grounded from watching TV for a week. No amount of begging and whining to your parents about injustice is going to pay off that debt for you. Fair or not, there will be no *Hannah Montana* for you for seven days.

How are you going to go to God now, all ashamed and dejected? Because in God's kingdom, Jesus has already suffered through something way worse than a week without TV — dying on the cross for you. God has not only already forgiven you, he's forgotten what you did. That doesn't mean it's all right for you to beat up on your little brother. It does mean you are not, in his eyes, a rotten sister. You are holy, and next time a holy person will call for her mom to usher the kid out.

## Do That Little Thing: SHOUT-OUT

Give God the credit for your holiness right now. Have you made a loner feel like part of the group? Tell her God gave you the idea. Have you said something encouraging to your struggling big sister? Let her know God was in on it. Did you do the dishes without being asked? Admit to your mom that God suggested it. Challenge yourself to see just how many shout-outs you can give to the Father.

# How Do You Know Who You Are?

*"What about you?"* [Jesus] asked. *"Who do you say I am?"*
Matthew 16:15

There you are, *so* nervous because you're going to a party or a class or a camp where you don't know anybody, and some grown-up says, "Don't worry. Just be yourself."

Now how in the world are you supposed to do that when sometimes you're not even sure who you ARE? It can be a hard thing to figure out, especially when other people are constantly telling you who you are *supposed* to be.

- Your teacher says you have to do better than you're doing.
- Your mother says you have to be nice.
- Your father says you have to be tough.
- The commercials on TV say you have to be skinny and blonde with blindingly white teeth.

Even if you could pull all of that off, would that be you?

There's a great way to figure out who really you are: get to know God, and he'll show you. It really can be that simple—so let's go to God this week and see how it's done.

# Sunday

> I tell you that you are Peter, and on this rock I will build my church.
> Matthew 16:18

How does that work—you knowing God and him showing you who you are? Let's look at a time when it happened.

Jesus was traveling around, not only healing people and giving them hope, but announcing that he was the Son of God and was there to give them life forever. But when Jesus asked his disciples, "Who do people say that I am?" they gave him a whole list of answers, like John the Baptist or the prophet Jeremiah.

But when Jesus asked, "Who do YOU say that I am?" Simon Peter answered, "You are the Christ, the Son of the living God." Simon Peter saw what Jesus did and listened to what he said, and he believed him. He knew who he was following.

And for that, Jesus said, "Now I will tell you who you are, Simon." He said from now on he was to be called Peter, which means "rock," and he would build his church. He told Peter he would have everything he needed for the job.

God is still doing that today. If you notice what he does and listen to what he says through Jesus in the Gospels, you will find out what it means to be you, what your purpose is in this life, how God is going to help you do what he has put you here to do.

He will show you just who you are.

## Do That Little Thing: QUIZ

Put a star next to each thing below that you know for SURE about God. Leave any you're still wondering about blank. (It's okay to have blanks. Getting to know God is a long process.)

____ He forgives absolutely everything wrong that I do, think, or say.
____ He forgets it all, too.
____ He loves me just exactly as I am this minute.
____ He created me for a reason.
____ He considers me part of his family.
____ He wants me with him forever.

The more stars you can honestly fill in as time goes by, the more you're going to understand yourself. It just happens that way.

# Monday

> God said to Moses, "I AM WHO I AM. This is what you are to say to the Israelites: 'I AM has sent me to you.'"
>
> Exodus 3:14

Wouldn't you love to get one glimpse of God so you would know what he looked like? People actually have seen God, and most of the time they didn't believe it was God they were seeing! Take Moses, for instance. God appeared to him as a burning bush and said outright that he was the God of his fathers, Abraham, Isaac, and Jacob. And what did Moses do? He "hid his face, because he was afraid to look at God" (Exodus 3:6).

Once he did believe he was seeing God, Moses was scared nobody would believe him. People, he knew, would ask him what God's name was; what was he supposed to tell them? That's when God revealed something huge about himself, not just to Moses, but to us. He said, "I am who I am."

God is. He just is, and that's all he needs to be. He requires no explanation. When Moses accepted that, God told him who he was—the leader and freer of the Israelites.

If you can say, "God IS, and I believe he is exactly who he is," then God will show you that you, too, are just who you are. He'll help you understand that there is no need to try to be what someone else tells you that you should be. In time, he'll show you what your purpose is, that thing that shows you all that you are. For now, just relax into the knowledge that who you are is exactly who you need to be.

## Do That Little Thing: FIND OUT

Ask your God-loving friends (grown-ups and kids) to fill in the blank for you: God is _____. You're probably going to get a lot of different answers, because each person knows God in a way that is special to him or her. What your friends say about God is what God is teaching them about themselves. Now you fill in the blank, and learn something about YOU.

# Tuesday

> I am God Almighty ... No longer will you be called Abram;
> your name will be Abraham, for I have made you a father of
> many nations.
>
> Genesis 17:1, 5

How many times do I have to tell you?"
Ever heard *that* from a parent, teacher, coach, or babysitter?
You've done the same wrong thing for about the sixtieth time, and
that person in authority says, "How many times do I have to tell you
not to do that?"

Although it isn't a good idea to actually *say* it, the correct answer
to that is, "Obviously, until I get it." That's the way God is with us.
He has to keep telling us the same thing over and over, because we
don't get it. See if this sounds familiar.

- God appeared to Abram, announced who he was, and Abram
  fell facedown.
- God gave Abram a new name that would better reflect the
  job he had for him.
- God gave him an important mission, one that would show
  people who he, God, is.

It's a hard thing to grasp, that God wants us to know him so
that he can use us to tell more people about him. But if you can just
understand it, just a little piece of it, God can use you in big ways.
So look for God today. You don't need to fall facedown when you
find him. Just know that he is God. He'll do the rest.

## Do That Little Thing: JUST THINK

Think about all the places and times you've seen God in the last two
days. It probably wasn't in a burning bush, but it might have been in
the "Oh, I get it!" you felt in math, or in your grandma coming home
from the hospital. Think about what those things showed you about
who God is. (Go back to Sunday's list for help.) He likes showing
himself to you.

"Who are you, Lord?" Saul asked. "I am Jesus, whom you are persecuting ... Now get up and go into the city, and you will be told what you must do."

Acts 9:5–6

You can understand God showing himself to Abraham, Moses, and Peter. But Saul?

Saul of Tarsus was not a nice man. He was a lot like the Pharisees you read about in the gospels, big on rules but not on love. When the early Christians were trying to spread the message of Jesus, Saul was out there throwing them in jail and sometimes even killing them. What they were doing was against Jewish law, and he wasn't having it.

So why on *earth* would God call on him, in the voice of Jesus, and give him the most important job in his new kingdom? Because God knew that Saul wasn't being his true self. He was doing what he'd been taught to do, what made him feel important and powerful. But he wasn't being who he was made to be.

Saul's true self was full of the very qualities God needed in a person in order to get the Jesus message out. Saul was smart and had great leadership skills. And when he was excited about something, there was no stopping him. All God did was say, "This is who I am, and now I'm going to show you who you really are, not who you think you are."

And—big surprise—Saul changed his name, from Saul, which means "asked of God," to Paul, which means "little." He could now be a humble servant of God, and feel pretty good about that. It always feels good to be your honest-to-goodness self.

## Do That Little Thing: GOD? CAN WE TALK?

In your quiet time with God, ask him if there are things you're pretending to be that you really aren't. Discussing it with God makes you feel safer about admitting that you only wear sparkly flip-flops because all the other girls do, when you'd really rather run around in tennis shoes. Or that you laugh at jokes that really aren't funny because you don't want to be left out. Just telling God about it can help you be more true to the real you.

# Thursday

God is greater than our hearts, and he knows everything.

1 John 3:20

Think back to when you first met your best friend. She was fun and happy, and she said such neat things about you. You couldn't imagine ever having a fight.

And then the day came when she said something to hurt your feelings or you found out she'd told a fib or you noticed she had a habit that got on your nerves. Did you think, "Now I know what she's *really* like"?

Why do we see the "bad" things in people as the "real" things, and the good things as just an act? God sees it in just the opposite way.

In today's verse, Paul says that God sees into our hearts where the love and the hope and the goodness are. When we mess up, that's the opposite of who we are. It's the result of our anger or our hurt feelings or our need to be noticed. What's true is when we show love in our actions. When we share our lunch with the kid whose mom didn't pack him one or stand between the bully and the girl who gets picked on every single minute — that's the truth about us.

Everything else is just an attempt to cope. When you really know God and talk to him every day, when you listen to him and obey his Word, you don't have to do wrong, stupid things to get attention or feel better. God gives the attention you need for the real you.

## Do That Little Thing: LISTEN UP!

Tell God about something you've done that really wasn't you. Something you did because you were mad or jealous or feeling left out. Ask God to show you what to do with those feelings of hurt and anger. Then pay attention in the days to come. You'll get your answer in some way you may not even expect, and you may find out something surprising about you.

# Friday

We know that we have come to know him if we obey his commands.

1 John 2:3

What color are your best friend's eyes? What's her favorite book? If somebody gave her a pony, what would she name it? You can probably answer all those questions without a second thought because you KNOW your BFF.

But how do you know if you really know God? Even if you hang out with the Father 24/7 and think you have a pretty good idea what he's like, it's hard to know for sure.

Try this rule of thumb: if you are doing what God commands us to do, you know him; if you're disobeying, you really don't know him at all. John says if you do any of these things, you don't really know God that well yet:

- hate your brother, or any other human being (1 John 2:9)
- crave (absolutely have to have) a lot of stuff (1 John 2:16)
- brag about what you have (1 John 2:16)
- believe people who tell you that Jesus isn't God's Son and you don't have to believe in him or follow him (1 John 2:22)

If you know and love God, you automatically:

- love your fellow human beings.
- care more about people than stuff.
- give God credit for what you have.
- love Jesus for all that he was and is.

Nobody does all of that perfectly, but if you're doing it most of the time, that's a good sign that you really do know God—and at this very minute he is showing you who you are too.

## Do That Little Thing: YOU CAN SO DO THIS!

Look at the four things above that people do when they know and love God. Is there one that you know you don't do most of the time? Could you make a change there, just a little one? If it's going to happen, you'll need God, but just identify what you need to do and then pray. By trying you'll show that you know our God better than you thought you did.

# Saturday

To all who received him, to those who believed in his name, he gave the right to become children of God.

John 1:12

If someone says to you, "Who are you?" you probably answer with your name, first and last. Your last name identifies you as a child of somebody, a member of a family that is helping to shape how you grow up.

Let's say a baby girl is born very sensitive and shy. If she has parents who understand that some babies are just like that, they will help her as she grows up to get used to being around people. She will always be a little timid, but she'll know how to work with that. If she has parents who think there's something wrong with being shy, they'll tell her not to be such a crybaby and push her to be outgoing. She might be able to cope with new situations, but she'll always think there's something bad about being the way she is.

Since there are no perfect parents, it's a good thing that before we are their children, we're God's children. Whatever qualities we have, they're the real us. We can use them to love people and serve God. We can be our true selves because we belong to God's family.

So what does that mean? It means open up your arms wide and embrace God, the Father who made you and loves you and gave you Jesus to guide and save you from being somebody you aren't.

## Do That Little Thing: SHOUT-OUT

Tell somebody that you like to talk to what you've learned in this lesson — that you were made to be your child-of-God self. That will be practice for the next time someone tries to tell you who you ought to be. You'll be able to tell them that Jesus was — and still is — the only perfect child of God, and he's the only one you're going to imitate, just by following his lead. When you can do that with ease, you know you're on your way to the true you.

# You Are Good — As Long As You've Got God

*I have the desire to do what is good, but I cannot carry it out.*
Romans 7:18

I'm not going to talk back to my mom anymore," you tell yourself. Yet within the hour you're toe-to-toe with her, eyes rolling, mouth spewing out, "Mo-om—no!"

"From now on, no more gossip," you tell your best friend. But before the day is through you hear yourself saying, "I don't mean to talk about her, but..."

What is that about? Why—like Paul in today's verse—do we not do the good we want to do, but instead the evil we don't want to do (Romans 7:19)? Are we just plain bad?

Paul says no, we aren't bad. The reason we make bad choices is because we're trying to cope with a messed-up world. Talking back to your mom is how you keep from feeling like everything is out of your control—because so much of it is. Gossiping is a way to feel like you belong, because it's scary to think of being an outsider.

Is there anything you can do about that? Absolutely. That's what this week is about: understanding that you were made for good. You've got God.

# Sunday

Hate what is evil; cling to what is good.

Romans 12:9

Ever been so engrossed in a video game, a DVD, or a book that your mom had to call you eight times just to get your attention? When it comes to something you're totally into, your powers of concentration put nuclear scientists to shame.

That ability to focus is a God-given gift and we all have it to some degree. But not all of us use it for one of its most important functions, and that is to focus on God.

We're not talking 24-hour prayer. You'd starve and flunk out of school. Focusing on God means, as today's verse says, "Cling to what is good." Cling—the way a baby koala hangs onto its mom.

When you get so irritated with your mother that you think your head is going to explode, it won't work just to say to yourself, "Be respectful. Don't talk back." You have to hang on to the right words with everything you have. "Mom," you can say through your teeth, "I'm so mad I'm about to say something evil. Can I go to my room and calm down?" Once there, you can hug your Bible, or throw yourself down on the bed and cry to God. Do what you have to do to hold onto honor for your mom.

"Cling" is an active word. It requires effort. Good isn't going to grab you and drag you back from evil. But once you hold on, you've got God. So start strengthening your clinging muscles!

## Do That Little Thing: QUIZ

Check off all the good things you'd like to do this week.

\_\_\_\_ Treat my brother(s)/sister(s) better.
\_\_\_\_ Be more respectful to my parents.
\_\_\_\_ Be kinder to kids who don't fit in.
\_\_\_\_ Pray more.
\_\_\_\_ Gossip less.
\_\_\_\_ Be less all-about-me with my friends.

Choose one to cling to this week, and ask God to help you hold on.

# Monday

I want you to be wise about what is good, and innocent about what is evil. The God of peace will soon crush Satan under your feet.

Romans 16:19–20

W hat is the deal with your parents not letting you watch R-rated movies or late night TV, and banning violent video games? Come on—that's realistic stuff. Don't you need to learn what the real world is like?

The real world? What's this you're living in now? The fake world? Just because something is dark, evil, and wrong doesn't make it real, and it sure doesn't mean it's true. Yes, it's important for you to know what drugs can do to you so you'll avoid them. You need to be aware that it isn't safe to wander around outside by yourself at night. It would be wrong for your parents not to make you aware that driving drunk is dangerous. But you don't have to see drug addicts, child snatchers, and drunk drivers to get that. In fact, those images can be hard to erase from your mind.

You have a much better chance of bringing out the good in yourself by learning about good things. Get an education in the things Jesus focused on—helping the poor, taking care of the hurting, encouraging the bummed out. Learn how to do that, and you'll be too busy for evil!

## Do That Little Thing: FIND OUT
What did you choose to cling to in yesterday's quiz? Why?

_____

_____

_____

_____

_____

_____

_____

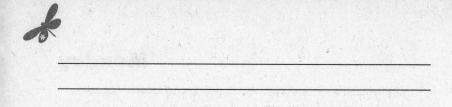

_____

_____

_____

_____

Ask a God-loving grown-up how you might learn more about that good thing. Then educate yourself. Become a specialist of Good!

# Tuesday

Solid food is for the mature, who by constant use have trained themselves to distinguish good from evil.

Hebrews 5:14

Think about something you've learned to do well or are working on. Maybe it's dribbling a soccer ball. A dance move. A new piece on the piano. Long division. How did you get it right? Did you read a book about it? Have somebody tell you how to do it? Watch someone else do it? Those things might have helped. But didn't you master that skill by *practicing*?

It's impossible to get really good at step-ball-change without putting on your tap shoes. Nobody ever played in a recital without hours at the keyboard first. It's the same with learning to do good. You can read the Bible, listen to sermons, and hang out with good-doing people all you want, but you won't even begin to bring out the goodness in yourself unless you practice.

It's tough. There are no "goodness scales" to pound out, no worksheets to sweat over. You just have to "be good" again and again. Make the right choice even if it isn't the popular choice. Refuse to get dragged into something you know isn't right. Create safe, healthy, fun situations to replace hazardous-to-your-health ones that put people down.

You'll make mistakes. Just start over and try again. It's the only way to train yourself. God's right there, coaching you.

## Do That Little Thing: JUST THINK

Close your eyes and imagine yourself doing one of the things you came up with yesterday for "learning about good." Think of all the ways it could possibly play out. For today, just think and pray. Tomorrow, do. Repeat often!

# Wednesday

Do not be misled: "Bad company corrupts good character."
1 Corinthians 15:33

Have you ever had a friend your parents weren't so crazy about? That girl who cussed? The one who dissed people behind their backs? Maybe you saw her better qualities, or you insisted you could help her. You may have even pulled out the argument that Jesus hung out with bad dudes, so why shouldn't you?

First of all, it shouldn't be a news flash that you are not Jesus. You're learning to imitate him and learn from him, but "learn" is the important word. You are not yet strong enough to spend time with way un-Jesus-like people and hold your own. It's hard enough to cling to the good when you *aren't* surrounded by people who think evil is a blast. It's almost impossible to be around someone who cusses and not start thinking a few swear words yourself. A really cool girl who is hilarious when she's talking trash about someone else can be irresistible. You're going to laugh—and then you'll join right in.

That doesn't mean you should hate those people. It just means you don't need to spend a lot of time with them. If you have to, because you're in the same class or on the same team, tell them how you feel about swearing or put-downs and give them a chance not to do those things around you. Then surround yourself when you can with God-lovers, and your goodness will blossom.

## Do That Little Thing: GOD? CAN WE TALK?

In your quiet time with God, talk to him about someone whose goodness isn't blossoming. Ask for God's strength and wisdom for him or her. God can do what you can't.

# Thursday

Each man [and woman] should give what he has decided in his heart to give ... so that in all things at all times ... you will abound in every good work.

2 Corinthians 9:7-8

Look at me, being all wonderful."
Maybe those exact words have never crossed your lips—that would *so* be bragging—but if you're like every other human being on the planet, you've at least thought something like that. You make the sour-faced lady in the nursing home smile, and you feel pretty good about your sweet self, right? It's easy to forget that God put that sweetness in you in the first place.

In fact, God has a whole system in place when you do something good:

- God gives you the idea to give of yourself—to share your lunch or give up recess to tutor somebody.
- You give generously.
- You feel really good about it.
- You want to give some more.

And God smiles, because that's what God had in mind all along.

## Do That Little Thing: LISTEN UP!

Since God gives us our good ideas, it makes sense to listen for them. In your quiet time, pay attention for suggestions about the goodness you've been trying to develop in yourself since Sunday. God has just been waiting for you to ask.

# Friday

He who began a good work in you will carry it on to completion.
Philippians 1:6

D on't start something you can't finish."
"You can't do that until you finish this."

"No, you can't take up the clarinet (gymnastics, tennis) because you've already quit guitar, ballet, and soccer, and we have a thousand dollars' worth of equipment gathering spiderwebs in the garage."

We're all guilty of not following through with something in our lives. We human beings abandon a lot of things as we seek and search for things we enjoy and are good at. Since God isn't human, he doesn't do that. God doesn't start what can't be finished. He has a total plan for everything and he's going to see it through.

Take you, for instance. He has begun a good work in you. That's obvious. You're reading and using this book, aren't you? That's just one sign that God has started you off on a journey. He can take you all the way down your path. All you have to do is pay attention, watch for the signs, and follow them. God won't give up on you. God never quits.

## Do That Little Thing: YOU CAN *SO* DO THIS!

It's time to take a step in that area of goodness you chose Sunday. You've started to educate yourself. You've listened for God's directions. Now take a deep breath and do that little thing. Read to your little brother. Ask your mom if you can help her fold the laundry. Say hi to the girl everybody laughs at. Stop a rumor. Give your friend a compliment. Spend five minutes telling God you love him. Do it. It's a good thing.

# Saturday

Let us consider how we may spur one another on toward love and good deeds ... let us encourage one another.

Hebrews 10:24–25

When you think about it, you belong to several groups: the family you live with, your extended family (grandparents, aunts, uncles, cousins), your class, your whole school. You might be a member of a Sunday school class — in fact, a whole church. If you play sports or take lessons or you're involved in activities, you have a team, a class, a squad, or a troop. It would be pretty lonely without your groups.

It would also be really hard to become your good self all alone, without other people. Even you and God together won't pull it off, just the two of you. God has set it up so that we need each other.

Jesus gave his disciples the job of speading his message. Paul (who wrote the letter today's verse is in) took friends with him to build the faith — Silas, Timothy, Barnabas, Priscilla, Lydia. He always talked about "we" and "us," and his letters were to big groups of people.

For you to be the best you possible, you need other people who are trying to do the same thing. And they need you. Encourage your friends when they have to stand up to a bully. Cheer them on when they turn their backs on bad choices. Sit with them when they're disappointed because nobody gets them. Be there for each other — because you weren't made to do it alone.

## Do That Little Thing: SHOUT-OUT

Did you take that small step toward goodness yesterday? Did anyone help you — by saying, "You can SO do this" or "Good job, girlfriend"? Go to your "cheerleader" and tell him or her how it went. Then celebrate your accomplishment together — you two and God. He's SO good!

## Messenger Girl

> Go into all the world and preach the good news to all creation.
>
> Mark 16:15

Isn't it just way hard to say good-bye to somebody you love being with? You've just had a great vacation with your grandparents, and you can hardly hold back the tears when they drive away. You're Daddy's Girl, and you get cranky when he goes off on a business trip. Your best friend moves away, and you feel like life as you know it has come to an end.

The only thing that makes it better is to have a plan for what to do next while you're getting over the sadness. We'll make a scrapbook of your trip, your mom says. You can email Dad every night, and in the meantime, let's go out for ice cream. Go have a good cry, and then we'll invite all your other friends over to begin to fill the gap.

You can imagine how the disciples felt when Jesus was getting ready to ascend into heaven. What helped at that moment was the "next thing" he told them to do. He gave them the Great Commission — told them to go out and spread the word about him to everyone. This, he said, is what you must do for me so that everyone will have what you have. This is the only way you can fully receive my gifts.

That was pretty strong stuff — and it still is. The Great Commission is for everyone who believes in the Message and life of Jesus. We can't keep the goodness to ourselves.

"But I'm just a kid!" you may say. And your point is? There is much you can do as God's Messenger Girl. This week, we'll explore your options.

# Sunday

How beautiful on the mountains are the feet of those who bring good news.

Isaiah 52:7

Beautiful feet? Are we talking pedicure here? This verse actually refers to messengers in biblical times who ran from the scene of a battle to bring news of the outcome to a waiting king and his people. Folks must have loved those feet that ran so hard and so far to bring them news, especially when it was good. And how cool is it to be the bearer of great news? Don't *you* love to greet somebody with "Guess what?" and watch her face break into a smile when you tell her the best thing ever?

As God's messenger, you can do that all the time, because you have the ultimate good news. As the verse goes on to say, you can:

- "proclaim peace"—Tell your friends to focus on God-things and there won't be all this gossip and hurt feelings and high drama in the girls' restroom.
- "bring good tidings"—Tell them they don't have to worry about being good enough, being popular, and fitting in, because God loves them, and when they know that, they will shine with the inner light that brings people right to them.
- "proclaim salvation"—Tell people all they have to do is believe God saves them from the trap of sin and wants to be with them always, even after they die.

That's better news than even a Snow Day!

## Do That Little Thing: QUIZ

What is the part of the Message of Jesus that you love the most? Put a star beside it here.

____ God loves me, no matter what.

____ All God expects of me is to love him and my neighbor and myself.

____ Jesus already took the punishment for my sin; God doesn't punish me — he just forgives me every time and tells me to sin no more.

____ God has a plan for me.

____ God will help me get through and grow from any hard times I have.

____ I can look forward to being in heaven with God at the end of my life here on earth.

Let whatever you starred be your Good News for this week. Now let's learn how to spread it.

# Monday

How, then, can they call on the one they have not believed in?
And how can they believe in the one of whom they have not
heard? And how can they hear without someone preaching to
them? And how can they preach unless they are sent?

Romans 10:14–15

Okay, you get the point. If everybody is going to get the Message, somebody has to tell them. But does that somebody have to be you?

Let's see. *What if that girl will never go to a Sunday school picnic if you don't invite her? What if that kid will never know what Christmas really means unless you show him? What if that group of girls will always think Christians are stuck-up goody-goodies unless you show them what you're really made of?* There are certain messages to particular people that God has put in your to-do list. If you wait for somebody else to do it, (a) that's so much longer for the person to go without the good news, and (b) you will miss out on the blessings that come to you when you share. Run, right now, and say, "Guess what?" with that precious piece of good news.

## Do That Little Thing: FIND OUT

Take the part of the Good News you decided on yesterday to a God-loving grown-up and ask how he or she would share that with someone. You might even practice on her — over a snack, of course!

# Tuesday

Think of what you were when you were called. Not many of you were wise by human standards; not many were influential; not many were of noble birth.

1 Corinthians 1:26

You might be all set to share the Good News with somebody—and then you start thinking about your pastor, who preaches those long sermons, half of which you don't even understand; or your Sunday school teacher, who can quote the Bible faster than you can text message; or that evangelist on TV, who gets so worked up about the Gospel he practically cries. It's enough to make you give up before you start. How are you—a kid!—supposed to speak for Jesus? You didn't go to seminary. You aren't even a grown-up!

You don't have to be any of those things to be a Messenger. You are, in fact, the exact kind of person God uses. It's all in 1 Corinthians 1:27-28. Haven't you ever felt like you were:

- "foolish"?—"You silly thing!"
- "weak"?—"You're just a kid—and a girl, even."
- "lowly"?—"I'm just in elementary/middle school. Nobody pays attention to what I say!"
- "despised"?—"I'm not exactly the most popular girl in my class."

Why would God use you as a messenger? Because you know you're only able to do anything good that you do because of God, which means you won't brag about how wonderful YOU are. You're *just* the girl for the job.

## Do That Little Thing: JUST THINK

Imagine youself (foolish, weak, lowly, and despised) sharing your special part of the Jesus Message with someone who is foolish, weak, lowly, and despised, too, and really needs to see what God can do. Dream it. See it in your mind. Feel it in your soul. Get ready.

# Wednesday

I came to you in weakness and fear, and with much trembling.
My message and my preaching were not with wise and per-
suasive words, but with a demonstration of the Spirit's power.

1 Corinthians 2:3–4

That's *Paul* talking. Paul, who wrote all those wise letters, whose
words we turn to so we can sort out what we're supposed to do
as Christians. If *he* was scared when he first started delivering the
Message, if he felt like he didn't know what he was doing, how are
*you* supposed to be a Messenger?

The same way Paul did—just by showing people what God's
spirit is doing in your life. It's okay if you're nervous (okay—freaked
out). Maybe you don't know exactly what to say or you're afraid
people are going to make fun of you, think you're a geek. You might
be convinced that you'll be too pushy and turn people off totally.

Don't worry. Know that God's Holy Spirit is in you. It's who
you are. You can demonstrate that with your life. As St. Francis of
Assisi, a great messenger of Christ, once said, "Preach the Gospel
always. If necessary, use words."

## Do That Little Thing: GOD? CAN WE TALK?

In your quiet time with God today, talk about how you can *show* that
piece of the Message he's sparkled in your heart. Tell God any ideas
you have. Express your fears about putting yourself out there. Ask for
strength and wisdom and protection from people who aren't ready
to see. God loves to discuss that stuff.

# Thursday

> They received the message with great eagerness and examined the Scriptures every day to see if what Paul said was true.
>
> Acts 17:11

You're on Day 173 of this book, which means you've read a little more than 175 verses of the Bible. Out of 66 books, that's such a teensy part of the whole Message. Even if you read this entire book to a Jesus-seeker, would that be enough?

Relax. God isn't asking you to give every person you share with the *whole* Message. Even Paul didn't do that. He got people started, and then it was up to them to read and study and get to know God by knowing Jesus.

So just share your piece (from Sunday) with as much enthusiasm as you can. Live it. Be it. Encourage people to check it out for themselves. God will take care of the rest.

## Do That Little Thing: LISTEN UP!

Ready to get out there and be God's messenger girl? There's one more thing you need to do before you get those beautiful feet moving. Get quiet with God and ask if your plan, your thoughts, your ideas for sharing are what he wants. It's easy to get in his way, so listen for the little niggly warning signs that this is about you, or that you're about to act like the boss, or anything else that keeps the Good News from being good. Look at anything that makes you uncomfortable. Talk to a grown-up about it if you need to. God wants you to be perfectly clear — because this is big news you're carrying.

# Friday

Go, stand in the temple courts ... and tell the people the full message of this new life.

Acts 5:20

The apostles were the first messengers for Jesus, and they totally had it going on. They were healing the sick and drawing more and more people to the faith. The Jewish high priests and associates who didn't believe the Message were jealous of all the attention the apostles were getting and had them arrested and thrown in jail.

Anybody just out there preaching their own thing would have spent one night in a smelly, rat-infested prison cell and decided it wasn't worth it. But when an angel of the Lord sprung them from jail and said, "Get out there and keep talking," they went straight to the temple and in front of everyone went right back to teaching.

It may not be that hard for you to stand up for what's right and tell people it's God who works in you. But doing that could put you in social danger. You could end up in the prison of the unpopular. Will there be an angel of the Lord available to help you?

You can count on it. If you're sharing what God gives you to share, God will not leave you locked up all alone. God frees. So keep running with the Good News.

## Do That Little Thing: YOU CAN *SO* DO THIS!

You're ready. You have a message. You're the one to carry it. You don't have to be a professional preacher. You don't even have to be totally sure of yourself. You can show with your life and share with your words the Good News of love and forgiveness. Your God-loving friends have shown you how and God has coached you. Now go do that little thing.

# Saturday

> Can anyone keep these people from being baptized with water? They have received the Holy Spirit just as we have.
>
> Acts 10:47

There's a chance you haven't done your sharing yet. Maybe you haven't had the opportunity or you chickened out. It's okay because there's a reason, and it isn't that you're a wimp. Maybe you're thinking you can't do it because you haven't been going to church all your life. Maybe you haven't been baptized yet or you're not used to talking about what you believe because your friends aren't there yet.

You know what? If you feel pulled to what you've been reading in this book, you too can be a Messenger for Christ. It isn't a closed club. Peter made that clear when non-Jews felt the Holy Spirit and wanted the whole Jesus-life. "We're no better than they are," he said. "Baptize them!"

Not ready to share yet? Then just learn all you can about the Message. Become part of a community of Jesus-lovers. Pray and get to know God personally. Just doing those things will show God to someone, maybe without you even realizing it. You'll know when you're ready to tell what you know. You were made for it.

## Do That Little Thing: SHOUT-OUT

Whether you've shared your piece of the Message with someone, or you're still preparing yourself, give God the credit. Grab a friend and say, "Guess what God did with me today!" and then tell her — even if it's just the tiniest thing. Guess what? You just shared the Message. Go messenger girl!

# You Are a Child Who Needs God

You are the children of the Lord your God.

Deuteronomy 14:1

Y ou treat me like a child!"

Ever said that—or thought that—to your parents, or anybody else who doesn't recognize that you are practically an adult (give or take a few years)? It's not like you can't make up your own mind about things, right? You can make a peanut butter and jelly sandwich, make your bed, put together an outfit that doesn't scream "Little Girl!" Why can't they give you some credit for your maturity?

If you think that from time to time, imagine what was going through the heads of the people Moses was talking to when he said, "You are the children of the Lord your God." They were grown-ups who had just spent forty years in the desert looking for the Promised Land. At least some of them must have thought, "Who are you calling a child?"

But Moses knew, because God told him that all of us are children in God's eyes because we don't always know what's best for us and even when we do know, we don't always act like it! This week is about accepting that, to God, we are always kids—his kids. And it's about finding out what a huge and wonderful thing that is for us. So get ready to curl up in God's lap and learn what it really means to be one of God's children.

# Sunday

> Whoever humbles himself like this child is the greatest in the kingdom of heaven.
>
> Matthew 18:4

Maybe you're the slickest goalie the soccer league has ever seen or the only one among your cousins who can touch your nose with your tongue. And then somebody comes along who can do it better. That person is so good at it that you have to just stand back in awe and say, "Wow."

When that happens, you're *humbled*.

Jesus chose the disciples to be his closest friends, which would make anybody feel like they were all that. One day they even came to him and said, "Who is the greatest in the kingdom of heaven?" (Matthew 18:1). They probably expected him to say, "Oh, definitely you guys."

Instead, Jesus called a little kid over to stand with him and said, "I tell you the truth, unless you change and become like little children, you will never enter the kingdom of heaven" (Matthew 18:3). Not only would they not be the greatest, they wouldn't even get in! He didn't mean they should start sucking their thumbs. He said they needed to be humble, like that little boy or girl who looked up at him with big ol' eyes and knew he or she was loved and safe.

No matter how old you get, or how tall, or how good at fractions, you will always be a child of God. God is in charge, and without him you really can't do a good thing. Look to him with wonder, run to him when you're hurting, hug his neck (in your mind!) when he gives you a gift. If you don't, you'll miss out on so much.

## Do That Little Thing: QUIZ

Check off all the reasons you still like being a child.

\_\_\_\_ Somebody fixes my breakfast, lunch, and dinner

\_\_\_\_ Somebody hugs me before I go off to school/start my day

\_\_\_\_ Somebody takes care of me when I'm sick

\_\_\_\_ Somebody buys me Christmas presents

\_\_\_\_ Somebody celebrates my birthday with me

\_\_\_\_ Nobody lets me act like a brat

\_\_\_\_ Somebody helps me with my schoolwork

\_\_\_\_ Somebody goes to my soccer games, recitals, plays, or parent/teacher conferences

\_\_\_\_ Somebody listens to my problems and helps me solve them

\_\_\_\_ Somebody tucks me into bed at night

\_\_\_\_ Somebody loves me no matter what I do

# Monday

What son is not disciplined by his father?

Hebrews 12:7

When you tell your mom or dad that some kid you know is an absolute brat and needs somebody to straighten him out, do your parents immediately go to that child's house and ground him?

Hello! No! That's not their kid!

Only the real parent is responsible for getting a kid into shape. Teachers may help, along with coaches and grandparents, but at the end of the day, it's up to the mom and dad—the ones who love him, know him, care how he turns out.

God is the ultimate Father, the one who parents even your dad. He cares enough to discipline his kids. Otherwise, we'd all turn out to be shoplifters or permanent couch potatoes. Although "discipline" isn't everybody's favorite word, it's really one of the best reasons to accept that you are God's child, because "discipline" doesn't just mean "you're grounded." To be disciplined by God means:

- to spend time with him every day.
- not to clutter up your life with a lot of unnecessary stuff that keeps you from thinking about God.
- keeping his commandments to love him, your neighbor, and yourself.

When God the Father disciplines you as his child, he inspires you to stick to those things, make time for them, make a place for them. And when you do, you get closer to him. So close you're in his lap. And that's where he wants you.

## Do That Little Thing: FIND OUT

Ask your God-loving grown-up friends what their spiritual disciplines are. If they aren't sure what you mean, show them this page and talk about praying, reading the Bible, giving away possessions, or things like that. Maybe some of the things they tell you will be disciplines you'll want to adopt to bring you closer to God's lap.

Both the one who makes men holy and those who are made holy are of the same family. So Jesus is not ashamed to call them brothers.

Hebrews 2:11

The neatest thing about being a child of God is that you get to have Jesus for your brother. He's the Son of God, right? And since you are God's daughter, well ...

That is cool on a number of levels:

- If you have a big brother who sticks up for you and makes you feel special, but isn't always there, you have Jesus who is always available to look after you and have late night talks.
- If you have an older brother who is none of the above, Jesus fills the gap.
- If you have a little brother you are crazy about, now you know how Jesus feels about you as his little sis.
- If you have a younger brother who drives you nuts, you know how amazing Jesus is to put up with you, his younger sister, without screaming, "Get away from me, you brat!"

You have the perfect brother who is not ashamed to call you his fellow sibling. You're part of the same holy family he belongs to, even if on earth you have no brothers and sisters at all. Didn't life as a child of God just get a lot less lonely?

## Do That Little Thing: JUST THINK

Imagine sharing your childhood with your brother Jesus. What would it be like when you get scared at night? Or when you're nervous about a new situation? Or when you're faced with kids who aren't being so nice to you? Think about him always being there to both boo-hoo and giggle with. Get a picture in your mind of being your silliest self and him laughing with you instead of at you. Keep that image, those thoughts, that picture — because they're for real. Your brother Jesus is all of those things. He's sharing your childhood with you.

# Wednesday

Everyone born of God overcomes the world.

1 John 5:4

Have you noticed that temptations dangle in front of you like piñatas hanging from the ceiling, waiting to be smacked open?

The opportunity to cheat on a test. The urge to juice up that rumor a little, and then pass it on. The need to smack your brother because he's being a mini-moron.

How are you supposed to resist all that stuff?

One of the benefits of being a child of God is that your Father makes you able to overcome. You are filled with his Spirit, which makes you strong enough to turn your eyes away from Straight-A girl's paper so you won't copy it. It gives you the wisdom to bite your lip instead of passing on gossip. It tells you that decking your brother, no matter how annoying he is, isn't going to make him less moronic.

Your mom and dad didn't just give you all the rules when you were born and expect you to remember and follow them all. Neither does God. Just as they tell you over and over (and over!), so God fills you, strengthens you, talks to you again and again, day after day. After all, you are his child. He wants you to overcome the sin of the world that separates you from him, so the two of you can be closer. And when God wants something, he can make it happen.

## Do That Little Thing: GOD? CAN WE TALK?

What is one temptation you'd like to overcome right now, this very minute? Write it here or keep it firmly in your head.

_____

_____

_____

Tell God that temptation is hanging over your head, just waiting for you to reach up and grab it. Ask him to please help you pass it up, or even better, knock it out of the way. If you and God have had this discussion before, that's okay. Remember, he's there over and over, again and again, because as his children, we need him. We need him badly!

# Thursday

You are no longer a slave, but a son; and since you are a son, God has made you also an heir.

*Galatians 4:7*

Do you know the word *heir*? Not to be confused with hair, *heir* is pronounced without the "h" so it sounds just like "air." An heir gets (inherits) all of someone's money and property when that person dies. Usually the heir is the son or daughter, and when someone is wealthy, his children expect that when he passes on, they will be very rich indeed.

A slave, on the other hand, can't expect anything when the master dies. In the days of slavery, a master owned slaves as if they were property, not people. He didn't love them as he did his children, and he sure didn't leave them anything after he was gone.

You are not God's slave. He doesn't think of you as property that he owns. He loves you and wants you to be taken care of. Since you are a child of God, you can expect to receive everything that he has to give. You are, then, an heir to everything God has for you.

It's still possible for you to be a slave, though, to things like popularity, the desire to have a whole lot of stuff, the need to be in charge all the time. Those things can own you, force you to do things you know in your heart are just wrong. If you're a slave, you get nothing. Knowing God through Jesus can set you free of those things and make you an heir. Then you get everything. Easy choice, huh?

## Do That Little Thing: LISTEN UP!

Close your eyes and get quiet. Do you hear any chains rattling? Not real chains, of course, but the inner sound of things that might be keeping you from being free. Listen. Does the clanking of your thoughts tell you that it's time to stop trying to get into the "cool" group, and make some true friends? Does it say you might want to stop badgering your mom for yet another new cell phone, and help her with the little kids instead? Listen. And then shake off those chains. You're the only one who can. God's there to help.

# Friday

> In my Father's house are many rooms ... I am going there to prepare a place for you.
>
> John 14:2

You're (hopefully) not thinking about getting married any time soon, but when you do have daydreams (or nightmares!) about settling down with a great guy someday, you more than likely picture the two of you in a home of your own with some kids in the back-yard playing on the swing set.

Back in biblical times, a Jewish girl had a different vision. She knew that when she got engaged, her husband-to-be would go to his dad's house and get a room ready for them, because it was the custom for the bride and groom to move in with HIS family after the wedding and live there to raise their kids. A bride knew her fiancé really, really cared about her when he prepared a special, perfect-for-her place in his father's house.

That's what Jesus meant when he said to the disciples, "I am going there (to my Father's house) to prepare a place for you. I will come back and take you to be with me." And what a place it was: heaven.

That's the promise in being God's child. You get to "marry" Jesus—become his true love and spend your whole after-this-life with him—and live in the Father's house in heaven.

So not only do you get to spend life here as the daughter of God, but you can look forward to that special place he has prepared for you when you go to be with him forever. That's a lovely dream you know will come true.

## Do That Little Thing: YOU CAN *SO* DO THIS!

Make a list — or draw a set of pictures — of all the special places God has prepared for you here, in your lifetime already. Your haven of a room? The place on the beach or lake you go to every summer? Your grandmother's convertible? Your dad's lap? With all of those in front of you to make you smile, you can begin to imagine what heaven will be like. Makes you want to stay real close to God, doesn't it?

# Saturday

Dear friends, now we are children of God, and what we will be has not yet been made known.

1 John 3:2

What do you want to be when you grow up?"

"I think you're going to be built just like your mother."

"Do you think you'll keep playing the piano (dancing, ice skating, playing basketball) when you're older?"

Grown-ups talk about stuff like that, but who really knows what you're going to be, or even what the next phase of your life is going to look like? It might be kind of a bummer if you did, because there would be no surprises.

God the Father seems to like surprises, because we totally have to rely on him to help us discover who we really are. But one thing being a child of God does tell us: "We know that when he [Jesus] appears, we shall be like him, for we shall see him as he is" (I John 3:2).

The more you accept that you are God's daughter, the clearer it is that when Jesus does return, you're going to recognize him — and you're going to be just like him. He is, after all, your brother. He does free you from being a slave to your own sinful stuff so you can be an heir like him. He is getting your room ready for you.

Everyone who spends this life getting closer and closer to God will be just like Jesus. No bullies. No hurt feelings. No excluding and gossiping and worrying and grabbing for stuff. Just the brothers and sisters of Jesus, hanging out in God's house. Who would want anything else?

## Do That Little Thing: SHOUT-OUT

Who do you want to tell that you are a child of God? A fellow sister or brother? Somebody who doesn't have much of a family and needs one? Choose somebody who will "get it" and share your joy. Make it a "family" picnic or pizza night or snuggle-in. Celebrate that you are heirs with a whole lot to look forward to.

# PART III

# HOW DO YOU GET TO BE A HOLY CHILD OF GOD?

> We ... are being transformed into his likeness with ever-increasing glory, which comes from the Lord, who is the Spirit.
>
> 2 Corinthians 3:18

Remember those fairy tales you used to hear or watch on DVD when you were a kid (or maybe even just last week!)? There was always something being transformed into something else—a boy into a donkey or a frog into a prince or a beast into a drop-dead-gorgeous babe. It was make-believe, but it made for a great story.

But here's something that isn't pretend: you are right this very minute being transformed. Seriously. You are being changed from who you think you have to be to get along in this world, into the real you who is more and more like Jesus every day.

We're not talking magic. We're talking about the Spirit of God, which comes to you through Jesus and curls around inside you, slowly turning you into a brighter, more beautiful version of who you are now.

That might sound too fantastic to believe, which is why we're going to spend the next thirteen weeks showing examples of people who were transformed in that very way. As you read and wonder about them, you're going to see yourself transforming, too, little by little, moment by moment. It won't be magic. It will be true—the truest story you'll ever hear.

## Two Sisters, One Hot Guy

> Now Laban had two daughters; the name of the older was
> Leah, and the name of the younger was Rachel. Leah had
> weak eyes, but Rachel was lovely in form, and beautiful.
>
> Genesis 29:16–17

That sounds like a fight waiting to happen, doesn't it? Two sisters, one squinty and cross-eyed, the other a candidate for America's Next Top Model. Can't you just see the stuff that went on in their growing-up years?

People saying, "Isn't it a shame about Leah's eyes? Now Rachel, she is a knock-out." Enough of that and Leah was probably ready to knock *Rachel* out.

Kids making fun of Leah, but crowding around Rachel, wanting to be her friend—as if they, too, could become beautiful just by hanging around her.

As they got older, boys asking Leah to set up a meeting with Rachel, and never noticing that Leah had her attractive features too.

Who would have blamed Leah if she resented her sister, Miss Thing? The jealous curl to her lip probably didn't do anything to improve her appearance, which only made things worse.

And nobody could really criticize Rachel for thinking she was all that from time to time. You don't hear how much prettier you are than your poor, funky-eyed sister all your life and not believe it just a little bit.

That's the scene we start this week with—two sisters who aren't in the best place. Let's see how God transformed them. And how he can do the same in you.

# Sunday

When morning came, there was Leah! So Jacob said to Laban, "What is this you have done to me? I served you for Rachel, didn't I? Why have you deceived me?"

Genesis 29:25

Remember Jacob, a good guy you read about in Week 4? When he went out looking for work, God not only blessed him with a job at his Uncle Laban's successful sheep farm, but he also presented him with a beautiful young woman—Laban's daughter Rachel.

The minute Jacob saw her, he went over to her and kissed her and started crying. That was some serious love at first sight. Jacob went to work for Rachel's dad, promising that he would work for him seven years in return for Rachel as his wife.

When you think about how old you'll be in seven years, that will give you an idea what kind of sacrifice Jacob made to have Rachel. When it was over, Jacob went to Laban and said, "Okay, I'm ready to marry her."

Laban threw a major wedding, complete with the traditional veil for the bride. But behind that veil was not Rachel, but Leah. Jacob didn't find out until the next morning that Laban had married him to the wrong girl. Laban pulled this trick because he didn't think it was fair for the younger sister to marry first, and he was really worried that nobody was ever going to get past Leah's "weak eyes" and want her for his wife.

Can you even imagine how everybody felt? If there isn't some major transformation soon, this story isn't going to have a happy ending. Stay tuned.

## Do That Little Thing: QUIZ

Check off any of these areas where you feel resentful — you just know this isn't fair at ALL:

\_\_\_\_ Your brother or sister gets more attention, or gets away with more, than you do

\_\_\_\_ A parent makes decisions that make YOU want to scream

\_\_\_\_ A teacher treats some students better than others in your class

\_\_\_\_ Everybody flocks to the girls who are "perfect." You have nice qualities too, but nobody notices

\_\_\_\_ Some girls just seem luckier than you are

Keep these handy as we go through the week. You might just see some transformation happen.

# Monday

> When Rachel saw that she was not bearing Jacob any children, she became jealous of her sister.
>
> Genesis 30:1

Jacob didn't just let Laban get away with his trick. He demanded to have Rachel as his wife. So Laban worked it out—if Jacob promised to work for him seven *more* years, he could also have Rachel. After fourteen years, Jacob had two wives.

Poor Leah. It was obvious that Jacob didn't love her, that his heart belonged to Rachel. God saw Leah's pain and blessed her with children—one boy after another, until she had four. She kept thinking Jacob would start to love her because she was giving him sons, which was a big honor back then.

It was the first time ever that Leah got to have something her sister didn't—because Rachel wasn't producing any children—and Rachel was jealous. Now she knew how Leah felt all those years. She wasn't going to have that, so she let her maid, Bilhah, have two sons for Jacob. "I have had a great struggle with my sister," she said, "and I have won." Can you stand it?

Not to be outdone, Leah let *her* maid, Zilpah, bear two sons for Jacob. And after that, she herself had two more sons and a daughter for Jacob. The count was now Leah, 9, Rachel, 2. Finally, God "remembered Rachel," and she had a son of her own. "God has taken away my disgrace," she said. But was she satisfied with that? Are you kidding? She named her son Joseph and then said, "May the Lord add to me another son."

Was there any hope that these two women were ever going to stop competing with each other and simply be who they were made to be? God saw some hope. Read on.

## Do That Little Thing: FIND OUT

Ask your God-loving grown-up friends if they ever competed with anybody so hard that it got out of control. Maybe it broke up a friendship or came between brothers or sisters, or even put God out of the picture. You *can* learn from other people's mistakes — so get into their stories. You're sure to see how they've been transformed since then.

Then Rachel and Leah replied, "... Surely all the wealth that
God took away from our father belongs to us and our children.
So do whatever God has told you."

Genesis 31:14, 16

Tricking Jacob into marrying Leah wasn't the last nasty thing
Laban did. He also tried to cheat Jacob out of the flocks that
belonged to him. God didn't allow that, which really ticked Laban
and his sons off. Finally, Jacob decided not to put up with it anymore, and, with God's help, he formed a plan. He decided to take
Rachel and Leah — and all of those kids! — back to his own home.
He was worried that Rachel and Leah would be upset about leaving,
but *finally* the two agreed on something. They told Jacob they were
behind him all the way.

Because Laban was a hard man, Jacob took his considerable family away secretly in the middle of the night. Rachel made off with
her father's household gods (small, portable idols that she worshiped
because she hadn't given up her pagan background yet).

When Laban discovered his family was gone he went after them,
demanding to know why Jacob would do such a "horrible" thing.
Jacob laid it all out for him, until Laban really couldn't say a whole
lot. But he was still upset about the missing household gods and
accused Jacob of stealing them. Rachel kept them hidden until her
father finally gave up and let them go. At last Rachel saw that she
needed to think about somebody besides herself. Finally she and
Leah teamed up to support the family. The transformation had
begun.

## Do That Little Thing: JUST THINK

Go back to those resentments you checked off on Sunday's quiz.
Choose one and think about what it would take for you to let go of
that and work with the person you're jealous of or have issues with.
What would be more important than staying mad? What would feel
better than clinging to that's-not-fair? This might take some imagination, but remember, it took the fear of being separated from their
husband and kids that turned Rachel and Leah around. Think big.

# Wednesday

> They gave Jacob all the foreign gods they had and ... Jacob buried them.
>
> Genesis 35:4

Rachel, Leah, and Jacob got away from Laban and made peace with Jacob's long lost brother Esau (whom you'll remember from Week 4), and had a few other adventures along the way that could have cost them their lives. At last God told Jacob to settle in Bethel and build an altar there, which meant they were to worship him and only him, and he would protect them in their new home.

Jacob had become a great leader for his family, and he knew that it was only because of God that they were still together and alive. He told everybody to get rid of their foreign gods, get cleaned up, change their clothes, and help him build an altar.

There's nothing in the chapters before this that says Rachel ever got rid of those household gods she ripped off from her father. If she still had them, she, like everyone else, took them to Jacob so he could bury them. It was time to turn her life completely over to the God who had saved her. Time to bury the old and get on with the new.

That must have meant Rachel buried her old issues with Leah, too, because those are never mentioned again. There was no more fighting over Jacob, no more competing for who could have the most babies. They just settled in Bethel, and God blessed them.

Living in obedience to God did it. They were blessed with a new place to live safely and in freedom. They were different women because God transformed them. Now they were who they were always meant to be.

## Do That Little Thing: GOD? CAN WE TALK?

Now that you've decided what resentment you'd like to let go of, and you've imagined what it might take to get you to do that, talk to the Father about how much better it would be to dump the jealousy now than wait until something forces you to. Ask for his help. Promise your obedience, even if it's hard. Tell him you're willing to bury the old stuff. He'll give you the shovel.

# Thursday

A nation and a community of nations will come from you, and kings will come from your body.

Genesis 35:11

When you think about what a messed-up bunch Jacob, Rachel, and Leah were when they first met, it's pretty amazing to see them at this point in the story. God came to Jacob—actually appeared to him. How cool is that? God blessed him and told him that he was going to turn that slew of kids—there were eleven of them now—into not just one nation, but a whole community of nations. Some of the children and grandchildren and great-grand-children of Jacob and Rachel and Leah were going to become kings and lead those nations for God.

That was the promise God made to Abraham and Sarah, who had Isaac, who married Rebekah, who had Jacob. God was doing what he said he'd do, and while he was doing it, he was transform-ing the people he used to do it. None of them was perfect—least of all Rachel and Leah, who spent the first half of their lives trying to outdo each other and hating each other's guts. And yet he changed them into who they really were, the mothers of kings.

You can trust that God can change you into your true self too—because he will. In fact, he's doing it right now. You have no idea what is starting within you this very minute. Cool, isn't it?

## Do That Little Thing: LISTEN UP!

Do something a little different today. Instead of listening to God, which hopefully you'll do anyway, listen to yourself. Hear what you say, what you think, all the noises you make inside and out. You might find that some of those things surprise you with their grown-up-ness, their almost-adult wisdom, their hint of who you're becoming. Write them down if you want, or just savor them. It is delicious to discover that you are not all that you are going to be.

# Friday

> As she breathed her last — for she was dying — she named her
> son Ben-Oni.
>
> Genesis 35:18

Just when you're getting to like and respect Rachel, she dies.

But it wasn't totally a sad thing. First of all, remember in Monday's reading, the minute Rachel gave birth to Joseph she asked God for another son. She was giving birth to that second son when she died. Benjamin became the leader of a strong tribe that you'll hear about again and again in the Bible.

Jacob loved her until the end. He set a pillar on her grave that stayed there for a long time. Many, many years later the prophet Samuel told a future king, Saul, to go to Rachel's tomb, where his journey to being "changed into a different person" (1 Samuel 10:6) would begin. She was never forgotten.

Her son Joseph, as you learned back in Week 4, was one of God's most obedient sons, who made a huge difference in the lives of everyone he touched. Rachel lived on in him.

Who would have thought that beautiful young girl who fought with her sister and tried to outdo her in the baby department would turn out to be the inspiration for so many? It didn't happen overnight. It wouldn't have happened at all if it hadn't been for God. But it happened. And it's been happening to God's daughters ever since. Get ready, because something just like that is happening in you too.

## Do That Little Thing: YOU CAN *SO* DO THIS!

You knew this was coming, didn't you? It's time to get busy letting go of that resentment, that jealousy, that urge to compete in an unhealthy way. Think about what your God-loving friends have shared with you. Consider what you may have heard from God, perhaps in that almost-grown-up voice that spoke up in your head. Then take a step. Tell that girl you're jealous of that she's a really great soccer player. Ask your big brother for help with your math homework, even though it kills you that everybody thinks he's this genius. Ask your dad to assure you that he loves you just as much as he does your little sister, even though she got the dimples. Just do it. It will transform you — into You.

# Saturday

A voice is heard in Ramah, mourning and great weeping,
Rachel weeping for her children and refusing to be comforted,
because her children are no more.

Jeremiah 31:15

Centuries after Rachel died—we are talking hundreds of years—Rachel's name came up again. Here's why. It gets a little complicated, so try to hang in there.

- Rachel had Joseph, who had two sons, Manasseh and Ephraim.
- Their grandfather, Jacob, blessed them and said they would become great and would father two groups of nations named after them.
- Ephraim and Manasseh did turn out to be the two most powerful tribes in the northern kingdom of Israel, but they were taken over by the Babylonians and the people were taken into captivity.
- So when Jeremiah says you can hear Rachel crying for her children, it's his way of saying that the whole kingdom mourned as it passed through Ramah on its way to Babylon.

Rachel herself did a lot of crying in her life. It makes sense that Jeremiah would use her name to help people understand the great tragedy of the exile. She sacrificed a lot. But her name lives forever. And she still helps us understand how we are being transformed.

## Do That Little Thing: SHOUT-OUT

Do you feel like you've changed a little this week? Maybe you took that step to stop resentment, or you understand God a little better, or you just know you aren't always going to be the person you are today. Whatever has happened, share it with somebody you know will understand. And don't forget to give God the credit. He's working hard in you.

# WEEK 28

## Judge Deborah

Deborah, a prophetess... was leading Israel at that time.

Judges 4:4

Wait a minute. Did you say Deborah? As in a female? Leading Israel?

Kind of makes you look twice, doesn't it? Most of the other kings and prophets and important people you read about in the Bible are men. Deborah was definitely a woman, and a pretty smart one at that. But how did she get to be in charge?

At that time, the Israelites had finally—FINALLY!—entered the Promised Land. All they had to do was run out the Canaanites, who were a pretty messed up bunch, and make the new land a kingdom for God. There was no need for an earthly king, because God was in charge. They just had judges who helped sort things out when people got things confused.

And, boy, did they. Instead of getting rid of the Canaanites, the way God told them to, they settled in with them, married them, adopted their gods, and pretty quickly forgot that they were supposed to be living totally for God.

It was up to Deborah, during her term as judge, to straighten some of that out. She had to be transformed from "just a woman" into a leader who could turn her people away from the bad decisions they were making against God. This week, her story will get you up and moving on some "judging" you might need to do.

# Sunday

She held court under the Palm of Deborah ... and the Israelites came to her to have their disputes decided.

Judges 4:5

Ya gotta love Deborah. No stuffy courthouse (or tent!) for her. Unlike the male judges who held court in a city gate where people probably felt nervous and uncomfortable, she put everybody at ease by parking herself in the shade, outside, where people could just join her and talk out their problems.

There are a couple of other things you're going to love about Deb.

- Her name means "bee," which makes you think of honey, right? In Hebrew it also refers to the sweet juice of the dates, which grew on the palm she sat under.
- The justice Deborah handed out was as sweet as the date juice (honey), and people knew that. She wasn't there to make people feel small. She was there to make things fair for them.
- She was the only judge who was also a prophet. Having that special connection with God made it even easier for her to see the right thing to do.

We're starting off with Deborah already doing a good job for God, but that doesn't mean she couldn't still grow. You, too, can go along for a while making good choices, growing up as God's child. And then all of a sudden, a situation will come up that really challenges you to move to the next level. That's what happened to Deborah. You'll learn more about her tomorrow.

## Do That Little Thing: QUIZ

How do you think you're doing as a child of God? Check off the statements below that are true for you. (Don't be too hard on yourself!)

\_\_\_\_ I talk to God.
\_\_\_\_ I listen to God.
\_\_\_\_ I think about what God wants me to do.
\_\_\_\_ I do what I think God wants me to do.
\_\_\_\_ I check my actions with what's in the Bible.

_____ I really, really love God.
_____ I try to love other people the way I love myself.
_____ I ask God for forgiveness when I don't do the above.

You're doing better than you thought, aren't you? God has given you a good start. Who knows what great things are going to happen from here!

Because of the way you are going about this, the honor will not be yours, for the Lord will hand Sisera over to a woman.

Judges 4:9

M en. They ask you for advice and then when you give it to them, they don't want to take it. Just ask your mom about that!

Or read about Deborah (Judges 4:6–24). The Israelite warriors wanted her to tell them how to conquer the Canaanite army led by a guy named Sisera. So Deborah told Barak (a warrior of Israel) to take 10,000 men to Mount Tabor while God lured Sisera right into a trap.

The instructions came straight from God, but did Barak listen? Negative. He whined and said he'd only go if Deborah went with him. There's a brave man for you. Deborah said, fine, but he wasn't going to get the credit for the victory. A woman was.

So Deborah was transformed from a quiet prophetess under a palm tree into a warrior. She went with the 10,000 men because that was what had to be done, what with Barak wimping out. God uses the people who are willing to become more than they are right now. You're a mini-woman. Read on to see how you can become a warrior too.

## Do That Little Thing: FIND OUT

Ask your God-loving adult friends to tell you about a time when they had to take on a new role because somebody else couldn't (or wouldn't) do it. Find out if they felt like somebody different in the process.

# Tuesday

"Stand in the doorway of the tent," he told her. "If someone comes by and asks you, 'Is anyone here?' say, 'No.'"

Judges 4:20

God didn't only make Deborah brave; he made her clever. With her riding off to battle with Barak and his 10,000 buddies, you'd think her prophecy that the honor of victory would go to a woman meant that woman was her. Hmmm ...

Finally listening to Deborah's instructions from God, Barak led the army to Mt. Tabor and scared the daylights out of Sisera and his men. Sisera—another "brave warrior"—abandoned his chariot and took off on foot. The Israelites got everyone else while Sisera hid out at the home of Jael—a woman.

She agreed to hide him. Covered him up. Gave him milk. Told him she'd keep his whereabouts a secret. And when he went to sleep, she cheerfully stabbed him with a tent peg, and he died.

Deborah was right. The honor of getting rid of the evil Sisera went to a woman. And on that day God took care of the enemy Canaanites and saved Israel.

Sometimes it takes a woman to do a man's job, so be ready for your transformation, which hopefully won't involve tent pegs!

## Do That Little Thing: JUST THINK

Can you think of things that usually only boys get to do? Things you might like to try, but you haven't yet because you thought they weren't for girls? Whether it's going fishing with your dad instead of shopping with your mom, or seeing how good it feels to burp as loud as you can — try it. God doesn't want you to limit yourself to what the world assumes is "the girl thing." You sure didn't see Deborah doing that.

# Wednesday

When the people willingly offer themselves — praise the Lord!
Judges 5:2

How do you celebrate when you've done something that is, quite frankly, incredible? When you get a 100 percent on a test or score your all-time high in goals or nail your solo in a recital, do you go out for ice cream? High-five everyone in sight? Do a cartwheel?

What you probably don't do is make up a song about it (although if you do, all *right!*) But when a major victory was scored in Deborah's day, it was common to write a piece of music to celebrate. Usually it told the whole story of what happened, just like you do for your friends when they weren't there to share the thrill with you. Always the song included praise for God, who made the whole thing happen, and Deborah was right there with that. She was brave and clever and loyal, but she gave God all the credit.

That's the best transformation there is.

## Do That Little Thing: GOD? CAN WE TALK?

Today, get together with God and talk about the last big thing you did (big to you, at least), that screamed for celebration. Celebrate with him — making him the guest of honor. He won't mind if you eat his cupcake for him. Songs are optional!

# Thursday

Village life in Israel ceased, ceased until I, Deborah, arose, arose a mother in Israel.

Judges 5:7

Have you ever looked back in time and thought, "Wow ... this is so much better than it used to be"?

Maybe you've been in a new school for six weeks and you suddenly realize you have friends, you feel at home, and you're so much happier than you were that first strange day. Could be you've felt that way when your new baby sister or brother stopped screaming all night or you finally recovered from the worst case of chicken pox in medical history. Good is so much better when you compare it to how bad things used to be.

Deborah sang about that — about how before the victory people couldn't live normal lives in the villages because enemies were always marching through their streets and setting up camps on their lawns. Then she'd followed God's instructions and helped the Israelites fight back and restore peace. How very cool for her to see how her willingness to be transformed made life so much better for her people.

That's the best part of something good: the memory of you and God working together for change.

## Do That Little Thing: LISTEN UP!

Listen to your past. Go back into a memory of a tough time or just a hard day. Relive the things you knew you had to do to better that day in the principal's office, or that week your dad was in the hospital. Hear in your head how you're a little different now because of those things. That is the best.

# Friday

May all your enemies perish, O Lord! But may they who love
you be like the sun when it rises in its strength.

Judges 5:31

G reat job, girl!"
Yes!

"Now, this is the kind of work I expect from you from now on."

Oh.

That's the thing about improving, rising to the next level. Once
you've made an A in math, baked (rather than charbroiled) a batch
of cookies, or emptied the dishwasher without argument, everybody's going to expect you to keep doing it forever and ever. Amen?

And why not? You've shown you can do it. You're a bit of a different person now. Why shouldn't this be the start of a new pattern?
Transformation isn't about one fine performance—like the Israelites obeying God and putting down the king of the Canaanites. It's
about becoming more like your true self so you will always rely on
God to help you defeat your enemy—be it the Mystery of Math or
the Demon Arguer.

So, yes, when you change, so will other people's expectations
of you. But that will only make you better and better. Forever and
ever. Amen.

## Do That Little Thing: YOU CAN *SO* DO THIS!

What little victory have you (and God) achieved lately? Did you
refrain from telling your sister to shut up? Sit through a whole church
service without getting up to go to the bathroom, get a drink, floss
your teeth? If you could do it once, you can do it most of the time.
Start the pattern today by doing it just one more time. You'll rise in
strength like the sun!

# Saturday

Then the land had peace forty years.

Judges 5:31

Well, what do you know?
The Israelites got it right, and look at that: they finally had some peace. And for a whole generation. That means all the kids born that year grew to be 40 years old—older than your parents, probably—without enemy soldiers threatening them. They could actually eat, sleep, learn, play, and grow without fear.

You've never had to be afraid of a war breaking out in your neighborhood, but you may have seen your share of "battles." Maybe your parents fighting—sisters and brothers at each other's throats— drama among the girls at school. Think about the butterflies in your stomach, the sweaty palms, the wide-awake-at-night *that* causes, and then multiply it by a thousand. That's how it feels to live in a war-torn country like Iraq or Darfur.

To people there, and to the Israelites, peace is and was a precious thing. The Israelites had it because of a woman named Deborah, who was willing to be transformed by God into who she needed to be.

You can be the cause of peace in your battles too. Just ask God to let you be transformed. There is no end to what you can do.

## Do That Little Thing: SHOUT-OUT

You're being transformed right now. Look back at your answers this week. Think about the steps you've taken. Now tell an important person in your life what God's doing — even if he's merely giving you the courage to talk about it. (A palm tree is not required for this conversation, but some honey might be nice.)

## From Nobody's Girl to Everybody's Mom

Naomi returned from Moab accompanied by Ruth the Moabitess, her daughter-in-law, arriving in Bethlehem as the barley harvest was beginning.

Ruth 1:22

You met Ruth back in Week 21. She was the one whose husband died, but she didn't go back to the safety of her own family. She took her widowed mother-in-law back to *her* home, in a different country. It was bad enough for Ruth, just leaving the only home and people she'd ever known. But if you'll recall, she and Naomi had to travel alone across dangerous desert, risking death from thieves and wild animals.

They weren't even sure what kind of welcome they were going to get when they arrived. Naomi had left her people years before. Would they even remember her, much less still love her? And Ruth was a foreigner. People were way suspicious of strangers.

As we pick up Ruth's story now, she was frightened and poor, though determined to take care of old Naomi. You'll see by the end of this week how God changed her—and her life.

# Sunday

Why have I found such favor in your eyes that you notice me — a foreigner?

Ruth 2:10

Who gets all the attention in your life? Your list might look something like this:

- my little sister who pitches fits
- my older brother who's this football star
- the girl in my class who has, like, every outfit they sell at Limited Too

It seems like the people who get noticed are the ones grabbing for the spotlight—whether they deserve it or not! Wouldn't it be nice if someone looked your way and said, "Wow—you are so good. Hey, everybody, have you met this girl? She's like the most obedient, well-behaved kid."

Probably not gonna happen. And yet you never know. Ruth just quietly did her thing—picking up leftover grain in the fields all day so she could feed Naomi. But Boaz, the land-owner, who was actually one of Naomi's relatives, saw that she was special. He told her where to get the best leftovers, made the men who were drooling over her stay away, and offered her water whenever she was thirsty.

"Why me?" Ruth said.

Why anyone else? Boaz knew the sacrifice she'd made for Naomi, how she was basically giving up having a life of her own to help her mother-in-law. He thought Ruth should be rewarded.

It's worth it to quietly do the right thing without expecting applause or even thanks. It's where transformation begins.

## Do That Little Thing: QUIZ

Put a check next to things you do that don't get noticed much.

\_\_\_\_ I get myself ready in the morning (without a cattle prod)
\_\_\_\_ I do my best in school
\_\_\_\_ I help my teacher
\_\_\_\_ I help other kids
\_\_\_\_ I never push in line
\_\_\_\_ I obey the rules
\_\_\_\_ I share my stuff
\_\_\_\_ I let my sisters and brothers be first
\_\_\_\_ I do my chores without whining
\_\_\_\_ I do my homework
\_\_\_\_ I pray

Now smile, just because you do those good things. Sometimes that's enough.

# Monday

"The Lord bless him!" Naomi said to her daughter-in-law. "He has not stopped showing his kindness."

Ruth 2:20

It can be scary when the grown-up who's in charge isn't there any more. You wonder who's going to take care of you when parents get divorced, or the cool teacher quits to go have a baby (the nerve of her!).

Even grown-up women in Ruth's day felt that way. When Naomi's husband died, she, like all widows, had to depend on her male relatives to take care of her. But both her sons had died, and she wasn't sure when she returned to Bethlehem if her kinsmen there would do the job.

What a huge relief it must have been for her the day Ruth came home and told her Boaz was feeding her, giving her extra stalks of barley, and protecting her from the other workers who thought she was cute. It was the first time Naomi felt any real hope in a long time.

Had Ruth done anything big to give her that hope? She was just being loyal, doing what she had to do — but she changed Naomi's life. You just never know what difference the small things will make. Best to keep doing them, right?

## Do That Little Thing: FIND OUT

Ask your God-loving adult friends if they ever suddenly found themselves taken care of — especially when they didn't expect it. You may hear stories of modern-day Ruths and Boazes, stories that will inspire you to keep on doing those small things.

# Tuesday

This kindness is greater ... You have not run after the younger men.

Ruth 3:10

Have we mentioned that Ruth was a cutie? And young? Most of the guys who worked for Boaz had checked her out, and she basically could have had any one of them she wanted.

Boaz, on the other hand, was closer to Naomi's age. Sure, he was rich, but he'd probably given up on the idea of marrying a beautiful young woman long ago. We're thinking *he* was showing *Ruth* all this kindness, but when she showed him that he was the one she chose to be with, he thought *she* was the kinder one.

That's the way it works when people keep doing the good, right thing. They just can't outdo each other. They simply continue to be kinder and kinder. And as they do, it becomes more and more natural. It becomes part of them to be generous and thoughtful and all those things we can't just wake up one morning and decide to be.

See who you can try to "out-do" in the kindness department this week. You'll be amazed at the change in you.

## Do That Little Thing: JUST THINK

Think of someone who is always kind to you. Is it your teacher, who never ceases to understand your issues with spelling? The lady next door who lets you watch the Disney Channel at her house because your family doesn't get cable? The girl on the bus who shares her Lifesavers with you every single day?

Now think of something kind you could do for that person. Better yet, come up with a whole list. Try to "out-do" him or her. And the more you can do without that person knowing it's you, the more fun it will be. There's going to be kindness all over the place!

# Wednesday

Don't let it be known that a woman came to the threshing floor.
Ruth 3:14

Has the boy thing started in your school or group yet? You know, a girl "liking" a boy, and then getting somebody to find out if he "likes" her, and then the word getting out to, like, the whole school—and the girl getting embarrassed and the boy being all, "Shut UP!"

It can get out of control. Boaz didn't want any of that going on with Ruth. She'd taken a big risk coming to him and showing him that she wanted to be with him. He wanted no teasing, no rude remarks, no rumors started by the other guys. So Boaz did what *every* guy should do for the girl he loves—he protected her reputation.

That made Ruth feel special. (Because she was. Because every girl is.) It gave her confidence. She was transforming from shy little grain-gatherer to almost-wife. All it took was God, working in a man like Boaz, and a girl like Ruth soaking it all up.

What does this mean for you? As you begin to notice that boys aren't always absurd little creeps, be sure you spend time with the ones who care what other people say about you, that want them always to speak the truth. The Boazes make the best boy-type friends.

## Do That Little Thing: GOD? CAN WE TALK?

Ask God to show you someone whose reputation you could help protect. Are there rumors circulating that you know aren't true? Do kids just assume things about a girl without really knowing her? God can help you be a Boaz for some wonderful Ruth. How cool would that be?

# Thursday

Although it is true that I am near of kin, there is a kinsman-redeemer nearer than I.

Ruth 3:12

Boaz loved Ruth. Ruth loved Boaz. They were good to go, right? In those days it was more complicated than that. When a woman's husband died, it was the responsibility of the closest male relative to marry her. Naomi liked Boaz for Ruth, so she hadn't told Ruth there was a closer male relative she should ask first.

But as crazy as Boaz was about Ruth, he couldn't ignore the law. He had to go to the other guy first and see if he wanted Ruth. It must have been scary for Boaz, Ruth, and Naomi. What if the guy said, "Sure, I'll take her"? Everybody would be miserable — including the guy himself who didn't even know Ruth. She would have been just another one of his wives.

God was totally in charge, though. The other relative didn't want to mess up his nice life by bringing in yet another woman. He gave his sandal to Boaz (a sign that he was turning over the "property" to him), and Boaz was free to marry his precious Ruth.

Don't you love a happy ending? This one came about because Boaz used his integrity, even though it was risky. That's how transformation happens.

## Do That Little Thing: LISTEN UP!

Integrity is like your conscience — that little voice in your head that says, "Yes, you could cheat, but don't," or, "Sure, you could tell a lie and get out of this mess, but I don't advise it." Listen for that voice today. Heed what it tells you. Be transformed.

# Friday

He will renew your life and sustain you in your old age.

Ruth 4:15

"One more thing."

You may have heard that from the conscience-voice we talked about yesterday.

You help your mom by tucking your little brother in. You give him something to drink. Read him a story. Listen to his prayers. And as you slip out of the room to go do your homework or watch some TV, he says in that quivery little voice, "I'm scared. Can I have a hug?"

You could say, "I've done enough. Go to sleep." But your This-Is-God voice says, "Do this one more thing."

In Ruth's case, you may think she really *had* done enough. There couldn't *be* one more thing to do, could there?

There was.

Ruth and Boaz got married and had a baby named Obed (poor kid). And what did Ruth do? She *gave* the baby to Naomi, so she would have a "kinsman-redeemer" to take care of her. All the women said, "Naomi has a son."

Was there no end to what Ruth would do to keep her promise to Naomi? Evidently not. She just kept growing kinder, more loyal, more godly. That's what happens when you're transformed. You just want to do more and more, because you're changing, growing, becoming more the amazing you that you were created to be. It makes every sacrifice worth it.

## Do That Little Thing: YOU CAN *SO* DO THIS!

Helped anyone lately? Is there one more thing you could do? Did you let that never-gets-it-together kid borrow a pencil yesterday? Could you give him a few to keep today? Did you give your scared little brother a hug last night? Could you sit with him until he falls asleep tonight? Do that little thing.

# Saturday

Obed [was] the father of Jesse, and Jesse the father of David.

Ruth 4:22

Before we leave Ruth, you might want to know that she was rewarded for all her sacrifices — and not just with having that great guy, Boaz, for a husband. Her "prize" lasted longer than her lifetime — all the way to today.

When Obed (Ruth and Boaz's kid) grew up, he had a son named Jesse. Jesse later had a son named David. Remember David? All the way down through the generations, the promise was whispered by God that the Messiah, God's Son, the Savior of the world, would come from David's line. Straight from Ruth. She left her home, risked her life, worked to scrape together food, married an old man, and gave up her baby. In the process, she was transformed, from a scared young widow to a great-times-42 grandmother of the Son of God, our Jesus.

What can you say to Ruth except, "Thank you."

What can you do, except be as loyal and loving as she was?

What can you be, except transformed?

And you can be. Just like Ruth, you were created by God, you are loved by him, you have been given a purpose that somehow points to Jesus. You may not have to leave your family or risk your life to do it, but you'll make sacrifices too. If you make them with love and loyalty, trusting that God is behind it all, you will become all that you were made to be. And that, God's Daughter, is what you're here for.

## Do That Little Thing: SHOUT-OUT

What's the most fabulous thing you've learned this week as you've lived Ruth's story with her? Tell somebody about that — just that one thing that has stuck with you, that you will probably remember for a long time, that one thing that might even at this moment be transforming you.

# WEEK 30

## From No Lunch to All You Can Eat

> Whenever Hannah went up to the house of the Lord, her rival provoked her till she wept and would not eat.
>
> 1 Samuel 1:7

Got any plans for the kind of woman you want to be? Maybe a businesswoman in a great suit, carrying a leather laptop case. Perhaps an artist in a long flowing skirt, showing paintings in your own gallery. Or could it be a doctor in a white lab coat, saving lives one medical miracle at a time?

Maybe you've pictured yourself as a mom with a baby on each hip and several more playing in the backyard. That was the only dream women in biblical times had. From the time they were little girls they imagined themselves having little sons and daughters to sit at their tables and play at their feet and grow into fine grown-up people who themselves would have families. It was all about that.

So when a woman wasn't able to have children for some reason, it was not only sad; it was considered a disgrace. Surely she must have done something wrong, people thought, or God would have blessed her with the one thing that made her life worthwhile — children.

That's where we find Hannah. She was one of the two wives of Elkanah. His other wife, Peninnah, had children, but Hannah had none, and Peninnah couldn't leave it alone. She did everything she could to make Hannah feel bad about not being a mom — until Hannah was so upset she wouldn't even eat.

Let's spend this week watching Hannah's transformation from a very, very sad beginning.

# Sunday

Don't I mean more to you than ten sons?

1 Samuel 1:8

Have you ever wanted something so bad that it didn't matter what else you had; if you didn't get this one thing you were going to be miserable? It probably wasn't a horse or an iPod or a Barbie Dream House. It was more than likely a best friend, a job for your dad, or a cure for your grandmother's cancer. No matter how many A's you made or how many trips you took to Toys R Us, you felt a big hole where your happiness used to be.

That's how Hannah felt. Her husband Elkanah loved her (more than he did his other wife, the nasty Peninnah), and he thought that should be enough for Hannah. But how could it be, especially with Peninnah giving her grief and people whispering that Hannah was a disgrace? Hannah couldn't be happy, not with her arms aching to hold her own babies in her arms.

It's hard to imagine how God could use a weeping, broken woman like Hannah, but he did, by transforming her. So no matter what you may be weeping for right now, have hope. God is doing something important inside you.

## Do That Little Thing: QUIZ

Put a star next to the item on this list that you want more than anything.

I want:

____ My family to be happy
____ To do well in school
____ Someone I love to be healthy
____ Friends I can have fun with and trust
____ To feel safe
____ To feel like I belong
____ To know God is really there

Watch what happens to Hannah this week. If what you want is a good thing for you, you may have a Hannah experience, too.

# Monday

> She made a vow, saying, "O Lord Almighty, if you will only look upon your servant's misery and remember me, and not forget your servant but give her a son, then I will give him to the Lord for all the days of his life."
>
> 1 Samuel 1:11

How do you get what you want? Stomp your feet? You probably outgrew that when you were two. Grab for it? More than likely you gave that up when you learned to talk. Steal it? Hello!

When you want something, you ask for it. You don't keep your Christmas list a secret and just hope someone guesses what you'd like to find under the tree.

If what you want is not a physical thing, like the list on yesterday's quiz, it's hard to know who to ask to provide it for you. Saying to your mom, "May I please have a best friend?" is no guarantee you're going to get one. The only one you can ask for such things and expect results from is, of course, God.

That's what our Hannah did. Stricken with sadness and shame, she went to God and sobbed and begged, "in bitterness of soul" (verse 10). *Please, Father*, she cried, *all I want is a son.* And then Hannah went a step further. She said if God would bless her with a baby boy, she would give him back to God, to work for him his whole life.

*What?* Wasn't that kind of a rash promise to make? She wanted a baby so bad, but she was willing to give him up? That tells us something about Hannah. She didn't just want a baby so she could be like all the other cool moms. She wanted offspring so they could serve the God she loved. Sounds like if you want to be transformed, you have to be pretty unselfish. Don't worry. You have it in you, just like Hannah.

## Do That Little Thing: FIND OUT

Ask some parents that you know why they had kids. Be ready for some funny answers, but some pretty impressive ones too. Keep a list. It will tell you a lot about the desires God puts into people's hearts.

# Tuesday

In the course of time Hannah conceived and gave birth to a son.
1 Samuel 1:20

Have you noticed that when you ask God for something, he doesn't just swoop down his almighty hand and make it happen? Most of the time, he uses other people, and that was the case for Hannah too.

While she was weeping and praying in the Lord's house, a priest named Eli (remember him with the rotten kids?) saw her. At first he thought she was drunk because her lips were moving but no sound was coming out. As if this poor woman didn't have enough problems, there was somebody accusing her of bringing wine into the temple and boozing it up!

Hannah didn't just slink off in shame. She stood up for herself and told him that she had been praying out of "great anguish and grief" (verse 16). That must have really gotten to Eli, because he told her to go in peace, that God would grant her what she had asked of him.

Now, it was God who answered Hannah's prayer — she did have the son she so longed for. But Eli went to God for her, too, because Hannah was honest about her feelings. She didn't pretend it was okay for her to be childless. She didn't hide the grief that was tearing her apart.

God doesn't want us to put a happy face on something that aches inside us. Our feelings are there for a reason. Sharing them with people who love God, too, is the first step toward healing.

## Do That Little Thing: JUST THINK

Think about feelings you might be hiding, pretending they aren't there. Do you know why you don't share them with someone who would understand? Are you afraid they'll say you're silly or wrong to feel like you do? Go to God with them first. That may give you the courage to share them with another person who just might be able to help you. You never have to be ashamed of a feeling. It's part of you becoming more you.

# Wednesday

> Now I give him to the Lord. For his whole life he will be given
> over to the Lord.
>
> 1 Samuel 1:28

"If you'll just help me get out of this, God, I promise I'll never do it again."

Most of us have prayed that prayer at one time or another. And most of the time, we mean it. We really do intend to stop lying if God will just clear up this one fib. You are so sure you're going to do your homework from now on, if God will just make the teacher forget to collect it today.

But what happens when a prayer like that is answered? You probably have to own up: you forget the promise you made and eventually find yourself right back in that same bad spot again. Sometimes it's a bummer being human, isn't it?

You couldn't blame Hannah if she had been totally human when baby Samuel was born and "forgot" she'd vowed to turn him over to God. But when Samuel was still pretty little, she took him to Eli, the priest, and made good on her promise.

Can you even imagine what it must have been like for her to put her little boy into Eli's hands? She had to — she'd made a sacred vow. Makes you want to be careful what you promise God, doesn't it?

But here's the deal: Hannah made that promise because she wanted to, because she knew it was right, because it was put into her heart by God. She was no longer weeping, no longer grieving. She was being transformed.

## Do That Little Thing: GOD? CAN WE TALK?

Talk to God about promises you've made, whether you've kept them or sort of forgotten them or hoped *he* would forget (like *that's* gonna happen!). Ask for forgiveness, if you need to, or strength to hang in there with your vows. Just talk to God until you find out what he wants you to do with those promises. Then do that little thing.

# Thursday

My heart rejoices in the Lord; in the Lord my horn is lifted high.

1 Samuel 2:1

You've been crying for hours. You've used up a whole box of Kleenex and your eyes are swollen into slits. Your pillow is soaking wet with your tears. It doesn't seem like the world will ever be right again, so why stop crying?

And then some sun breaks between the slats of the blinds in your bedroom. You can smell the nachos your mom just took out of the microwave. Somebody turns on the stereo, and there's your favorite song, begging to be danced to.

Maybe you'll get up and at least look at the nachos. Watch your sisters twirl around the room. Empty your trash basket full of soggy tissues.

Yeah, before you even get out of your room, you're smiling again. And doesn't it feel good? Even better than before you started wailing? Rising from grief makes you want to run and dance and eat— and in Hannah's case, sing.

With Samuel placed in Eli's arms and her promise to God fulfilled, Hannah burst into a song. She rejoiced with everything she had, and not in her baby son, but in God, who gave her this precious gift that she wanted to share. Kind of makes you want to burst into song, doesn't it?

Go ahead. There's always something to rejoice in the Lord for, because you are always being transformed.

## Do That Little Thing: LISTEN UP!

Close your eyes and get quiet before God. What song do you hear in your head? Whatever the tune (be it "Shine, Jesus, Shine" or "Happy Birthday"), put some praise words to it, so that you can rejoice in the Lord just for continually making you YOU!

# Friday

> May the Lord give you children by this woman to take the place of the one she prayed for and gave to the Lord.
>
> 1 Samuel 2:20

You put your clothes away without being asked (okay, nagged, threatened ...), and your mom gives you a big ol' hug and an extra brownie.

You straighten the books on the classroom shelves that everybody has trashed, just because you want to, and your teacher gives you bonus points and a place at the head of the line.

Sometimes the more you give, the more you get back, even when you don't expect it. Sometimes. Not always. Some people will take what you give as if you owed it to them and never even say thank you. But it's never that way with God.

Take Hannah. She was so grateful to have a son, she gave him up to God. She even rejoiced in that. And every year she made a little robe for Samuel and took it to him when she and her husband went to the temple. She didn't expect anything in return except the joy of knowing her son was going to serve God all his life, and in a major way. But God had a surprise for her.

One year when Hannah and Elkanah (her husband) took the trip, Eli told Elkanah that Hannah would have other children. And boy did she ever—two daughters and three more sons. She had a houseful of young'uns so she didn't have to miss Samuel so much.

You just can't out-give God. You can try—and that's kind of fun—but he will always have the last word, the final gift. How lovely for Hannah. How lovely for you.

## Do That Little Thing: YOU CAN *SO* DO THIS!

What was the last blessing you received from God? You won't have to think very far back, because the blessings happen every hour, every minute almost. Pick one — be it a night without bad dreams or a hummingbird at your feeder. Then see if you can give something back to God for that — give your mom an extra hug or give up the front seat to your brother even though it's your turn. Wait. Watch. See if another blessing doesn't come right back at ya. That's SO God.

# Saturday

The boy Samuel continued to grow in stature and in favor with the Lord and with men.

1 Samuel 2:26

What makes your mom break into a grin? What brings those happy mother-tears to her eyes?

Your baby brother says, "Mommy" for the first time. Your older sister gets accepted to a good college. You bring home a report card that calls for a trip to Chuck E. Cheese's.

Nothing makes a mother happier than for her children to do well, even in the smallest ways. You kids are part of your mom. She's spent years taking care of you and helping you grow so you can become all that God wants you to be. When you show signs that it's happening, it's as much a success for her as it is for you.

Seeing Samuel grow up in the temple with Eli serving God, and hearing everyone say what a fine young man he was must have been huge for Hannah. He was everything she'd hoped he would be, maybe more, and that was enough to make her happy for a lifetime.

But there was more, and she knew it because she sang about it in her song. She sensed that Samuel was going to be a great man, and he was. He followed God every step of his life, and anointed a king and helped Israel grow into the nation God wanted it to become. Imagine Hannah's smiles and her happy mother-tears, so unlike the ones she wept as we started our week with her. Yes, Hannah was truly transformed.

Transformation into happiness is what God wants for all of us.

## Do That Little Thing: SHOUT-OUT

Tell your mom how glad you are that you're her kid. Tell her you thank God that you got her for a mom. Shout it out. Then get ready for the smiles. And it wouldn't hurt to have the Kleenex ready too.

## From Boy to Da Bomb

A son named Josiah will be born to the house of David.

1 Kings 13:2

Before you were born, your mom probably had an ultrasound that showed you swimming around inside her womb. The doctor may have looked at the screen and announced, "You're going to have a girl."

That was maybe four or five months before you were born. Josiah's birth was announced three hundred *years* before he made his entrance into the world. Why such a big deal?

Because by the time Josiah came along, Israel was a mess, with people worshiping foreign gods and the Assyrians taking over and everybody forgetting God. People needed to know that somebody was coming along who was going to straighten it out.

At the time the announcement was made, nobody believed the prophet who made it. Until, that is, the King reached out a hand to get to him and it shriveled up right before everyone's eyes. That was a serious prophecy.

You'll spend this week getting to know this Josiah who showed up three centuries later. His transformation will get you wondering what you, a tween, can do for God's kingdom. Trust me.

# Sunday

Josiah was eight years old when he became king.

2 Kings 22:1

Excuse me—did you say "eight years old"?

Uh, yeah. He didn't actually start acting as king until he was sixteen, but still.

Sounds like a glamour gig, doesn't it? People waiting on you hand and foot, doing whatever you tell them or else you'll chop off their heads. Fortunately, young Josiah didn't take advantage of the situation (although he probably ordered a special date smoothie from time to time): According to the Bible, "He did what was right in the eyes of the Lord and walked in all the ways of his father David," who was a godly king. Unlike the kings before and after him, Josiah wanted to do what God wanted him to do, "Not turning aside to the right or to the left" (verse 2). He didn't let anybody influence him in the wrong direction.

It would have been natural at such a young age to want to show off or get everybody's approval or have everything he wanted, just because he could. Kings a lot older than he was had done it! But Josiah's transformation started the minute he officially took the throne. He made a decision—it was going to be God all the way.

You're at least eight years old. You can make the same choice—that you're going to do what's right and not let anybody pull you off track. And that you're going to depend on God to help you. You can do it.

## Do That Little Thing: QUIZ

If you were king (or queen), which of these things would you do?

\_\_\_\_ redecorate the palace

\_\_\_\_ buy a whole new wardrobe with matching crowns

\_\_\_\_ surround myself with smart people

\_\_\_\_ figure out what was best to do for the kingdom

\_\_\_\_ cry because I was so overwhelmed

If we left out something important, write it here: _____

_____.

HINT: This has something to do with the Great King of all Kings.

# Monday

In the eighteenth year of his reign.

2 Kings 22:3

When Josiah was twenty-six years old things really got rolling. He'd been doing what was right by God and walking in the ways of David since he was eight. Now he was ready to make some changes.

As you know by now, the temple was the center of life for the people of God. If you didn't have a temple, you really weren't living the way God wanted you to. And in Josiah's time, the temple was in ruins. Josiah decided it was time to restore it, and he put everybody to work. He got the money together, hired carpenters and stone-layers, and had people buy materials. It was a huge deal, and Josiah had it all covered.

Although he'd been getting rid of the foreign gods and their religious practices before that, the rebuilding of the temple was Josiah's first big statement that things were going to change. They definitely did, as you'll learn tomorrow. It had to start with something very definite, something physical, so people would get it. Who says you have to be old to be wise to influence people or to make good changes? Sometimes the younger you are, the easier it is to be transformed so that God can use you.

And that's exciting news for YOU.

## Do That Little Thing: FIND OUT

Ask your God-loving grown-up friends how old they were when they first realized they really knew something about God. Ask them to think about an adult saying to them, "I never thought of it that way."

# Tuesday

When the king heard the words of the Book of the Law, he tore his robes.

2 Kings 22:11

What do you do when you get really bad news? Throw something? Burst into tears? Go into a funk?

You probably don't tear the clothes you're wearing, but that was the custom in Josiah's time. Whenever a person felt great emotion, he ripped his garment, especially if it had anything to do with a crime against God. Maybe it's a good thing we don't do that these days, or we would all be walking around in shredded jeans.

Josiah had good reason to be upset. While they were restoring the temple, the workmen came across the Book of the Law, which God handed down through Moses so long ago. The Israelites were supposed to be living by it all that time, but most of it had been forgotten. When Josiah's aide read it to him, it put him in some pretty serious pain. It was obvious why so many things had gone wrong in the kingdom—the people weren't following God's laws.

Well, du-uh. But Josiah didn't stop at grieving. He went straight to a prophetess to find out what this meant for him and for his people. He's a great role model for doing your best. When you find out you're not quite there yet, go ahead and get emotional, and then do something about it. Transformation takes place that way, whether you're eight, twenty-eight, or eighty.

Don't rip your jeans. Just get moving.

## Do That Little Thing: JUST THINK

Think about the last bad news you received. You found out you were getting a less-than-wonderful grade in science? Or you found out your favorite aunt was sick? How did you respond with your emotions? Cry? Chew somebody out? Curl up in a ball?

Now think about what you did about it. Did you try to get more information? Did you figure out a way to fix it? Did you have to just accept it?

# Wednesday

Because your heart was responsive and you humbled yourself before the Lord ... I have heard you.

2 Kings 22:19

I can see you're really sorry, so I'm not going to punish you this time."

Aren't those beautiful words? It's wonderful to hear them when you've accidentally done something wrong, or you just weren't thinking when you did it, but you'd do just about anything to take it all back.

Those words must have been especially welcome for Josiah. The news from the prophetess wasn't good. God said he was going to bring disaster on Israel because they'd forgotten him and worshiped other gods. He was ticked off and planning to destroy everything. But because Josiah tried to find out what God wanted and was so upset when he discovered how disobedient the people had been, God promised to spare him. God told him that he would be long gone, peacefully dead and buried, before the disaster came. He wasn't going to have to see it.

All God wants is for us to try to please him because we love him. If we love him, it's going to upset us when people mess around on him. But we aren't going to be punished for other people's mistakes. That wouldn't transform us so God could use us. And God continued to use Josiah, as you'll see tomorrow.

## Do That Little Thing: GOD? CAN WE TALK?

Talk to God about anybody you know who really doesn't get him, who is acting like God doesn't count or doesn't care about what they do. Ask God how you can help. And know that you already have, just by showing up to talk about it with a heavy heart.

# Thursday

The king ... renewed the covenant in the presence of the
Lord — to follow the Lord and keep his commands ... with all
his heart and all his soul.

2 Kings 23:3

I'm already late so I might as well not go at all." "I'm already getting a D, so why study anyway?" "I've already had too much sugar today, so one more candy bar isn't going to hurt."

Sometimes it seems like you've already messed up so badly, there's no point in even trying to make it right. But you can look at those statements and know they're ridiculous. It's better to go late than never. A good test score can always raise a grade. One fewer candy bar *will* make a difference for the cavity situation.

Of course, the bigger the mess-up, the harder it is to see how it could be saved, but Josiah had vision. Instead of giving up because God had already said Israel was going to fall to disaster, he called all the people together and read to them the newly rediscovered Book of the Covenant. (They must have been there for days!) He renewed the covenant and told the people he was going to follow the Lord and keep the commandments with all his heart and all his soul.

That was all it took. The people pledged right after him. From now on, it was all going to be about God, the one true God. They had broken their promise to him, but they were making it again. Even though they were a mess. Even though their destruction had already been predicted.

The transformation of a whole nation had begun.

## Do That Little Thing: LISTEN UP!

Try to hear in your head any promises you've made to God that you haven't exactly followed through on. Maybe you won't hear any. Maybe you'll just hear God's whisper in your thoughts — you're doing fine. If you do hear the sound of promises breaking, make them again. You can do that. God allows renewals.

# Friday

Not since the days of the judges who led Israel ... had any such Passover been observed.

2 Kings 23:22

YOU: Mom, I promise I'll feed him and walk him and clean up his poop.

MOM: I've heard that before. I don't think so.

Ever had a conversation like that with your mom when you fell in love with a puppy? Maybe you've had a similar discussion over a kitten, dance lessons, or an aquarium for your room. Too often moms are right—kids do make promises they don't follow through on. So do grown-ups.

Josiah was not one of those. The minute he made the promise to God that he and his people were going to follow him from then on, he went into action. He removed all the pagan articles from the temple, did away with the pagan priests, got rid of all non-Jewish sacrifices, and no longer allowed fortune tellers and psychics.

He didn't stop there. He used all that new extra space and time to do something for God. He once again had a Passover, the feast God established back when the Israelites escaped from Egypt, and which the people had totally forgotten about.

It was some party. Josiah provided thirty thousand sheep and goats, plus three thousand cattle, all from his own possessions. The celebration went on for seven days, as well it should. There was a lot of time to make up for. A lot of praise to God. A lot of love. That's what people do when they know they've been transformed.

## Do That Little Thing: YOU CAN *SO* DO THIS!

Clean out something in your life, whether it's your disaster of a backpack that shows you don't care that much about doing your best, or the group of kids you hang out with who aren't really good for you. Put away from you all that gets between you and God. Then celebrate the new space and freedom. It doesn't have to go on for seven days, but it should at least include thanks to God for a bit of a new start.

# Saturday

Neither before nor after Josiah was there a king like him who turned to the Lord as he did — with all his heart and with all his soul and with all his strength.

2 Kings 23:25

S he was the best one we ever had."
That could be said about a way-cool teacher, the ultimate baby-sitter, the bank teller who always has treats. What is it that makes some people stay in your mind long after they've moved on?

That unforgettable teacher knew everybody's name by the second day. The babysitter never watched TV when you wanted to play. The bank teller even had biscuits for your dog. "The best ones" do more than anyone expects them to do, because they love who they're doing it for.

Josiah was the best king Israel had had for centuries for those same reasons. He loved God and went all out to show him, from cleaning up the entire kingdom to rebuilding the temple. From renewing the covenant to bringing back the blessed Passover. That's why Josiah didn't have to stick around to see his people go down because of their past bad behavior. Yes, he died in battle, but that was a great honor, and his spirit went to join David's where he could spend the rest of his time in peace. That was his reward for being one of the best ones.

What "best one" are you? The best friend your BFF ever had? The most co-operative student a teacher could wish for? The smiling face that bank teller always looks forward to seeing? You are the best in some way, because God is transforming you.

## Do That Little Thing: SHOUT-OUT

Who's the best one in your life for some reason? Whether he's the best-ever dad or your all-time best friend, tell her (or him) what makes her the best. Tell her you're so glad God made her so special. Throw in a biscuit for good measure.

## WEEK 32

## From Beauty Contestant to Queen of Her People

Let the girl who pleases the king be queen.

Esther 2:4

- She was only 15 or 16 years old.
- She was taken away from her home to be with people who wouldn't accept her if they knew who she really was.
- She competed in a beauty contest where there was a lot more to win than a crown.
- She saved her entire people.

Sound like a girl you'd want to read about? That's Esther, our transformed Bible friend of the week. Close to your age, she experienced something most women don't see in their entire lifetimes. Esther herself could never have accomplished what she did if she hadn't allowed herself to be transformed by God.

And you want to know the bizarre thing about her story? Never once is God mentioned in the Book of Esther. You'll find him this week, though, because he's so there. So are you. Get ready to put yourself in Esther's place for seven heart-pounding days.

# Sunday

Let a search be made for beautiful young virgins for the king.

Esther 2:2

Your name is Hadassah, although you are also known as Esther, which means "star." You don't feel much like a star. Your parents died when you were little and you live with your cousin Mordecai, who is nice to you and takes good care of you, but he isn't like a mom and dad. You're lovely and have a nice figure, though, and you're pretty happy growing up, hoping to someday marry and have a family.

And then one day King Xerxes' men come into your neighborhood, announcing that the king is looking for a new queen and they are to round up all the beautiful young girls for him to choose from. You think it might be nice to be included in that, but it isn't so nice when you find out you have no choice. You've been picked and you're going, leaving Mordecai and going to live in the palace where you'll undergo beauty treatments for twelve months and compete with a whole bunch of other girls for the king's love. This isn't what you had in mind for your life.

Not only that, but you are a Jew, and King Xerxes is not. If he finds out about your heritage, he might not be so happy. Cousin Mordecai has told you not to breathe a word of it to anyone. It's hard enough being homesick. On top of that, you can't even be your true self with the new people you're meeting. This is hard. Very, very hard.

## Do That Little Thing: QUIZ

What would be the hardest thing for you about being in Esther's situation?

____ Being separated from your family
____ Not being in your familiar surroundings
____ Having to lie about your background
____ Worrying about whether the king would like you
____ Not having a choice about any of those things

Keep that in mind as you and Esther begin your transformation.

# Monday

Before a girl's turn came to go in to King Xerxes, she had to complete twelve months of beauty treatments prescribed for the women.

Esther 2:12

This must be what a piece of chicken feels like when it's been marinating for a year—six months with your skin in oil of myrrh, six with your hair in cinnamon perfume. You have been dipped, massaged, powdered, and shadowed until you can't remember what you looked like before you came to the palace. Sure, Hegai, your beauty coach, really likes you and has given you special food and seven maids and even put you in the best place in the harem.

But what if it's all for nothing? There are a *lot* of girls here, all preparing themselves in the same way. The king is only going to pick one of you for his queen. The rest will spend their lives hanging out here in the palace, never having the husband and family you always dreamed of.

One thing keeps you from feeling hopeless, and that's Cousin Mordecai. Every day he walks back and forth near the courtyard where you're staying to find out how you are and what's happening to you. It makes you feel less homesick and more confident, just knowing somebody who cares about you is nearby. You wish he could go with you tonight when you are presented to the king. He would help you smile, remind you that you are still the same girl who came here a year ago. Or are you?

## Do That Little Thing: FIND OUT

Ask your God-loving adult friends if there was ever a moment when they realized they'd grown up a little, and something would never be the same again. Find out whether it was sad or exciting, or maybe both. Don't forget to ask if your friends felt like God was close or very far away.

# Tuesday

The king was attracted to Esther more than to any of the other women.

Esther 2:17

You can't believe it. Truly, this has to be a miracle.

The king liked you. No, he loved you, almost from the first moment he saw you. You saw the spark in his eyes when you swept into his chambers, trying not to look like you were about to shake right out of your skin. His smile made your teeth stop jittering. His voice stopped your knees from clacking together.

And the announcement that you were going to be his queen stopped your heart, right in your chest.

So here you are, at your own wedding banquet. The crown sits on your head. You are surrounded by the envious girls the king didn't choose — but they can't hate you. You have somehow won the favor of everyone who has seen you. A great feast, a glittering banquet hall, a life of luxury as a queen all lie before you.

It's everything a girl could dream of. But it's still hard. You miss your home — you miss being able to say, "I am a Jew." At least you get to see Mordecai, who is never far away. It's a comfort, because somehow you know this moment is going to pass. You hope you're ready for what the next moment brings.

## Do That Little Thing: JUST THINK

Think about a moment that was so wonderful, you wanted to hold onto it so it wouldn't get away. Was it one Christmas Eve when everyone's eyes sparkled with the tree lights? The instant you put on your first pair of ice skates? The moment you realized Jesus was real? Savor it. Remember how it looked and sounded and smelled. Be there again. Such moments are gifts from God. They help transform you.

# Wednesday

Mordecai found out about the plot and told Queen Esther, who in turn reported it to the king.

Esther 2:22

You thought you loved Cousin Mordecai before, but you could never have been more grateful to him than you are at this moment.

Even after you became queen, Mordecai continued to stay close by, and you continued to follow his instructions, just like you always did when he was bringing you up. He is at the gate every day, which was why he overheard those two royal guards, Bigthana and Teresh, plotting to assassinate the king, your new husband.

Loyal Mordecai told you right away, and you have run to the king. Breathless, you find him and pour out the story. He must investigate, you tell him. You are so frightened that he will be killed.

He believes you. Thank goodness, he believes you. He takes you into his arms to thank you, but you assure him it was Mordecai, not you, who saved his life. After all, where would you be without Mordecai's wisdom, loyalty, and love? You can't do it alone. No one can. Not even a queen.

## Do That Little Thing: GOD? CAN WE TALK?

Talk to God about the wise adults in your life. Thank him for the ones who are always there for you. Or ask him to send you someone who might understand something you're going through. By the time you're finished talking, you'll probably realize he's your Mordecai, always nearby.

# Thursday

Who knows but that you have come to royal position for such a time as this?

Esther 4:14

Does the drama ever end?" you ask yourself.

There is now more trouble, all because of that evil Haman. You have known since the king made Haman the highest of his royal officials that he is power-hungry and up to no good—especially when he made it a rule that everyone has to bow down to him at the gate. It's been downhill ever since.

Mordecai refused to bow down, which sent Haman into a rage that made you afraid for your cousin. But Haman isn't content to kill just Mordecai. He wants to kill *all* the Jews, *your* people.

Your stomach ties into yet another tight knot as you learn that Haman has persuaded the king to allow him to do away with all the Jews because they have customs and beliefs different from the king's. You can hear your people weeping in the streets. You can see your beloved Mordecai at the gate, dressed in the sackcloth and ashes of mourning, even as a messenger arrives with a request for you. Mordecai is begging you to go to the king and ask for mercy for the Jewish people.

Fear races through you. Your husband doesn't even know that you are a Jew. And if you go into his presence without being called for, you could be put to death. But the words of Mordecai curl into your thoughts and whisper to your heart. What other chance do your people have? Perhaps this is why you are queen. You nod and send a message to Mordecai.

## Do That Little Thing: LISTEN UP!

It could be time for you too. Time to take a stand, speak your mind, start something new. Listen today for that small voice that gives you good ideas. Pay attention to it. Is God telling you to put a stop to teasing at the lunch table? Or to tell your teacher there's cheating going on? Or to start a FaithGirlz Club with all the girls who are feeling left out? Who knows but that you have come for such a time as this?

# Friday

How can I bear to see disaster fall on my people?

Esther 8:6

There is nothing left to do. You fall at the king's feet and beg him to put an end to Haman's plan to destroy your people. And then you wait in anguish. If he extends his golden scepter to you, you may rise and state your case. If he does not, you will be put to death. You've never felt so terrified.

But you have done the right thing. Haman has been stopped and hanged, and Mordecai is now his trusted one. But Haman's order to kill all the Jews is still out there in the far provinces. You must continue to risk your life until the order is stopped and your people are saved. You must.

There is a sudden murmur in the court. You dare to look up, to see the golden scepter being extended to you by your husband, your king.

Scrambling to your feet, you plead with him. You ask for him to write an order overruling the dispatches that Haman wrote to destroy the Jews in all the king's provinces. Then you hold your breath.

Again there is a bustling of importance. The royal secretaries are summoned. The new orders are given, and Mordecai seals them with the king's ring. As the official sounding words are dictated and written, you catch just a few—the ones that say that your people may now gather and protect themselves. They are free. And somehow, so are you.

## Do That Little Thing: YOU CAN SO DO THIS!

Does someone you know need a person to stand up for her? To defend her? To ease the teasing she suffers from? Can you be that person, even if you risk a little teasing yourself? If so, do it. Do it soon.

# Saturday

Esther's decree confirmed these regulations about Purim, and it was written down in the records.

Esther 9:32

You lean out from the balcony and breathe in the sweet smells of the cakes as they waft up from the feast below. Music floats with it, and laughter, and joy — the joy of your people celebrating their freedom. Beneath you the women dance, the men throw back their heads in pleasure, and the children dash among the tables at their games. In the swirling skirts and happy bearded faces and tables overflowing with food you see what has arisen from the days of fasting and prayer and fear.

Where once there was danger lurking in every corner, there is now the light of liberty.

Where yesterday there was shame, today there are heads held high.

Where for so long there has been anger and bitterness, there will always be the sweet memory of this day.

They must never forget, you decide. This feast must be held every year. You will call it Purim, and it will be two days of joy and feasting, days for giving presents to each other and gifts to the poor. You want your people to celebrate this custom for all the generations to come, so that no one will ever forget the good that had been done for them.

"Mordecai," you say, "I want to issue an edict."

As he comes to you with pen in hand, you smile. You can do this. You are the queen. And now at last, you feel like one.

## Do That Little Thing: SHOUT-OUT

Declare your own celebration, in honor of the good that is being done for you right now, as God transforms you, slowly and very surely, into the queen you will become. Even if you merely open a bag of tortilla chips for the fact that you are learning when to keep your mouth shut, invite someone special to join you. Tell him or her that this is all about God, and then pass the chips.

## From Boils to Spoils and Back Again

> This man was blameless and upright; he feared God and shunned evil.
>
> Job 1:1

If you bring home a good (okay, great) report card, you get a trip to Baskin-Robbins.

If you bring home a lot of great report cards, you get promoted to the next grade.

If you get promoted twelve times, you graduate from high school.

Isn't that the way life is? You do your best, and you get rewarded. Only the kids who mess around, don't do their work, and cut class end up without ice cream or a diploma. Right?

Well, not always. Sometimes really bad things happen to really good people, like Job, our transformed Bible friend of the week. There was nobody better than Job, seriously. He did *everything* right. And yet everything that could go wrong for him, did go wrong.

Why is there a story like that in the Bible? Because bad things happen to everyone, and all of us need to know how God wants us to handle those things. After all, it's the bad stuff in our lives that turns us into the good people we're meant to be. Get the Kleenex. We're going in.

# Sunday

Stretch out your hand and strike everything he has, and he will surely curse you to your face.

Job 1:11

Consider your little brother or sister, or some other itty-bitty kid you know. Aren't they just the cutest, sweetest things in life as long as everything goes their way? Keep them supplied with sippy cups and cookies and funny-face-making, and they're precious angels. But take away the pacifier or say they have to take a nap, and they'll pitch a fit that can start an earthquake.

People can be like that with God, too. As long as everything is going fine, they're all about God and how wonderful he is. But when things fall apart, they're all over him with, "Why are you doing this to me?"

In the story of Job, Satan and God were talking about that very thing. God asked Satan if he'd checked out his servant Job, who was more blameless and upright than anyone on earth. Satan said, "Sure he's good. Why wouldn't he be? He has everything going for him." Satan bet God that if he took everything away from Job, Job wouldn't be so crazy about God any more. God took him up on that and gave Satan permission to do anything he wanted to Job, as long as he didn't take his life. He bet on Job's loyalty and love.

So here we are with a Bible friend who has everything and who is about to lose it all, even though he hasn't done anything wrong. How does that transform someone? Sometimes that's exactly what it takes. We'll find out why.

## Do That Little Thing: QUIZ

Check off the things God might say about you right now. (Don't stress if you only check one or two. Remember, it's all about transformation.)

\_\_\_\_ You love him.

\_\_\_\_ You love other people, even the ones it's hard to love.

\_\_\_\_ You love yourself because God made you.

\_\_\_\_ You try to do the right thing.

\_\_\_\_ You ask God to forgive you when you mess things up.

# Monday

In all this, Job did not sin by charging God with wrongdoing.

Job 1:22

Satan wasted no time bringing tragedy into Job's life. First, all of his oxen and donkeys—the animals he needed to keep his farm going—were killed by traveling merchants.

The messenger wasn't even finished giving Job that news when another arrived, telling him lightning had struck all his sheep and servants, burning them up.

While he was still speaking, yet another messenger came and said Job's camels and the servants accompanying them had been slain by a tribe passing through.

Basically Job's entire operation had been wiped out. He could have started over, but Satan wasn't having it. A final messenger brought the news that a mighty wind had come along and struck Job's house. It had collapsed on his sons and daughters who were there feasting, killing them all.

Most of us have to admit that if that happened to us, we would shake our fists toward heaven and shout, "Why have you done this to me, God?"

But Job simply tore his clothes in grief (the custom, remember?), and then fell to the ground in worship. Worship! "The Lord gave and the Lord has taken away," he said. "May the name of the Lord be praised" (Job 1:21).

You may have heard the expression, "She has the patience of Job." This is what that means. And you haven't seen anything yet.

## Do That Little Thing: FIND OUT

Ask your God-loving adult friends if they have ever felt like God was giving them someone else's share of life's troubles along with their own. Get them to tell you honestly if they kept their faith in God every minute, or maybe even for a few seconds put the blame on God. Remember not to judge—not all of us are Job!

# Tuesday

Shall we accept good from God, and not trouble?

Job 2:10

The suffering we've seen in Job's life so far should have been enough proof for Satan, but, then, he *is* the source of all evil, so he didn't stop there. He went back to God and scoffed. He hadn't even gotten started with Job yet. Losing your animals, even your kids, was one thing. But what was Job going to do when his own skin was afflicted? God reminded him once again to do as he wished to Job, but he must spare his life.

Poor Job might have wished he *would* die after what Satan did to him. He was covered with painful sores from the soles of his feet to the top of his head. He suffered from nightmares and lost so much weight he looked like a skeleton. His pain was constant, and he looked—and smelled—so horrible no one wanted to be around him to comfort him.

Even his wife said, "Why are you still blessing God? Curse him and die and get it over with!"

Most of us would say she had a point. But Job saw something we can all learn from. He said, "Can we just take the good things God gives us and not accept the troubles too?" Hey, if we're going to accept the gift of God's presence in our lives, we have to take the whole package. Read on. Job shows us how.

## Do That Little Thing: JUST THINK

Has there ever been a time when you thought something wasn't so bad — until it happened to you personally? Maybe you didn't see what the big deal was about being sent to the office — until you were sitting there face-to-face with the principal. Or you thought crying over a bad grade was silly — until you saw that F on your math test. One thing's for sure; you're probably a lot more sympathetic now. You've already begun your transformation.

# Wednesday

I will say to God: "Do not condemn me, but tell me what charges you have against me."

Job 10:2

As things went from bad to worse, Job still didn't curse God. Through scabs and bad breath and the loneliness of being without his kids, he never once told God he was a lousy Father.

But that doesn't mean Job didn't ask a few questions like these:

- How come wicked people get away with murder, but when I try to do good, I get sent all these problems?
- Why did you make me if you were just going to destroy me?
- What did I ever do to you?

Job's friends didn't think he should be asking questions like that, but God understood, and he still does. He doesn't expect you to say, "Oh, well, such is life" when everything falls apart. He wants you to come to him with everything that's on your mind, including your demands of, "What is UP with this?!" That's called a relationship.

## Do That Little Thing: GOD? CAN WE TALK?

Got any questions for God right now? Do you want to know why your grandfather had to get sick just when you were learning how to play chess with him? Or why you can't dance with your feet the way you do in your mind? Ask anything you want. God wants to talk.

# Thursday

Miserable comforters are you all! Will your long-winded speeches never end?

Job 16:2-3

Job did have some friends who sat with him. That's nice when you're going through a rough time. Unlike your friends, who would bring you microwave popcorn and DVDs and tell you what was going on at school, Eliphaz, Bildad, and Zophar brought advice.

"God's scolding you for some sin, but you've always been so good, God isn't going to destroy you."

"You must have done something REALLY bad. Beg for mercy."

"Accept that this is your fault and move on."

Wouldn't it hurt even more to have your friends tell you that you had nobody to blame for your strep throat and your broken arm and your dead goldfish but yourself? It made Job imagine that God was angry with him, that he really had done something to deserve a plague of boils and lost children.

Here's the deal for us: we can't explain suffering, and trying to doesn't bring comfort to people in the middle of it. Job's friends didn't know the deal God had with Satan, or they wouldn't have told him it was all his fault. We don't have all the information God does, either. All we have is love.

## Do That Little Thing: LISTEN UP!

Keep your ears open for someone who's suffering, whether it's the cries of a girl your age with school, family, and friend issues, or a grown-up who has troubles the adults stop talking about when you come into the room. Then just be there, perhaps with a smile and a cookie and a hug. Leave the advice to God.

# Friday

After Job had prayed for his friends.

Job 42:10

Job did *what?* After listening to those three jack their jaws at him for seven days about how he must have messed up—when all he needed was some Neosporin and a few hugs—he *prayed* for them?

This is Job we're talking about. He is our model for dealing with the really hard things in life, so watch what he did.

After God told Job he hadn't done anything wrong, he dealt with Eliphaz and Bildad and Zophar. God was angry with THEM for not speaking the truth about him. He made them go to Job and sacrifice a burnt offering, and only if Job prayed for them would he not deal with them as they deserved, treating Job like that.

It was up to Job then. Don't know about you, but most people would have turned to their "friends" and said, "Neener, neener, neener—now get OUT!" If Job had, God would have dealt harshly with Eliphaz, Bildad, and Zophar, and why not?

Because Job was a godly man. He understood that they didn't have the big picture, that they were doing what they thought was right, even if it was wrong. What really mattered now was that God still loved him. In fact, that was all that mattered. And it still is.

## Do That Little Thing: YOU CAN SO DO THIS!

Pray for someone who hasn't been very nice to you. Go ahead, you can do it. Just go to God and ask him to forgive her, to cut him some slack, to help you let it go. After all, what matters is that you and God are talking, and that God loves hearing from you.

# Saturday

The Lord blessed the latter part of Job's life more than the first.
Job 42:12

Things must have seemed so bad to Job that nothing would ever be right again. But then there was God.

God made Job prosperous again. He gave him twice as much as he had before. All his brothers and sisters and friends came to him and comforted him. And each one gave him a piece of silver and a gold ring. Nice.

Next God provided Job with fourteen thousand sheep, six thousand camels, a thousand yoke of oxen, and a thousand donkeys. With the animal situation taken care of, God gave Job seven sons and three daughters, and nowhere in the land were there women as beautiful as Job's daughters.

Who would have thought Job would live a hundred and forty years and see his children and their children to the fourth generation? When he died, he was "full of years."

So what was all that suffering about? It was there to show us what to do when trouble strikes. Trust God. Don't turn on him. Remember that bad things do happen. Go ahead and ask God questions. Don't let friends' attempts to set you straight get you off the track with God. Know that God loves you. No matter what happens, your life will always be full as long as, like Job, you never lose touch with God.

## Do That Little Thing: SHOUT-OUT

Whatever is getting under your skin right now — a little friend itch or a big family pain or anything in between — tell someone your life is still full in spite of it, because you've got God. Feels good to say it, doesn't it?

# WEEK 34

## From Hunkdom to Wisdom

Young men without any physical defect . . . and qualified to serve in the king's palace.

Daniel 1:4

Do you know any young people who are pretty close to perfect? Seriously, are there teenagers in your family or your church who match Daniel's description: "Without any physical defect, handsome, showing aptitude for every kind of learning, well-informed, quick to understand."

It really does seem like some people start off with everything already together. They're gorgeous, smart, funny, and definitely have it going on. Why do people like that need to be transformed?

Daniel, our Bible friend of the week, was such a person. When the people of Judah were sent to Babylon in exile, the Babylonian king, Nebuchadnezzar, decided to take advantage of the incredible people who were now living in his country. He called for all the smart, good-looking young guys to be brought in and trained for his service. Daniel was one of those chosen.

It was a definite bummer to have to serve this foreign king who had dragged Daniel's people away from their homes and ripped off the treasures of their temple. So, perfect as he was, Daniel was faced with a situation that could have transformed him for the worse. This week you'll see how he dealt with the change in his life. As always, it will teach you something about you, too.

# Sunday

Daniel resolved not to defile himself with the royal food and wine.

Daniel 1:8

Imagine you're at your friend's house, and she offers you a soda and a bag of mini-donuts for an after-school snack. You know there's enough sugar and fat in that fare to hype you up and drop you down and leave you too sluggish to do your homework, all in the time it takes to catch a rerun of *iCarly*. You can eat it, or you can ask if you can have some baby carrots and a glass of orange juice instead.

Sounds like an easy choice. But what if your friend is hurt and says you're a food snob, or her mother says you can't come over any more if you're going to be that picky about the menu? Now imagine you're in the *king's* kitchen saying, "The food you're offering me is going to ruin my body. I'm not eating it."

That's what Daniel did. The king had all this rich food and wine he wanted his trainees to eat, but Daniel asked the chief official to give him and his closest friends ten days to eat only veggies and drink only water. "Then compare our appearance with that of the young men who eat the royal food," Daniel said (verse 13).

At the end of the ten days, Daniel and his friends looked healthier and better nourished than any of the other young men. It wasn't just a matter of eating the right foods. It was about Daniel staying true to the God-rules he'd grown up with. He didn't have to be home with his mother saying, "You WILL eat those vegetables or there will be no swordplay after supper." He was being put to the test, and so far he was passing. Sounds do-able, doesn't it?

## Do That Little Thing: QUIZ

Which of these rules could you break when you're away from home without anybody knowing?

\_\_\_\_ No sweet snacks between meals
\_\_\_\_ No soda with lunch
\_\_\_\_ No burping out loud
\_\_\_\_ No throwing away good food
\_\_\_\_ Eat the sandwich before the cookies
\_\_\_\_ No sugar after 6:00 p.m.
\_\_\_\_ No sugar-packed cereal for breakfast

Which of these do you need to start obeying even when nobody's watching?

# Monday

He urged them to plead for mercy from the God of heaven concerning this mystery.

Daniel 2:18

Daniel must have been feeling pretty good about himself. Not only did he prove that his diet program was better than the king's, but he got a lot of goodies from God, including knowledge and understanding of all kinds of learning. To top it off, God gave him the ability to understand visions and dreams.

No wonder King Nebuchadnezzar thought Daniel and his buddies were top shelf. He found them ten times better than all the magicians in his whole kingdom. Daniel had to feel secure that he was set for life.

But what Daniel didn't count on was the fact that the king was crazy. This guy had some really weird dreams that were waking him up at night. When he called in his usual dream-explainers, he said they had to guess what his dreams *were,* or off with their heads.

Come *on.* Nobody could do that, not even Daniel, who was called in to do what no one, of course, had been able to pull off. So much for Daniel feeling like he was all that. Fortunately, Daniel was wise enough to know that he could not do this by himself. He asked for, and got, a little more time, and he did what God wants all of us to do when we're faced with an impossible situation—go to our friends and get them praying.

Nobody can do the impossible—at least not without a LOT of help from God. One of the most transforming things is for us to realize that.

## Do That Little Thing: FIND OUT

Ask your God-loving adult friends if they have ever faced the impossible. You're sure to get stories, because everybody has, and probably more than once. Find out what they did, if they prayed, how it turned out. By the way, God came to Daniel in a dream of his own and revealed what was going on with the king. Otherwise, that would have been the end of the story!

# Tuesday

If we are thrown into the blazing furnace, the God we serve is able to save us from it.

Daniel 3:17

King Nebuchadnezzar was so grateful to Daniel for interpreting his dream and basically saving him, he put him into a high position in his court. It paid to be one of Daniel's friends, because the king gave his three buddies Shadrach, Meshach, and Abednego great jobs too.

That would have been the happy ending, except that, again, the king was slightly mental. Even after he told Daniel, "Surely your God is the God of gods and the Lord of kings" (Daniel 2:47), he had a ninety-foot golden idol built and ordered that whenever people heard certain music, they had to bow down to it.

Word got back to the crazy king that Shadrach, Meshach, and Abednego were ignoring the order. No way were they bowing to anyone but God. Daniel's transformation had affected them too.

Of course, King Neb went into a rage and told them he was throwing them into a fiery furnace. "Go ahead," they said. "Our God will save us. And even if he doesn't, we're not serving your stupid no-god idol."

At that point, the *king* was transformed from their biggest fan to their worst enemy. Into the furnace they went, in heat seven times hotter than usual. It was so hot it burned the guards, but the three friends of Daniel came out without so much as a scorch mark. Transformation reaches beyond one person. When the king realized this was no false God, it affected thousands.

## Do That Little Thing: JUST THINK

Do you have friends who have influenced you in a good way? Maybe you're taking better care of your teeth because your best friend's are so nice and white. Or perhaps you pay more attention in class because that girl you admire always has the right answer. Think, too, about how you may be influencing someone else to the good. Yeah, God is transforming you in ways you hadn't even thought of.

# Wednesday

You did not honor the God who holds in his hand your life and all your ways.

Daniel 5:23

The expression, "I saw the handwriting on the wall," means someone gets a hint of what's about to happen and takes action. That expression comes from the Daniel story.

King Nebuchadnezzar had been driven out to live with the wild animals until he admitted that God was the true ruler of the universe. He finally did, and he died with his sanity restored. But the Babylonians went on being party animals under the new king, Belshazzar. At one of his particularly wild banquets, he brought out the gold goblets King Neb had stolen from the temple in Jerusalem and had people drinking wine out of them and praising the gods of silver and gold. And then—a human hand appeared and wrote on the wall.

Daniel was called for because nobody else could read what the hand had written. He refused all promises of rewards and simply read: You, Belshazzar, didn't learn from what King Nebuchadnezzar finally realized, that there is one God and he is to be worshiped and obeyed. You are going down.

That very night, King Belshazzar was slain.

Daniel knew, and we can, too, that until people get that God is in charge, they're not going to have the at-peace lives they so long for. There will be bad dreams and craziness—and even handwriting on the wall.

## Do That Little Thing: GOD? CAN WE TALK?

Ask God if there's some message staring you right in the face that you aren't getting. Give him some suggestions and see if they ring true for you — like, "If I would just pray, I'd feel a lot closer to you, wouldn't I?" or "If I tried to see it my mom's way, I wouldn't fight with her so much, would I?" Something may become as clear to you as handwriting on the wall.

# Thursday

> Three times a day he got down on his knees and prayed, giving thanks to his God, just as he had done before.
>
> Daniel 6:10

No good deed goes unpunished." Have you heard adults say that? It isn't always true, but it was in Daniel's case.

Before he was bumped off, King Belshazzar made Daniel the third-highest ruler in the kingdom. Other staff members were NOT happy about that, and in their jealousy they plotted to have him killed. However, they didn't just hire a hit man. They persuaded the new king, Darius, to publish an edict that anyone who prayed to anybody besides the king himself would be executed.

Talk about a set-up. It was well known that Daniel prayed three times a day, and that he wasn't going to stop. He wasn't arrogant about it—he went up to his room. But the jealous men found him there, down on his knees, and told on him to the king.

Darius didn't want to have Daniel killed. He was probably the best thing that had ever happened to the kingdom. But he had made a royal decree, and to go back on it would make him seem weak. However, Darius said something when he sent Daniel off to the lion's den that summed up Daniel's whole transformation from boy-child with big muscles to wise, respected court official. He said, "May your God, whom you serve continually, rescue you!" (verse 16).

The best sign that other people are seeing the good changes in you is when they say, "Will you pray for me? God listens to you." Thank him for that.

## Do That Little Thing: LISTEN UP!

Listen today for the signs that God is working in you. Hear them in the things other people say to you. "I *have* to talk to you." "Will you pray for me?" "Can you help me?" That means your transformation is obvious to other people. How fantastic!

# Friday

> I issue a decree that in every part of my kingdom people must fear and reverence the God of Daniel.
>
> Daniel 6:26

The night King Darius threw Daniel in the lion's den and sealed it up so Daniel couldn't possibly get out, the king didn't eat, sleep, or have any entertainment brought in. You think? He was having a trusted friend chewed up by the king of the jungle, for Pete's sake!

The sun was barely up before the king was at the den, calling to Daniel, hoping God had saved him. That probably doesn't make any sense to you. Why did the king put him in there in the first place?

It was all about pride, which is something Daniel didn't have. He knew it wasn't his own strength that was going to keep him safe from the lions. If he was going to live through the night, it was going to be because of God. The cool thing is, the king knew that too. At the mouth of the den, King Darius called out, "Daniel ... has your God, whom you serve continually, been able to rescue you from the lions?" (verse 20). Imagine his joy when Daniel was lifted from the den without a scratch "because he had trusted in his God" (verse 23).

It wasn't just Daniel who was saved. It was King Darius and all the people who heard his new decree that they were to fear and revere Daniel's God. That's because Daniel was never all about himself. He was about the God who has the power to transform. That's all it takes.

## Do That Little Thing: YOU CAN SO DO THIS!

Go back to Wednesday's "Do That Little Thing" when you talked to God about something you need to do that he's been telling you for some time. Take a baby step today. Pray (maybe even three times like Daniel). You don't have to go into a fiery furnace or a lion's den. Just do this very little thing, and see if it makes somebody else happy too.

# Saturday

Daniel, I have now come to give you insight and understanding. As soon as you began to pray, an answer was given.

Daniel 9:22-23

Have you ever been in a position where everything was going
your way? Just for a day—or even fifteen minutes!—nobody
was mad at you, people were loving you, you didn't feel guilty about
anything. It was just one of those I-want-to-hold-onto-this times.

In situations like that, you just want to hunker down and not
disturb it, don't you? Somebody might be having a problem over
there, but shouldn't you just be allowed to enjoy your wonderfulness
over here for a while?

Daniel could have done that. He was a respected official in the
court, had the king's favor, and was rid of the guys who were trying
to have him killed. His own people loved him, too, because he'd
saved them from having to bow down to Babylon's gods, AND he
could see into the future through the visions God was giving him.

It was those visions that kept Daniel from lying back in his purple robes, eating dates, and basking in everyone's adoration. God
spoke to him through dreams about the end of time. Daniel himself
was good to go, but he was so frightened for his people, he begged
God to turn his anger away. God told him all that was going to
happen and reassured him, "Go your way till the end. You will rest,
and then at the end of the days you will rise to receive your allotted
inheritance" (Daniel 12:13). Transformation complete. And it can
be for all of us. Just go God's way until the end.

## Do That Little Thing: SHOUT-OUT

Gather in your mind all the things that are just right about your life at
this time. Make a list on paper if you want. Then tell someone who
loves God too how generous God is being to you. If it feels right,
pray together for anyone who isn't enjoying so many blessings right
now. What a great way to go.

# From Lowly to Holy

"How will this be?" Mary asked the angel.

Luke 1:34

God intended families to have a certain order: first you get married, and then you have kids. People don't always follow that, and in biblical times those who didn't were considered to be a disgrace. Girls were disowned by their parents and thrown out of the house if they became pregnant before the wedding.

Imagine Mary, then. She was no older than sixteen, engaged to Joseph, an older guy. She definitely wasn't well-off, but she had a secure future to look forward to—until she got a visit from an angel named Gabriel.

It was no small thing to have an angel come to you, and Mary was a little freaked out. Just think how she felt when Gabriel told her she was to become pregnant and bear a son for God. Who was going to believe such a story? Was Joseph going to refuse to marry her now? Was that happy future she hoped for ruined?

Angel or no angel, this could not have been a delightful surprise for Mary at first. And yet she allowed God to transform her into the most blessed woman who ever lived. Follow her story this week and once again learn how God is blessing you, too.

# Sunday

*I am the Lord's servant ... May it be to me as you have said.*

Luke 1:38

Sometimes it takes a minute, doesn't it?

You find out you've made the select basketball team, or that you've been picked to sing a solo, or that you now have your own room because your sister's going off to college. At first, you don't quite know how to react, except maybe to say, "No way! Are you serious?" It can be a few minutes, or even longer, before the news sinks in and becomes real.

That must have been what happened with Mary when the angel told her she was to be the mother of the Holy One, the Son of God. Her "How will this be?" was like your "Are you serious?" Gabriel went on to explain that the Holy Spirit would come upon her and form the child within her, which probably didn't help that much. Nobody was going to believe that. *She* was having trouble believing it.

But then God's messenger told her something she *could* wrap her mind around. He said that Elizabeth, her relative, was going to have a child in her old age. Everybody thought she'd never have kids, and yet she was six months pregnant. "For nothing is impossible with God," the angel said (verse 37).

That was the ticket for Mary. All right, then. Since she served God, she'd do whatever he asked of her, even the impossible. How incredibly brave. That's where transformation often begins, with accepting that God can do the impossible, whether anyone else believes it or not.

## Do That Little Thing: QUIZ

Check off anything that seems pretty impossible right now.

_____ Making it through a day without getting into some kind of trouble

_____ Getting through an evening without fighting with my brother or sister

_____ Understanding math (or science, or punctuation — you get the idea)

_____ Feeling like I belong

_____ Really believing that God is watching over me

_____ Really believing that God forgives me

Say, out loud, "God, may it be to me as you say." Then see what begins to happen this week.

# Monday

Mary said: "My soul glorifies the Lord and my spirit rejoices in God my Savior."

Luke 1:46-47

O—kay (big sigh). I'll do it."
Is that your usual answer to a request to take the dog out, unload the dishwasher, watch your little brother? You'll do what you're asked to do, but you don't have to be happy about it, right?

Mary was asked to do just a little more than the ordinary chores, and, as we've seen, she was baffled at first—who wouldn't be?

But then it became apparent why Mary was the one chosen. Not only was she willing to do whatever God asked her to do, no matter what other people might think (including Joseph!), but she was happy about it! It took a little while. She didn't burst into song about it until she went to visit Elizabeth, and Liz's unborn baby leaped for joy. That's when she was really convinced that this was a God-thing, and that's when she sang her famous song known as "The Magnificat" (Latin for "glorify").

Now it was all about God and how thankful she was that he had chosen her, a "nobody," for such a magnificent service. She went beyond her own good fortune and praised him for all he'd done for anyone who was humble and faithful before him. No wonder God chose her. Transformation begins with humility.

## Do That Little Thing: FIND OUT

Ask your God-loving grown-up friends if they have ever been HAPPY about being asked to do something that seemed impossible. This is a tough question and could require some thought, so have popcorn ready for munching during contemplation!

# Tuesday

She wrapped him in cloths and placed him in a manger, because there was no room for them in the inn.

Luke 2:7

Don't you hate it when you plan carefully for something, and everything still goes wrong? It rains on the day of your birthday party, or your little sister throws up on your dress in the car Easter morning because she's already eaten an entire chocolate bunny. It would be one thing if you'd done something to cause all that rotten stuff, but when it's beyond your control you have the urge to scream, "It's not fair!"

Mary may have had that urge the night Jesus was born. Just when it was time for her to deliver, the order went out that everybody had to go back to their hometown to be taxed. Great. A trip to Bethlehem in her ninth month. On a donkey, no less. And was there a hotel room to be found? Talk about unfair! She was about to give birth to the Son of God, and she and Joseph ended up in a stable (or even a cave, we're not sure) with the cows.

God definitely wanted the birth of Jesus to be "lowly," so that his rise to Savior would be even more miraculous. That meant that Mary had to be transformed, from an inexperienced girl into a woman who knew how to make the best of things. She didn't whine about the lodging situation. She just used fresh straw to turn a feeding trough into a crib and wrapped the baby in whatever cloths she could find. She began what has become one of the best parts of our Christmas celebration.

## Do That Little Thing: JUST THINK

Have you been proclaiming that something is "not fair!" lately? Think about whether you should do something about that injustice (like online bullying) or make the best of it. Picture yourself doing both. The images God puts in your mind will help you decide what to do — besides whine!

# Wednesday

> Mary treasured up all these things and pondered them in her heart.
>
> Luke 2:19

You've probably noticed that when somebody walks into a room with a baby, everything else stops and all the adults gather around. They even start to make strange noises and faces and generally turn into blithering idiots. You've probably done some of that yourself. Very few people can resist trying to make a baby smile.

Meanwhile, although the mom likes the attention her baby is getting, she worries about the germs people are blowing into his face, and whether he'll be able to calm down enough for his nap, and whether that one woman's "Are we gonna have a bab-ba?" is going to scar him for life.

A whole bunch of people came to see the Baby Jesus, hauling in lambs and perfume and all kinds of stuff he could have been allergic to. They were in a cave-turned-stable to begin with, so Mary probably wasn't up for much entertaining. It could have been confusing, upsetting, even frightening. But by now, Mary seemed to know what was happening, and she didn't turn people away or even just shrug them off. She examined all of it in her mind, and looked at it, and felt it. She was the first one to know the importance of this baby, and she wasn't going to waste a moment of the experience of being his mother. Transformation requires attention. So ponder away!

## Do That Little Thing: GOD? CAN WE TALK?

Ask God if there is anything in your life that he'd like for you to ponder. Are there things you're taking for granted, little pieces of life that would be so much more important if you were paying more attention? It could be your little sister, who is growing up so fast, or your friendships, which are a little ragged. Whatever it is, ponder it with God.

# Thursday

He went down to Nazareth with them and was obedient to [his parents]. But his mother treasured all these things in her heart. And Jesus grew in wisdom and stature, and in favor with God and men.

Luke 2:51–52

Have you ever heard new parents complain that babies don't come with an instruction manual? The Jews in the time of Jesus actually had one! Jewish custom and law spelled absolutely everything out, and Mary followed it in raising Jesus.

He was named on his eighth day. When he was forty days old, Mary and Joseph took him to the temple to present him to the Lord. And when he was 12 years old, they took him with them to Jerusalem for the Feast of the Passover. That's when Jesus began to do things that weren't covered in the instruction manual.

When Jesus' family left to go home to Galilee with a crowd, he stayed behind in Jerusalem, though they didn't realize it. At the end of that first day, the "I thought he was with *you*" began, and Mary and Joseph made tracks back to Jerusalem, where it took them three days to locate their son. You can imagine how freaked out they were.

They found him in the temple, sitting in the midst of the teachers, who were all amazed at his wisdom. Mary wasn't amazed — she was frantic. Jesus didn't get why she was so upset. "Didn't you know I had to be in my Father's house?" he said (verse 49). She tried to understand what he had to do — but she still raised him to be obedient. She had come a long way from the scared young woman who asked the angel, "How can this be?" She still didn't get it all, but she was growing deeper in acceptance.

## Do That Little Thing: LISTEN UP!

There are probably things in your life right now that you don't get, that you just can't understand (ya think?). Your cousin with Down syndrome. Moving every year for your dad's job. Having asthma. Listen for the sigh of acceptance inside you — that willingness to think, "I don't have to understand it. I just have to let it be for now." It could take more than one listening session. Some things even take a lifetime — so it's a good idea to get started now.

# Friday

His mother said to the servants, "Do whatever he tells you."

John 2:5

Who coaxed you into taking your first steps? Who took you to school your very first day ever and told you it was going to be fabulous? Who made you pancakes on the day of standardized tests and said, "You can SO do this." It was probably your mom. She knew what you could do and she saw that you did it. It's in the Mother Contract.

Mary, like most mothers, knew what her son was capable of — she'd been informed of it by an angel before he was even born. She wasn't going to let him pass up the opportunity to get started, and she found that opportunity at a big wedding reception.

Those parties could go on for days, and it was the responsibility of the one throwing the shindig to make sure there was enough wine for everyone. There wasn't much to drink but water or wine in those days, so there had to be plenty. If you ran out, it was way more than embarrassing. People would be talking for years about what a lousy host, lousy *person* you were.

This host ran out of wine, and Mary pointed that out to Jesus. What was he supposed to do about it? he asked her. But they both knew. Jesus said it wasn't time for him to perform a miracle yet, but being his mother, Mary gave him a little push. Turning to the servants, she said, "Do whatever he tells you." Water was, of course, turned into wine by Jesus. It was time to get this thing started.

## Do That Little Thing: YOU CAN *SO* DO THIS!

Go back to that "impossible" thing you turned over to God on Sunday. Has it begun to seem more possible, more hopeful, more doable? That's all it takes for you to make a step toward making it happen, whether it's by simply saying, "Okay, God," or rejoicing in it, or making the best of it, or treasuring it, or trying to understand it — that's a beginning. If necessary, get your mom to give you a push. It's in her contract.

# Saturday

When Jesus saw his mother there, and the disciple whom he loved standing nearby, he said to his mother, "Dear woman, here is your son," and to the disciple, "Here is your mother."
John 19:26–27

Who sits with you when you throw up? Who wipes the snot off your little brother's nose? Who spends all night singing to you when you have a fever? Again, that would be your mom. And she will always do that for you if you need her to. Ask your mother if her mom talked her through morning sickness when she was pregnant with you or pitched in when the whole family had the flu at once.

Moms don't stop being moms when their kids are grown up — and Mary was no exception. When most of the disciples had gone into hiding, Mary stood at the foot of the cross and waited with her son while he suffered. From the moment she found out that he was going to be born to the day he was crucified, she truly devoted her entire life to him. She allowed herself to be transformed into what she needed to be in order to fulfill that purpose.

God doesn't ignore that kind of devotion. Jesus stopped in the middle of his agony and made sure that his mother was taken care of — and that his beloved disciple had the joy of spending the rest of his life with that marvelous mother. She would always miss her son, but Mary would live on knowing that her transformation was complete. And that is what all of us long for.

## Do That Little Thing: SHOUT-OUT

Tell your mom that you're glad she's the one who was assigned to you. Better yet, don't just tell her; show her. Take care of her in some way, whether it's with a cup of tea or an offer to match up the socks. She transformed herself for you, and she's overseeing the transformation in you. She deserves some thanks for that.

## From Bouncing Baby to ... One Strange Dude

John's clothes were made of camel's hair ... His food was
locusts and wild honey.

Matthew 3:4

To say that they are "a little bit strange" is putting it politely. We're
talking about those scruffy folks you sometimes see on the street
who wave their arms and shout that the end of the world is coming unless we all straighten up. They're the people your mom steers
you to the other side of the road to avoid, murmuring that a little
medication probably wouldn't hurt that person.

But that exactly describes John the Baptist, who was sent by God
to get people ready for Jesus. He started off as the precious baby boy
who leaped for joy inside his mother, Elizabeth, when Mary showed
up, pregnant with Jesus. But by the time he was an adult, he was
dressing in camel hair outfits (some of the scratchiest stuff on the
planet) and existing on a diet of bugs and honey. He was, frankly,
pretty weird.

He had to be in order to get people's attention so they would listen up and make themselves ready to meet Jesus. So you get ready for
some weirdness this week, not just in John, but perhaps in you too.

# Sunday

You brood of vipers! Who warned you to flee from the coming wrath?

Matthew 3:7

In case you aren't up on your reptiles, a "brood of vipers" would be an entire pit of very poisonous snakes, with venom in their little snakey-fangs. That was a pretty big insult to be thrusting at the Pharisees. They were a group of educated men who told everyone they should keep the Law of Moses so strictly that it was often ridiculous—but they themselves broke the law in secret all the time, which made them hypocrites. They were so wrapped up in keeping the rules, they had forgotten about God's love and mercy. To John, they were like a bunch of poisonous snakes.

If somebody called you a viper, would you stick around to hear more? Probably not, unless the person saying it was so convincing he made you think about your weaknesses and failings and made you want to change them. In spite of his freaky appearance and far-out diet, John had that effect on people. He wasn't giving a feel-good-about-yourself message, but people came from all over Judea and confessed their sins to him and let him baptize them.

But John didn't take any of the credit for himself. Even when he had the Pharisees hanging their heads in shame, he said the guy they really needed to prepare themselves for was the one who was coming after him. Huh. Strange. Insulting. Brutally honest. And humble. Not a guy you necessarily want to hang out with for fun, but definitely somebody to learn from.

## Do That Little Thing: QUIZ

Do you have any of these viper qualities?

___ You gossip

___ You've spread a rumor

___ You criticize someone for something you've actually done yourself (only nobody knows)

___ You seem sweet, but you can say some pretty ugly things

___ You know all the rules, but you don't always follow them

There's a little viper in each of us. That's why you need to prepare the way for Jesus this week. You can do it — you have John the Baptist to show you, strange as he is.

He is the one who comes after me, the thongs of whose sandals I am not worthy to untie.

John 1:27

Think about the last time you were involved in a program at church, like the annual Christmas pageant or a project at school. You had your part, you knew what you were supposed to do—but did something bigger start to look like it might be more fun, get you more stage time, make you feel more important at the lunch table?

There is nothing wrong with dreaming of the next big thing you could do, as long as it doesn't rob you of the joy—and the importance—of what you're doing right now. Today, at this moment, your job is always to focus on what you've been given to do and stick to it until it's done.

John the Baptist knew all about that. He had one job, and that was to convince people to get the big sins out of their lives so they'd have room for Jesus in there when he came. He didn't wish he could be Jesus. He never claimed to be anything like him. In fact, he said he himself wasn't good enough to untie Jesus' shoes. He had a big enough job to do. So do all of us, right this very minute.

## Do That Little Thing: FIND OUT

Ask your God-loving adult friends if they've ever had to do background work for someone else. Behind the scenes in a theater, secretary to a big boss, bat boy? Ask them to be honest about how they felt. It might help you see just what a big sacrifice John the Baptist made, and how rewarding it actually was. It'll come in handy someday. Maybe even someday soon.

# Tuesday

I need to be baptized by you, and do you come to me?

Matthew 3:14

Isn't it fun to feel important? When you've broken your arm and everyone gathers around to look at your cast and hear how it happened? When you know the dance routine the best, and everybody looks to you to learn the steps?

What isn't fun is when somebody else breaks a *leg*, and hobbles in on crutches and takes all the attention. You try not to turn green with jealousy, but it's hard. The spotlight is such a warm and wonderful thing to be in.

John the Baptist would have felt like that when Jesus showed up, if he weren't so focused on exactly what God put him here to do. He was very successful at getting people to repent of their sins and change their lives. He was baptizing people in droves. He was the talk of the desert. But the minute Jesus came on the scene, he immediately turned all the attention on him. Even when Jesus gave him the huge honor of baptizing him, John said, "No, man, you're the one who should be baptizing me."

Outspoken and flamboyant as he was, John never let his ministry be about him. It was always about Jesus. Couldn't we all take our cue from him when we're feeling like we're all that?

## Do That Little Thing: JUST THINK

Think about what it's like when you have to back off and let someone else take the spotlight. Do you gracefully let it go? Go pout in a corner? Grab that spotlight back? Announce that the new spotlight holder is just trying to ruin your life? Don't beat yourself up. Just think about what you do, and consider how you might do more of a John the Baptist thing in the future.

# Wednesday

Are you the one who was to come, or should we expect some-one else?

Luke 7:19

"This is not what I expected." "I thought we'd be further than this by now." "Are you sure we're doing this right?"

Those kinds of doubts can crop up in your mind when things aren't exactly going the way you planned. It could even be happening as you work with this book. You might be thinking, "I should be feeling closer to God by now (or being nicer to my brother or getting more control over my arguing). Am I doing something wrong?"

John the Baptist was probably having some of those doubts himself. John was in prison for telling King Herod he was wrong to steal his brother's wife. John's disciples continued his ministry and kept him informed, but it didn't seem to him that Jesus was moving fast enough. You can't really blame John. He was in some dungeon, sharing lunch with the rats. Naturally he needed reassurance, so he sent his disciples to ask if he'd been right, that Jesus was indeed the Messiah.

Jesus wasn't upset with John for asking. He told John's disciples to report to him what they were seeing—him healing the sick and driving out evil spirits and relieving the suffering of the poor. He understood John's doubts, but he didn't want him to lose hope because of them.

If it was okay for John to have doubts, it's okay for you. Jesus is there for you, too, with all the reassurance you need. Just look around you at all he does, and know.

## Do That Little Thing: GOD? CAN WE TALK?

Talk to God about any reassurance you need — that he's real, that Jesus is still healing and curing and helping, that he still loves you. Tell him about your doubts, and ask him to let you see what he's doing. He wants to get those doubts out so you don't get tangled up in them.

# Thursday

Give me here on a platter the head of John the Baptist.

Matthew 14:8

After reading all the success stories of Daniel and David and Esther, it's hard to hear this one about John the Baptist.

John, as you learned yesterday, was in prison. King Herod might have just left him to spend the rest of his life there if he hadn't thrown himself a birthday party and watched his stepdaughter/niece dance for him. He thought she was so fabulous he told her she could have anything she wanted. That must have been some dance!

The girl, Salome (not to be confused with salami), went to her mother and said, "What should I ask for?" Her mom was ticked off at John for calling *her* a sinner, so she said, "Ask for John the Baptist's head on a platter."

Herod thought she'd want jewels, maybe a few more maids. But he couldn't refuse her, not in front of all his guests. So John was beheaded, and his head was brought in on a platter — like it was just another dish at the feast.

Doesn't that seem so unjust? That's the point. Speaking out for God and for what's right doesn't guarantee that nothing bad will happen to you. There will always be people who get angry at being told they're wrong, and some of those people are powerful. John knew that, but he spoke out anyway. His time on earth ended in a brutal way, but the lesson of his courage and godliness lives on in us when we face our own King Herods.

## Do That Little Thing: LISTEN UP!

Listen for that thought that says, "Speak out." Against the bully who keeps that shy girl from going to her locker. Against the popular kid who gets away with shoving people in the lunch line. Against your own friends making fun of that fourth grader's Little Mermaid backpack. Just listen, until you know what to say.

# Friday

Some were saying "John the Baptist has been raised from the dead, and that is why miraculous powers are at work in [Jesus]."

Mark 6:14

Salome and her mother might have felt less guilty with John the Baptist out of the picture, but King Herod didn't. His guilt was driving him crazy. Seriously.

Jesus continued to heal people and drive out the spirits that tormented them, and he sent his disciples out to do the same. His ministry was growing, and more and more people were believing in him.

But there were still some who, even though they saw what he did with their own eyes, couldn't accept that he could do those things because he was the Son of God. They said he was some prophet or something. One of the most popular opinions was that he was John the Baptist come back from the dead—even though John himself had always said it was Jesus who was the important one, the Savior.

Since King Herod was the one who had John the Baptist killed, his guilt drove him into thinking that, yes, John had come back from the dead. That must have scared the dickens out of him. Not a bad thing, really.

The point is, John wouldn't have wanted it that way. He wanted people to believe in Jesus, not him. We should listen to the echoes of his memory. He's still pointing us away from our guilty consciences, toward Jesus. Let's follow.

## Do That Little Thing: YOU CAN *SO* DO THIS!

Still wrapped up in guilt over your viper behavior (See Sunday's Quiz)? It's time to let it go. Turn your back on it just one time today — by buttoning your lip against one piece of gossip on the bus or telling your mom you lied about your math grade or whatever. Enough with just feeling bad about it. Do something.

# Saturday

What did you go out to see? A prophet? Yes, I tell you, and more than a prophet.

Matthew 11:9

What if your teacher told you the questions that were going to be on the big test, but you didn't look up the answers?

What if your mom said your grandmother was coming to take you shopping, and you could go if you got your room cleaned up—but you didn't remove so much as a cobweb?

The good news of an upcoming event is fun to hear, but if you don't do what you have to do to participate in it, the fun doesn't last long.

Jesus was worried about the people missing out on more than fun. He wanted them to be saved from lives of slavery to their messed-up ways. They weren't doing what they had to do, and it didn't have to be that way.

John the Baptist came, like your mom telling you about your grandmother's visit, to inform the people that Jesus was coming to save them and heal them and make their lives better. All they had to do to get ready was be truly sorry for the things they'd done wrong and want to do better. That was all.

And did they do it? Not all of them. Some of them loved hearing about all the good things Jesus was going to do, but they weren't willing to lift a finger to prepare. John the Baptist's words went to waste with them. Nobody can really know Jesus unless they're willing to give up all their bad stuff. It's a bummer that so many people are missing out when they don't have to.

## Do That Little Thing: SHOUT-OUT

Tell somebody what God taught you this week through that strange character, John the Baptist. Was it just the knowledge of your inner viper? A new willingness to work behind the scenes and let someone *else* have the spotlight? That it's okay to have doubts or to speak out even though somebody might not like it? The ability to knock your guilty conscience out of the way and just get rid of those inner vipers to make room for Jesus? Give God a shout-out for that. (And there's no need to don camel hair or eat insects for the occasion!)

# From Blockhead to Rock

> When Simon Peter saw this, he fell at Jesus' knees and
> said, "Go away from me, Lord; I am a sinful man!"
>
> Luke 5:8

At school when sides are chosen for basketball or a spelling bee, the "best" people always get picked first, right? The fastest, the smartest, or even just the most popular. If you want to win, you have to have the right people.

Jesus didn't operate that way. When he went out to call his disciples—the people who were going to be with him for three years and who would carry on his work when he was gone—he didn't look for the brightest and the most popular. It was hard to tell at first just what he *was* looking for, because his first pick, Simon Peter, was just a big fisherman with no education and not a lot of self-confidence. Not that there's anything wrong with catching fish for a living. Every time you eat a tuna fish sandwich you have to be grateful that somebody does it.

What was it about Peter that made Jesus choose him? Wouldn't it be good to know that if we want to work for Jesus too? Our first clue is in Peter's reaction to Jesus when he performed the miracle of loading the men's nets with fish that had escaped them all night. Peter said, "Go away from me, Lord. I am a sinful man." The closer a person gets to God, the more he sees his own flaws and sins. Peter had to know Jesus was God to feel his failings so sharply. That was all it took—knowing and believing. Let that be your start as you follow Peter through his transformation this week. Simply know and believe.

# Sunday

> They pulled their boats up on shore, left everything and followed him.
>
> Luke 5:11

Have you and your friends ever talked about what possessions you would grab if your house were on fire and you had to get out fast? No matter what you imagine taking with you, it's even hard to think about leaving the rest behind.

What if you were called to something that required you to take absolutely nothing that you owned with you? What if you had to drop everything and go? Leave your family and friends? Simply stop your life and start a new one?

Okay, so maybe you can't even picture it, but Simon Peter, James, and John didn't have time to think about it. When Jesus said, "Guys, don't be afraid. I want you to help me gather people instead of fish," they went with him. Nothing else mattered.

Right now, while you're still growing and learning, God won't ask you to drop everything—school (which you might not mind!), family (which you just couldn't do), friends (which—well, don't even go there). But he might ask you to abandon something so you can be closer to him. Will you be like Simon Peter and simply do that little thing?

## Do That Little Thing: QUIZ

Put a check next to any of these things you could let go of right now if it meant being closer to God:

____ A friendship that gets you into trouble sometimes
____ An activity that crowds your schedule with one too many things
____ A habit that isn't good for your health
____ An attitude that turns people off
____ A grudge that keeps you from forgiving

# Monday

> "You of little faith," [Jesus] said, "why did you doubt?"
>
> Matthew 14:31

What made you decide you wanted to play soccer or take dance lessons or jump off the high dive? You probably saw somebody else do it first and it looked like fun—and easy. But once you got started, didn't you find out you had a lot to learn?

Peter was that way about being Jesus' disciple. He really, really wanted to become like Jesus—but remember, Jesus didn't pick the sharpest tacks in the box as his students. Take the night Jesus sent the disciples ahead on a boat so he could go up onto a mountainside by himself and pray. When a storm came up on the lake, he got concerned about his guys and went to be with them in the boat—by walking across the water.

The disciples thought he was a ghost and freaked out. Jesus called out to them, in the voice they knew so well, but Peter said "Lord, IF it's you, tell me to come to you on the water."

IF—that word separates us from God all the time. If you really love me. If you really are God. If you can hear me. God understands our iffiness, just as Jesus understood Peter's and called him to come. Peter actually took a few steps on the water—and then he realized what he was doing, felt the wind, and got scared. Down he went, calling for Jesus to save him. Which Jesus did, of course, but he wanted to know as he caught Peter, "Why did you doubt?" He doubted because he had a lot to learn about faith. And so do we.

## Do That Little Thing: FIND OUT

Ask your God-loving adult friends what their "ifs" are or have been in the past when it comes to God. Share yours, too. We can all help each other with our iffiness.

# Tuesday

Peter said, "Explain the parable to us."

Matthew 15:15

Don't you love it when you're in class and you don't understand something but you're too embarrassed to raise your hand and say, "I'm totally clueless," and then somebody else does it?

That was one of the best things about Peter—he wasn't afraid to ask questions. He knew he was no scholar and he wasn't ashamed of that. He just wanted to learn all he could from Jesus, and if that was going to happen, he had to have things explained to him.

It didn't even seem to bother him when he asked a question and Jesus said, "Are you still so dull?" (verse 16). He probably got that Jesus didn't have forever to get all this stuff through to them, that he was bound to get a little impatient with his dullness. Peter didn't care how he sounded—he just wanted to know.

Let that be an inspiration next time you just don't get it and you're afraid if you ask, someone is going to say you're lame. Who cares? It's all about learning everything you can. Aren't you grateful to Peter for asking for an explanation of that parable—so you can understand it today? Yeah, he'd have been a great guy to have in class!

## Do That Little Thing: JUST THINK

Think about something you've been afraid to ask about. Is there something you want to discuss with your parents? Material you're struggling with in school? An issue you want to take up with your friends? Imagine asking your question or starting your discussion. Would it really be so bad if somebody said, "What?" While you're thinking, consider if there might be somebody else who wants to have that answer too.

# Wednesday

You are the Christ, the Son of the living God.

Matthew 16:16

Had one of those, "Oh, I get it!" moments lately? Like when multiplying fractions suddenly stops looking like the formula for rocket fuel, or that comma slides right into place without you even having to think about it. When you have one of those moments, you wonder why you didn't see it sooner. The reason is, of course, that you didn't know then what you do know now. You don't just "get it" unless you're paying attention, trying to figure it out.

While Simon Peter was bumbling around with his doubts and asking clumsy questions, he was learning. He watched, he listened, he wrinkled his forehead in deep thought. And when Jesus said, "Who do you say I am?" Peter didn't even have to think about it. He got it. "You are the Christ, the Son of the living God," he said.

He was the first one of the disciples to realize it and put it into words. Big, dense, tell-me-one-more-time Peter. So don't beat yourself up because you have to hear and see and do something over and over before *you* get it, especially in matters of Jesus. You're just doing the Peter thing—and it sure worked for him.

## Do That Little Thing: GOD? CAN WE TALK?

Tell God what you think you "get" about him, even if it's just "I know you're there." Ask him to fill you with more understanding, more I-get-its. And don't be afraid to ask him over and over again.

# Thursday

Peter said to Jesus, "Lord, it is good for us to be here. If you wish, I will put up three shelters."

Matthew 17:4

You can fix macaroni and cheese out of a box and make a mean peanut butter and jelly sandwich. Think you're ready to cook a whole meal by yourself for the entire family?

You fed your baby cousin her bottle while your aunt sat close by. Think you're ready to babysit alone for a whole afternoon?

Once you get a taste of something, it's easy to think you're ready for the whole enchilada, but most big skills take time to learn, and that's especially true of spiritual things. Learning to live close to God is a process that can last a lifetime.

Peter didn't know that yet when Jesus chose him, along with James and John, to go up a high mountain with him. There, they saw him glow with godliness as he talked to Moses and Elijah (long since dead). Jesus picked him because he was learning and growing, and Jesus knew he could trust him. But when he saw the three spirits together, Peter showed that he didn't totally understand it. He wanted to put up tents for them!

And that's okay. Faith is a journey, and who better than Peter to show us that, because he's so very much like us. Keep stumbling along. Every experience with God brings you closer to understanding.

## Do That Little Thing: LISTEN UP!

While they were up on the mountain, God said about Jesus, "This is my Son, whom I love; with him I am well pleased. Listen to him!" (verse 5). So do that. Listen for Jesus, wherever you are. Words of real love, of true faith, of genuine honesty are Jesus talking. Listen.

> Immediately a rooster crowed. Then Peter remembered the word Jesus had spoken … and he went outside and wept bitterly.
>
> Matthew 26:74–75

Is there anything worse than realizing you have totally let someone down? The disappointed sag in your little brother's face when you blow off his T-ball game to sleep in. The stiffness in your mom's chin when you forget her birthday. The drop in your dad's voice when you tell him you broke the remote because you were playing with it, just like he told you not to. Makes you want to melt into the floor, doesn't it?

What if it were Jesus you were letting down? Peter had that experience. After all he'd learned, all he went through with his Lord, he still denied even knowing him the night he was turned over to the officials. Jesus predicted it would happen. He said before the rooster crowed the next morning, Peter would have denied him three times. Peter said there was no way — so can you even imagine the guilt and the self-hatred he felt when he heard that cock-a-doodle-do, right after he'd said for the third time, "I don't know the guy"?

We can't be too critical of Peter, because most of us let Jesus down on a daily basis. Every time you disrespect your parents or laugh at a not-very-nice joke, it's like you're saying, "Jesus? Jesus Who?" So what can we learn from Peter? That we will make mistakes. That we can't brag that we won't. That when we realize what we've done it's going to hurt inside. That it's okay to cry.

Read on tomorrow to see how Jesus handled it. For now, know you're not alone.

## Do That Little Thing: YOU CAN *SO* DO THIS!

If you've let anybody down lately — and who hasn't — go to that person as soon as you can and set things right. Even if you've done it three times — even if you said you never would — apologize and see if you can make amends. Don't wait for the rooster to crow before you make a start.

# Saturday

Repent and be baptized, every one of you, in the name of Jesus Christ for the forgiveness of your sins. And you will receive the gift of the Holy Spirit.

Acts 2:38

I can never show my face there again." "I can never look her in the eye, ever." "We're going to have to move now, because my life here is over."

Even if you aren't a drama queen, you may have had one of those thoughts. Something so heinous, so embarrassing, so awful happens, you just think there's no going back. Of course, if that were true every time a person made a mistake, life as we know it would come to a complete halt. When people mess up royally, they have to do what they can to move on.

Peter is one of the best examples of that. After he denied Jesus and ran off and hid, you'd think he would have disappeared forever, trying to get away from the guilt that haunted him. Instead, he knew from his time with Jesus that this was a forgiving Lord. He stuck with the disciples during the three days Jesus was dead, keeping them together, not letting them give up hope. When Jesus rose from the dead and came to them, Peter told him without shame how much he loved him—three times to be exact—the same number of times he denied him before. Jesus showed Peter that he had forgiven him by giving him the most important job there was—to build a church from his teachings.

So on the day of Pentecost when the Holy Spirit came, just as Jesus promised, Peter stood up before everyone—the big, dense fisherman turned spiritual leader—and invited them all to receive the Spirit. It was a magnificent transformation. Who would have thought it?

## Do That Little Thing: SHOUT-OUT

Fill in this blank: Jesus can use me, even though I _____
_____.

Now tell someone you trust. Shout it out, Peter style.

## Changed in a Flash

> Saul began to destroy the church. Going from house to house, he dragged off men and women and put them in prison.
>
> Acts 8:3

The people God chose to do his work just kept getting more and more unlikely. He began with Abraham, who was practically a saint starting out, but things went downhill from there—the stuttering Moses, the little kid David, the big lug Peter. At least all of them loved God and wanted to serve him.

When it came to spreading the word about Jesus, God chose a guy who not only didn't love the Lord; he hated him. Seriously. Saul of Tarsus, our transformed Bible friend of the week, was a Jewish leader who was so angry with the followers of Jesus he was actively hunting them down and killing them. The first time he appears in the Bible (Acts 8:1) he was at the stoning of Stephen, giving his approval for his horrible death.

Why would God choose somebody like that? You'll find out this week. For now, just know that from where he started, Saul had no place to go but up. It gives you hope, doesn't it?

# Sunday

He fell to the ground and heard a voice say to him, "Saul, Saul, why do you persecute me?" "Who are you, Lord?" Saul asked.

Acts 9:4–5

You may have experienced this scene. A girl talks really big around her friends and the kids who are afraid of her, spewing out her threats, making everybody feel like they're two inches tall. Then a teacher comes along, asks her what she thinks she's doing, and she shrinks like a raisin, smaller than any of her victims. Doesn't it just make you furious? She *knew* what she was doing was wrong. Otherwise she wouldn't have known the authority was right, and she would have tried to take her out too!

Paul was on his way to Damascus with letters of permission from the high priest. These letters said that if he found anyone in Damascus who belonged to the Way of Jesus, he could take them as prisoners to Jerusalem. It was his biggest—and worst—job yet. But the minute the light flashed from heaven and he heard the Lord's voice, he *knew* who it was, and he *knew* what he'd been doing was wrong.

Maybe that was the first reason why God chose him to take the good news of Jesus to all corners of the known world—because deep in his heart, he *knew*. And when Jesus called him by name, he paid attention.

Do you *know* who's in charge? Pay attention this week. He might have a job for you.

## Do That Little Thing: QUIZ

Check off any of these ways that you *know* God's voice when you hear it, however you hear it. Don't be upset if you don't think you hear God. It will come — just keep listening.

____ I have a thought that I know didn't come from me.

____ I think something might be from God, and then someone else says the same thing to me, so I know.

____ I read something in the Bible, and it's like it was written just for me.

____ I get a special feeling inside me.

____ I find myself saying or writing something I know I didn't think of by myself.

____ I can actually hear God's voice.

# Monday

When he came to Jerusalem, he tried to join the disciples, but they were all afraid of him, not believing that he really was a disciple.

Acts 9:26

Well, duh! What did Saul expect? He'd been tearing around the country, killing their fellow believers, and now all of a sudden they were supposed to welcome him like he was one of them?

It wasn't an easy gig for Saul. He had to convince the other disciples that he was for real, that this wasn't a trick to get them to relax with him so he could round them all up and take them to prison—or worse.

Perhaps you've run into that yourself. You've decided to change some not-so-good behavior, and you try, but your family is suspicious. "This won't last," they say. "I give it three days and you'll be back to your old ways." Or maybe you know somebody else who was attempting to turn herself around. You don't want to be hurt by this person again, so you sit back and wait to see if she's for real this time.

That may be the second reason why God chose Saul to do this huge job. If he could show the disciples that he had really changed his heart, he could be trusted with the rest of God's people. This job wasn't for the wimpy, so Saul was put to the wimp test right away.

We can thank God he passed.

## Do That Little Thing: FIND OUT

Ask your God-loving grown-up friends if they have ever had to earn someone's trust back after letting them down — or out and out attacking them in some way. Get them to tell you if it was hard and how they went about it — and what part God played in putting things right again.

# Tuesday

For a whole year Barnabas and Saul met with the church and taught great numbers of people.

Acts 11:26

H e was an overnight success!" people sometimes say about a singing star or an actor. It does seem like all of a sudden that fabulous person sprang up out of nowhere and is now everywhere.

But it very seldom happens that way. Most of the time, successful people practice and train for years and work their way up singing at birthday parties and doing commercials where they have to dress up like dental floss. There might be a big break that launches a career, but it doesn't happen "overnight."

Even though God told Saul that he would be working for him from now on, Saul didn't take out on his own the next day to preach the gospel. Barnabas trained him and showed him how to spread the word in Jerusalem. Then he and Barnabas traveled together for a year, since Saul wasn't ready to go solo yet.

Saul was used to being the boss and having other people take orders from him. That must have been the third reason God chose him. If he could humble himself before men who knew more than he did, he could do the same with God. Makes you want to sit at somebody's feet and learn, doesn't it?

## Do That Little Thing: JUST THINK

Been thinking you're all that about something? The sport you play? An activity you're involved in? In your group of friends? Among your family members? Think about what you might learn from someone else in that area. Imagine yourself spending time asking questions and listening, instead of talking about what you know. Just think about it. If it seems right, do it.

# Wednesday

> We had to speak the word of God to you first. Since you reject it and do not consider your selves worthy of eternal life, we now turn to the Gentiles.
>
> Acts 13:46

Let's say you have some really great news. You're getting a puppy, or your family's going to Disney World on vacation, or your dad just got a job after being out of work for three months. You get online or pick up the phone or run next door to share, because that's half the fun of having something fabulous happen to you.

But what if your friends don't get excited for you? What if they say, "Oh, yeah, cool," and turn back to the TV? Do you deflate like yesterday's party balloon and keep the news to yourself after that? Or do you find somebody who wants to share your joy? (Even if it's your pet parakeet.)

God wanted somebody like Saul to spread his Good News, somebody who wouldn't give up when his own people, the Jews, said the News was no big deal. He wanted somebody who would say, "Fine, I'll take it to the Gentiles [the non-Jews]." That was the fourth reason God selected Saul, because Saul knew the work he was doing wasn't about him and his popularity. It was about the message of Jesus—and he would tell it to anybody who would listen.

God wants that from you too. After all, the news is just too good to keep to yourself.

## Do That Little Thing: GOD? CAN WE TALK?

Ask God if there's someone who needs the good news you have to share — through your smile, your "hi" when no one else speaks to her, your generosity with homework help, or half your double-chocolate-chunk cookie. Ask if God wants you to talk to her about him too. Get the details. This is God's favorite subject.

# Thursday

We too are only men, human like you.

Acts 14:15

Have you ever worshiped the ground somebody walked on? Seriously, in some weak moment, have you idolized a person other than Jesus? Would have done anything to meet him or her, but knew you'd die if he or she actually walked into the room? Sometimes that happens with movie stars or rock singers—you just get so stuck on that person, and you have to have all the posters and the CDs and the DVDs and the t-shirts. Usually you come to your senses before you set up an actual shrine in your room, but you can see how easy it is to fall into worship.

That happened to Saul (who was now called Paul) when he and Barnabas healed a man who had been crippled from birth. The man got up to walk, and the people called Paul and Barnabas gods. They were ready to offer sacrifices to them—which brings us to the fifth reason God picked Paul to do his work. Paul was having none of their worship. He told the people he was there for one thing, and that was to spread the good news about Jesus. That was the kind of focused person God wanted working for him, and he still wants that.

Got your eyes on God today?

## Do That Little Thing: LISTEN UP!

Listen for the things in your mind that you think about more than anything else. Is it making good grades? Having cute clothes? Getting more stuff? Or are there more Jesus-like things floating around in there? Ways to make your friends happy. Things you could do to grow wiser. Stuff you could do to help your mom. What you think about is what you'll worship.

# Friday

I myself in my mind am a slave to God's law, but in the sinful nature a slave to the law of sin.

Romans 7:25

Nobody's perfect.

But, come on, aren't there people who come pretty close?

What about Mother Teresa, the wonderful nun who ministered to the lepers in India? And Billy Graham, who has helped so many people to know about Jesus? Or even your grandma, who always seems to know the right thing to say and do?

Even they aren't perfect, but the thing that makes them special is that as good as they are (or were), they never thought they were any better than anyone else. Paul was like that too. He taught so many people about Jesus and started communities of believers and basically knocked himself out spreading the Word. And yet he called himself a sinner, said he couldn't do the good he really wanted to do unless he totally let go and let God work in him. Reason number six why God chose Paul: he never thought he was better than anyone else, and he totally counted on the grace of Christ to keep him on track. It's nice to know that even the most perfect people aren't perfect. Takes the pressure off, doesn't it?

## Do That Little Thing: YOU CAN SO DO THIS!

Choose something you really want to do in order to be a better person, and that you just haven't been able to pull off. Do you want to kick that lying habit? Stop being jealous of your sister? Take more responsibility for the kitten you begged for? Instead of trying to do that little thing, ask God to work inside you to help you change. Just ask. Just listen. See what happens.

# Saturday

One thing I do: Forgetting what is behind and straining toward what is ahead, I press on.

Philippians 3:13–14

Here we are at the end of our week with Paul. You've seen him transformed from a tyrant out to take down as many Christians as he could into the voice Christians now turn to when they want to understand what it looks like to live as Jesus wants us to. That may be the biggest change in a person in the whole Bible.

But Paul didn't consider himself to be "there" yet. He knew he had a long way to go before he was even close to being like Jesus. He started out behind anyway! Yet he didn't get discouraged. He didn't worry about his past mistakes; he didn't even stew about all the people he'd persecuted back when he didn't know Christ or understand what he was about. That would only have kept him from doing the work God wanted him to do. Instead, he looked ahead and kept trying to get better and better, with God's Holy Spirit inside him all the time.

You have made your own mistakes, but they are nothing compared to what Paul did in his pre-Jesus days. If Paul can put his past behind him, so can you. Forget it, even if nobody else will. Look ahead to the fabulous life God has planned for you. Be transformed. All it takes is trusting that God is at work in your life this very minute. So press on.

## Do That Little Thing: SHOUT-OUT

Shout this out to someone you trust: "I'm free!" Tell that person that you are shaking off all the old stuff that nags at you, that tries to pull you back. Chirp about the new stuff you're moving toward because the Holy Spirit is in you. Ask him or her to shout with you, because you are pressing on!

## Body-Building

> In the last days, God says, I will pour out my Spirit on all
> people . . . and everyone who calls on the name of the Lord
> will be saved.
>
> Acts 2:17, 21

The amazing individuals you've been reading about these last twelve weeks—people like Esther and Ruth, Peter and Paul—are not the only ones God has transformed. Anyone who believes in him through the message of Christ is changed into more and more of the person he or she was meant to be. Hopefully you've seen changes in yourself in these months, little differences that show you that God is at work in you.

But there's more. God doesn't just transform individuals, one by one. He creates great changes in whole groups, and that's what this final week of Part III is about. Probably one of his most amazing transformations ever took place when the early church was formed into the body of Christ. Get ready to see some body-building this week, and to watch your own spiritual muscles pump up, too.

Judge for yourselves whether it is right in God's sight to obey you rather than God.

Acts 4:19

What would it be like if the people who were in charge of you began telling you to do things you didn't think were right? If a teacher tried to make you say that the Bible was a bunch of hooey, or your after-school care person said it was okay to clobber somebody if she hit you first—it would be really hard to stand up and say, "I don't think so." You might do it, but you'd probably be at least a little nervous about the consequences.

That's the position Peter and John (two of the apostles) were in when they were called before the Jewish Sanhedrin—kind of like our Supreme Court. As Jews, Peter and John had been taught to respect these leaders and do what they said. But when the Sanhedrin ordered Peter and John to stop healing people in the name of Jesus, in fact, to stop talking about Christ, period, they couldn't obey.

That was a huge thing, especially for unschooled, ordinary men. But it had to be done in order for the new church, Christ's church, to understand who their new leader was. It wasn't the Sanhedrin; it was Jesus, the head of the body that was being formed. Transformation began.

## Do That Little Thing: QUIZ

Which of the following would you do if someone in authority said you couldn't even mention Jesus' name:

\_\_\_\_ Cry a lot.

\_\_\_\_ Tell him he was crazy.

\_\_\_\_ Do it anyway when that person wasn't around.

\_\_\_\_ Do it right out in the open and take the consequences.

\_\_\_\_ Realize I don't talk that much about Jesus anyway.

The good news is, you don't have to do any of those things, because from the time of Peter and Paul, the body of Christ has fought for the right to speak the name of Jesus.

# Monday

No one claimed that any of his possessions was his own, but they shared everything they had... There were no needy persons among them.

Acts 4:32, 34

Suppose you went into the cafeteria for lunch one day and the principal told everyone to put his or her lunch on one table so everyone could choose what they wanted to eat. That would be great for the kids who only brought a peanut butter sandwich and some carrot sticks. They could feast on somebody's brownies and somebody else's chocolate cookies and think they'd died and gone to heaven. But the kids who'd been looking forward to their private stash of treats all morning weren't going to be so excited about all that sharing.

In Jewish culture there was a definite difference in status between rich and poor—between those with the peanut butter sandwiches and those with the homemade brownies. If you were well-off, it was assumed God was blessing you, and if you were poor, you, or your parents before you, must have done something wrong. They had believed that for centuries.

It was a huge thing, then, for these new Christians to put all their possessions into one big pile so that everyone was taken care of. It meant they believed now that what Jesus said was true—it is not your material possessions that make you good; it is what you do for others and how you love them. Doing that showed major transformation. Think about making your lunch part of a buffet, and you'll get an idea just how big that was.

## Do That Little Thing: FIND OUT

Ask your God-loving grown-up friends if they've ever felt smaller — or bigger — than someone else because of what they did or didn't own. Talk about when that changed, when they realized it's not the having but the sharing that makes God happy.

# Tuesday

Brothers, choose seven men from among you who are known to be full of the Spirit and wisdom. We will turn this responsibility over to them and will give our attention to prayer and the ministry of the word.

Acts 6:3

Who seems to be more "important" in your church—the lady who takes care of the babies in the nursery or your senior pastor? In school, is it the principal or the woman who serves the pizza in the cafeteria?

We all tend to make some jobs more significant than others in our minds. We're more impressed if some girl's dad is a brain surgeon than if he's a bricklayer. But where would the brain surgeon perform surgery if there were no brick hospital? The principal can be hilarious over the intercom every morning, but that doesn't mean much at lunchtime when you're so hungry you're ready to eat your backpack. And could the pastor preach his sermon if the sanctuary were full of screaming babies?

In the Hebrew culture, just like in ours, some jobs were considered more impressive than others. But the followers of Jesus changed that. They saw that the widows and orphans needed to be taken care of, but the message of Jesus had to be spread too. So they divided up the jobs, making each one as important as the other. Who cared about status when there was so much to be done for God and his people?

Yes, really, who cares if somebody's a cheerleader and somebody else makes friendship bracelets and somebody else reads five books a week? If it's for the love of God and others, what difference is there?

## Do That Little Thing: JUST THINK

Think about what impresses you. A girl with cute clothes? One who is the queen of the soccer field? Somebody who rocks at math? As you go through those impressive people in your mind, consider what the early Christians found out — that there is so much to do in God's kingdom, everybody's important. Then go tell somebody with a "small" job that you appreciate what she does.

# Wednesday

The Most High does not live in houses made by men. As the prophet says: "Heaven is my throne, and the earth is my footstool. What kind of house will you build for me?" says the Lord.

Acts 7:48–49

Have you ever driven through a large town and seen mega-sized churches that look like college campuses? Maybe you even belong to one that has its own coffee shop and bookstore and gym. It seems like God *must* be in a place that huge and beautiful.

You already know from this book that the people of Jerusalem were all about their temple, and that was because God told them exactly how to build it and how to treat it with reverence. They actually believed that God lived in the temple and they had to go there (at least once a year if they lived far away) to show their love and respect for him.

Jesus changed that. He said that it wasn't about a place any more. He was the place. People could now come to him, anywhere, anytime, and be with God. He was the new temple.

That did not set well with the folks who didn't get Jesus yet. How dare somebody like Stephen, who spoke the words in today's verse, speak against the Holy Place? In fact, they stoned Stephen to death, and after that the Jesus-followers had to "go underground" and scatter so they wouldn't be killed too. But that didn't stop them from preaching and teaching. They just did it in places other than Jerusalem, which meant more people heard about the message of Jesus. It wasn't about a place any more — not then, not now.

## Do That Little Thing: GOD? CAN WE TALK?

Instead of going to your quiet place to talk to God today, try chatting with him wherever you are. On the bus, discuss silently what's going on in your life. Before your vocabulary test, whisper a request for a good memory and concentration. When you're bored out of your mind in the orthodontist's waiting room, ask God to fill your mind with something fun to think about. Like why people are so worked up about straight teeth!

# **Thursday**

When they arrived, they prayed for them that they might receive the Holy Spirit, because the Holy Spirit had not yet come upon any of them; they had simply been baptized into the name of the Lord Jesus.

Acts 8:15–16

Nobody had more ceremonies and feasts than the Hebrew people. You've read about Passover and Purim and the major weddings, and those are only a few. There was a ritual for everything, and people came to believe that if you went through the right motions, you were okay with God. Make the offerings and sacrifices, have enough wine at the wedding, you're good to go.

The early Christians knew Jesus didn't want it to be that way anymore. So even when people chose to be baptized—which meant they believed that Jesus was the Son of God and they wanted to devote their lives to him—that by itself didn't mean they were set for life—well, eternal life. They also had to be filled with the Holy Spirit, so that God was in them, showing them the way. That wasn't something they could get from a ceremony. They had to pray to be filled, and then get everything else out of the way, and open themselves up wide. Only then would their relationship with God be real. Only then would they be transformed.

## Do That Little Thing: LISTEN UP!

Listen for the Holy Spirit in you. What will you hear? It's different for everyone, but a feeling of strength or peace or thoughts of love and blessings, or the urge to do something kind or just for someone else — those are the sounds of the Holy Spirit. Hear and be grateful that you are filled.

# Friday

> You are well aware that it is against our law for a Jew to associate with a Gentile or visit him. But God has shown me that I should not call any man impure or unclean.
>
> Acts 10:28

Okay, so first you tell me not to hang around kids with bad reputations. Now you're saying I need to love them and pray for them and treat them like everybody else. What's up with that?

That's a confusing issue. It was for the early Christians too. The Jews had been taught all their lives that they were God's chosen people and must separate themselves from other "unclean" people. If a Jew went into a Gentile's house (a non-Jew), he was considered unclean and couldn't go to the temple until he purified himself.

That was so that God could train his people to devote their lives to him, like God is doing with you now. He didn't want them being influenced by non-Jews who could totally take them down the wrong path, and as you've read, that happened pretty easily! It can for you too.

But with the coming of Jesus, God wanted his message to be available to everybody, Jew and Gentile. It was a new thing for both of them, so they could go down the same path together. But the Jews weren't sure. Was it possible that they could still be clean before God if they went to lunch with Gentiles? That was a risk, and God understood that, which is why he gave Peter a vision to say it was okay. So, yes, pray for and be kind to the rough kids. The two of you may end up on the same path someday.

## Do That Little Thing: YOU CAN *SO* DO THIS!

No one at your age is ready to jump right into the middle of a group of cussing, stealing, cheating, disrespecting kids and minister to them. There are some adults who aren't ready for that! But what you can do is pray for people you know who aren't on the right path. And you can smile at them. And you can refuse to bad-mouth them in conversations with your friends. You can't be big buddies right now, but you can show Christian love. Try it.

# Saturday

I want you to know that through Jesus the forgiveness of sins
is proclaimed to you. Through him everyone who believes is
justified from everything you could not be justified from by the
law of Moses.

Acts 13:38–39

What if your mom and dad had a big book in which they wrote down everything you did wrong, since that first time they had to tell you "No"? And what if the more things were written down in there, the less they loved you?

Let's stop right there because that is worse than a nightmare. No parent does that—especially not God the Father. But the Jews believed that he did, that if they followed every one of the laws God handed down they were okay with him, but if they didn't, they were doomed. But who could ever keep all those laws? They were never going to be all right (justified) with God.

And then Jesus showed them that they couldn't possibly be right with God by doing everything perfectly. What they could do was believe that he forgave them and that as long as they believed in him the way Jesus taught them, they were never doomed. They were always all right. They were going to spend the rest of time with him.

It may have been hard to let go of obeying the high priests and believing in their wealth. It might have been hard to accept that each person was equally important to God. They had a tough time believing God wasn't just in the temple and in the rituals. It was nearly impossible for them to get used to hanging out with Gentiles. But this forgiveness, this acceptance by God, this they could handle. This transformed them.

## Do That Little Thing: SHOUT-OUT

Aren't you so glad the early Christians understood the transformation God was making in them? They're the reason you have your Bible, this book, your group of fellow believers, your joy at being forgiven for the mistakes you just can't help making. Tell somebody you trust just how glad you are. And if you don't have all those things, share that with someone too. She can help you.

# PART IV

## How Can I Be Me in an Un-Me World?

Though we live in the world, we do not wage war as the world does.

2 Corinthians 10:3

It's hard to read about Ruth and Esther and Deborah and not think, "I want to be like that. I want to be holy." But then you remember that they had God talking to them, and people coming to them for advice, and whole countries depending on them. You feel like just an ordinary person.

Here's the thing about the fabulous people you read about in Part III: they were all human. As you saw, they each started out clueless and were transformed into the people God meant for them to be. That can happen to you too. You (probably) won't be made queen, and you (may) not become a judge, and you (definitely) won't give birth to God's Son. But whatever it is God has sent you here to do and be, you'll need the same kind of closeness to God that Esther and Deborah and Mary had.

It isn't an easy thing to come by, that closeness, because the world gets in the way. It's not interested in your being your true godly self, and it tempts you with all kinds of things that get between you and God. It's tough to be aware and strong, but it can be done and God wants it to be done. That's why his Word shows you how. In our final thirteen weeks together, you'll find ways to be like the very-human people you've met here. You will be a fabulous, very-You YOU!

## The Big Ten

> These are the commandments the Lord proclaimed in a loud voice to your whole assembly there on the mountain ... He wrote them on two stone tablets and gave them to me.
>
> Deuteronomy 5:22

The Ten Commandments. Everybody knows those, right? Don't lie or steal or kill. They're such a part of you, you wouldn't dream of breaking them, so why do you even need them anymore?

Kids have been asking that since Moses first brought the Ten Commandments down the mountain. The answer is the same now as it was then. There had/have to be rules so people would live reverently before the God who gave them such a good life. They weren't going to just do that naturally, and, actually, neither are you.

This week you'll take a close look (like with a microscope!) at how the Big Ten really apply to your tween life, in ways you probably haven't thought of. You'll want to do that for the God who gives you a good life—a life that is set right and put-together, without a lot of worries and fears. So let's start with the basics for a set-right life.

# Sunday

Hear, O Israel, the decrees and laws I declare in your hearing today. Learn them and be sure to follow them. The Lord our God made a covenant with us.

Deuteronomy 5:1–2

On the first day of school, the teacher usually gives the classroom rules (which can take all of that day and part of the next!) and tells you what you're going to learn that year. Usually you're so busy trying to remember the rule for getting a bathroom pass and the consequences for sneaking a look at your text messages, you sort of miss the what-we're-going-to-learn part. But the thing is, the rules are there so you *can* learn. It would be a little tough to get fractions and commas and the states and capitals if kids were throwing spit wads and hanging from the light fixtures.

God gave his people ten basic rules so that they could learn essentially two things: (1) their duty to God and (2) their duty to their neighbors. He wanted them to know how to worship him and how to live in community with each other. Otherwise, that whole escape from Egypt and trip through the desert was for nothing.

As you start your journey to the real, godly you, try thinking of the Ten Commandments as your basic survival guide. You'll be glad you have it.

## Do That Little Thing: QUIZ

Write down the five basic rules of your house or your classroom. Think of the ones that keep the family or the class from running amuck — that if you didn't have them, your life would be pretty much chaos.

# Monday

I am the Lord your God ... You shall have no other gods before me.

Deuteronomy 5:6–7

Have you ever been so scared that you thought your teeth were going to shake right out of your mouth? You know, knees-knocking, palms-sweating scared? You might have gotten through it by focusing on one thing, one thought.

"If I can just talk to my mom."

"Only three more steps—now two, now one."

"Please, God—please!"

Focusing keeps us from running off screaming when things get scary. That's why God's first commandment was for us to keep our minds on him, and nobody else. He admitted he was a jealous God who wanted all of his people's attention and didn't want to share it with anybody. He even spelled it out:

- No making idols of any kind and worshiping them.
- No using God's name for anything except to call on him and praise him. (No, "Oh, my God!" when you're shocked or surprised.)
- Set aside a day just for God and rest.

God expects respect and reverence, but he knows it's hard because we can't see him. At least, not unless we follow the rules.

## Do That Little Thing: FIND OUT

Ask your God-loving grown-up friends how they keep their focus on him. Some may breathe prayers all day long. Others may wear a cross. Still others might play praise music in their cars when they drive. Keep a list. Some of their focus methods may work for you too.

# Tuesday

Honor your father and your mother, as the Lord your God has commanded you, so that you may live long and that it may go well with you.

Deuteronomy 5:16

You absolutely know you have to honor your mother and father. You wouldn't scream at them, call them names, out-and-out disobey everything they said, or wish they were dead any more than you'd jump off a bridge.

But what about the times when you know you're right and they're ... possibly ... wrong? Like when they hang around you and your friends. Or treat you like a baby. Or refuse to let you express your opinion. Or just don't see that what they've decided is so unfair.

That's when God asks you to honor them more than ever. To realize they're doing their best at a way-hard job (raising you!). To talk to them (when you aren't ready to pitch a fit) about the things they do that drive you nuts.

Flouncing to your room and slamming the door, yelling back, or venting to your friends won't solve parent problems. Talking it out might. And it's a whole lot more honorable.

## Do That Little Thing: JUST THINK

Imagine you are a parent. How do you know which of your kids is telling the truth? How do you always know what's going to be embarrassing to your daughter when she's changing so fast? It used to be okay to look at the stuff in her room. When did that change?

See how tough it is?

# Wednesday

You shall not murder.

Deuteronomy 5:17

The hair on the back of your neck is standing up, and your eyes have gone into slits. Why? Because *she* is passing by. She hasn't said anything—yet—but she will, and it will be all you can do to keep from ripping off the wallpaper. You know it's wrong to hate another human being, but at least it isn't as bad as murder, right?

Actually, when you despise someone, even for a minute or two, you feel the beginnings of the same kind of anger that drives people to hurt the people they hate. It's good to learn how to nip it in the bud, and fast.

Later in the Bible (Matthew 5:21–22), Jesus said don't let yourself get angry enough to even think about calling a person a name, because it's right up there with breaking out your semi-automatic weapon and taking aim. He said the minute you realize you have issues with someone, drop everything and go work it out (Matthew 5:23–25). Don't wait for someone else to settle it. Don't let it get that far. Deal with stuff before you start committing murder in your heart.

## Do That Little Thing: GOD? CAN WE TALK?

Go to God about anybody you, uh, sort of can't stand. Tell him you're sorry for feeling that way about one of his kids, but also vent about what led you there, because it's important to get that out to the one who understands. Ask him to help you find a way to forgive, to pray for, and to stop wishing the worst for that person. He will replace your hatred with love. That's what he does. He's God.

# Thursday

You shall not steal.

Deuteronomy 5:19

If you walk into your friend's bedroom and see that she has an outrageously cool poster you would die to have, you probably don't wait until she's gone to the kitchen to get popcorn, take it off the wall, and run home with it. Seriously—that would be stealing, and you don't steal.

But have you ever taken a longer-than-a-glance look at the test answer sheet the teacher left on her desk in plain sight? Or kept money you found in the hallway without trying to find out who it belonged to? Or pointed out that the girl who beat you in the spelling bee can't do math worth a flip? If so, you've stolen something from someone.

How can you get through life without committing theft, then? By changing the way you think about that "something" you want so much that you just take it. Jesus said (Matthew 6:28–30) that if you don't get all worried about having stuff, you won't be tempted to take it from somebody else. A cool poster, an A+, an extra ten dollars are nice to have, but they'll never give you the lasting feeling that being your best self can. That's a "something" you can never steal.

## Do That Little Thing: LISTEN UP!

Search your thoughts for the "I want" that may be driving you to steal. What makes you crave it so bad you can almost taste it and touch it? Once you recognize how much space it takes up in your mind, you won't be as likely to imagine yourself taking it!

You shall not give false testimony against your neighbor.

Deuteronomy 5:20

You have probably never been on an actual witness stand in a courtroom giving testimony that could prove someone's guilt or innocence. But have you ever:

- said something negative behind someone's back that you weren't sure was true?
- said something negative behind a person's back that you *knew* wasn't true?
- exaggerated while telling what happened to somebody?
- stretched a truth a little to get somebody who deserved it into trouble?
- kept your mouth shut while somebody else told something you knew was a lie?

Oops. You've given false testimony. One of the best ways to tell if your heart is really clean before God is to listen to what comes out of your own mouth (Matthew 15:18–19). If you aren't a reliable witness, it's time to clean up your act. God expects it of you.

## Do That Little Thing: YOU CAN *SO* DO THIS!

Is there someone you have stretched the truth or just plain lied about? Even if you believe she "deserved" it, or you assume everybody knows you were exaggerating, or you really don't think it's that big a deal, do the right thing. Follow the commandment. Go to her and confess. Tell the people you "witnessed" to that what you said wasn't exactly the truth. Do what you can to fix any bad situation you caused. Then go and sin no more: You can do this.

# Saturday

You shall not covet.

Deuteronomy 5:21

Do you ever feel jealous, even of your own best friends? Maybe they're pretty and talented and smart, and you're sure you're not any of those things. Does it sometimes make you wish they'd fail at something, just so you wouldn't feel like such a loser?

It's natural to want to have nice things and be the best. It's *coveting* to want that so much you wish somebody else didn't have it. Keeping yourself from coveting is one of the toughest of the commandments, but it isn't impossible. For starters, pray, pray, pray. Ask God to help you replace those thoughts with the truth, which is that God loves you and made you every bit as pretty and smart and talented as your friends in ways you haven't even discovered yet. Start looking for what shines in you. Make a list of the things you do well, down to the teeniest part. Develop those wonderful talents and qualities. You'll be so busy working on your own stuff, you'll spend less time on how much better you think everybody else is. You won't wish they'd fail, because you'll be succeeding. That's how the commandments work.

## Do That Little Thing: SHOUT-OUT

Tell somebody about all the things that you own that you treasure. Talk about the people in your life who love you. Share a list of the gifts and talents that make you who you are. Speak of the blessings in your life that make you secure and happy. Tell how grateful you are for your relationship with God. Once you've said all that, why would you want a single thing that someone else has?

## Cookies with Grandma

The proverbs of Solomon son of David, king of Israel ... for giving ... knowledge and discretion to the young.

Proverbs 1:1, 4

Do you know a really wise older person, somebody who's lived a long time and gathered a lot of knowledge about how to live? It could be a grandma or grandpa, or one of the ladies at church with bluish hair, or the guy who cleans your school. Whenever you're confused or befuddled, that person always has a snippet of advice that clicks in your brain and is worth more than a half-hour lecture.

Reading from the book of Proverbs is like sitting down with that person, sharing a plate of warm-from-the-oven cookies, and learning little pieces of life. You'll do that this week. You'll nibble on cookies of wisdom until they fill you up. After all, being wise about life isn't just for old people. How do you think *they* learned to be so godly?

# Sunday

Listen to advice and accept instruction, and in the end you will be wise.

Proverbs 19:20

Do you ever get the whole sweaty-palm thing going just before a new school year starts and think, "The teacher's going to think I'm stupid. I don't know any of that stuff yet!"?

Well, du-uh. Of course you don't know it yet. That's why you're going to school—to learn it. Nobody expects you to walk into seventh grade already knowing how to solve for X. All you have to do is be teachable.

That's what this proverb is telling you. Be a person who is open to all there is to learn. How do you do that?

- Listen to advice, instead of cutting in with, "Yeah, but—"
- Accept instruction, rather than saying, "Hello! I can figure it out for myself."

Looks like the first part of wisdom is accepting that you don't know anything and being ready to learn. It's a sure cure for those sweaty palms.

## Do That Little Thing: QUIZ

When it comes to listening to advice and accepting instruction, I:

____ hate to be told what to do and I say so.

____ sit there and pretend to be paying attention while my mind drifts off to Neverland.

____ listen, and then argue.

____ take it all in and then do what I want anyway.

____ listen to the advice and then try to use it.

# Monday

A fool gives full vent to his anger, but a wise man keeps himself under control.

Proverbs 29:11

"She makes me so mad!"
How many times have you said or thought that — either before, after, or during a major spitting fit? Your sister wears your best white sweatshirt without asking and spills chocolate milkshake on it. Your mom won't listen when you try to explain *why* you had to run through her petunia bed. Your best friend tells the world your deepest secret. And you blow.

Anger is a human emotion, and it sometimes serves you well. If you didn't get furious when someone was unfair to you, you'd let people trample on your feelings on a daily basis. Anger at big injustices, like racial prejudice and mistreatment of the poor, leads people to change those things for the better.

Anger doesn't serve you well when it gets so out of control you can't think straight. You smack your sister, talk back to your mom, tell your best friend you never want to speak to her again — and what have you accomplished? Our wise proverb doesn't say, "Never get angry." It advises, "Don't let anger control what you do." Tell your sister you expect her to wash that sweatshirt, and do it at something less than a full-out scream!

## Do That Little Thing: FIND OUT

Ask your God-loving grown-up friends if they ever had anger issues — ever said something in the heat of battle that they were sorry for. You'll find that even the calmest among us blows a gasket now and then — and learns from it.

# Tuesday

There is a friend who sticks closer than a brother.

Proverbs 18:24

If Miss Thing told her friend, Miss Almost-Thing, a lie about you, and you heard Miss Almost-Thing telling some other Wanna-Be-Thing in the restroom, and it hurt your feelings (big breath here), who would you go to for comfort and advice? Your best friend—or your brother?

Unless your brother is a saint among siblings, you would probably turn to your friend first, and she would do the same if it happened to her. Brothers and sisters can be close because they share parents and a history and a house, but there's all that rivalry for attention and arguing over front seats and remotes that keeps them from always being trustworthy with your deepest secrets. Besides, they aren't your exact age (unless you're twins), and you didn't get to pick them.

A true friend is one you select (or God picks for you), someone who is there for you and understands you maybe even more than a brother or sister could. A wise person values and treasures that kind of friend—and she tries to be one.

## Do That Little Thing: JUST THINK

Picture your best friend. Remember all the things she does for you, from sharing Oreo middles to listening to you complain about your brother for the bajillionth time. Keep those thoughts in a mental treasure chest. Now fill hers up, too.

# Wednesday

Pleasant words are a honeycomb, sweet to the soul and healing to the bones.

Proverbs 16:24

"Sticks and stones may break my bones, but words can never hurt me."

Whoever said that didn't know what he was talking about. When you get hit with a stick, you get a bruise, it heals, and you're good to go. If you get hit with a "You're such a loser. Why do you even try? Just go away!" that hurt lasts a long, long time. It makes you doubt yourself. It might even make you start acting like a "loser" because you think, "Hey, maybe *I am* one."

People constantly spew words that hurt, so that it's hard not to join in, just to keep from being wounded yourself. You might not even mean to sting someone with what you say, but playful teasing can turn into hurtful taunting, an innocent joke can become a mean jab, a funny retort can cut into someone in a tender place you didn't even know was there.

That's why it's wise to use your words in ways that heal. Instead of "You're such a klutz," try, "I trip over stuff all the time. You want some help?" Rather than "Shut up!" go with, "Could you hang on a minute? I need to think."

Words can hurt. Wise words never do.

## Do That Little Thing: GOD? CAN WE TALK?

Ask God to do a little tongue training with you. Ask him to get it ready to speak only healing words and to apologize if any hurt escapes from it. Then listen. His words are honey-sweet.

# Thursday

Let another praise you, and not your own mouth; someone else, and not your own lips.

Proverbs 27:2

You did it. You got straight A's. Won first place. Were chosen Most Valuable Player. You're amazing—and you want to tell somebody.

That's natural. What's the fun in doing well if you can't share your success? It only stops being fun for everybody else when you go on and on, unable to talk about anything but your own fabulousness, until people start yawning and claiming they have to go bathe their cat.

It's awesome to have people congratulate you and gaze at you in wonder over your accomplishment. But a wise person waits for someone else to bring it up, to say, "I heard you made all A's—wow!" or "Congrats on making MVP. That rocks." That feels even better than proclaiming your own greatness. Wisdom always feels better.

## Do That Little Thing: LISTEN UP!

Listen for God's praise, his pride in you. Feel his pleasure in the fact that you've stopped whining — that you broke up an argument at school — that you can finally spell "rhinoceros." After a session like that, you won't need a lot of praise from anybody else.

A gossip betrays a confidence; so avoid a man who talks too much.

Proverbs 20:19

No doubt you've been in on a scene like this. A group is crowded around one girl who has a juicy story to tell about somebody who isn't present (because if she were, this wouldn't be happening). Everybody leans in as Gossip Girl fills them in on the details of Absent Girl's less-than-wonderful deeds. There may even be gasping and murmurs of, "No way. Are you serious?" It's a magic moment for Gossip Girl because she is the center of attention. She is important. And you feel pretty significant too, being part of the group she is trusting with this information —

Oops. Stop right here. You're about to trip over that word "trust." What about Absent Girl, who trusted Gossip Girl with her secret? What about all of you, who now know her secret and can tell it to anyone you want? And what about Gossip Girl? Can you trust her with *your* secrets?

Absolutely not. If she gossips about someone *to* you, she'll gossip to someone else *about* you. A wise person doesn't trust a gossip — and she doesn't become one.

## Do That Little Thing: YOU CAN *SO* DO THIS!

Plan ahead to stop gossip in its tracks. If you know a Gossip Girl, let her know you won't be listening to or spreading any of her stories. If you know someone's being gossiped about, simply let her know she can trust you — and then be worthy of her trust. If you yourself are a Gossip Girl, ask God to forgive you and help you find true things to talk about today. You're a great storyteller, so tell a God-story instead.

# Saturday

Become wise by walking with the wise; hang out with fools and watch your life fall to pieces.

Proverbs 13:20 MSG

So what makes you wise? Being teachable. Controlling your anger. Valuing your friendships and being a valuable friend. Using only healing words and staying away from gossip. Refusing to brag about yourself.

Those are only a few of the cookies-with-grandma morsels found in the book of Proverbs. There are hundreds more, which seems overwhelming. So just remember this—your best chance at becoming wise is to hang out with wise people.

Surround yourself with friends who don't talk about you behind your back, who know how to comfort you and laugh with you, who don't brag about themselves all day. Look for grown-ups who are always learning new things themselves, and who encourage you with their words, and who don't lose their tempers at the tiniest things. They have great wisdom. Find folks, no matter what their age, who love God and want to live as Jesus did and are truly themselves. Be with them, and you, too, will become your wisest you.

## Do That Little Thing: SHOUT-OUT

Have you found a wise person? Tell everybody about him or her, how God is working through this mentor. If you haven't found one, shout out to God for someone to fill that role. The right person will hear you.

# Food, Fame, and Fun

> Jesus was led by the Spirit into the desert to be tempted by the devil.
>
> Matthew 4:1

God set it up. It had to happen. Jesus had to stare temptation in the face without blinking.

It happened to the Israelites when they were in the desert, remember? They had to face hunger and fear and impatience and trust in God through it all. But as you'll also recall, they didn't do so well. They were always grabbing the next idol that came along and doing things their own way when they thought God was taking too long. They proved that they couldn't resist temptation and keep God's commands.

That's why God sent Jesus, making him human just like the Israelites, just like us, and putting him to the same test. Jesus did a whole lot better.

This week you'll see Jesus being tempted by the devil in three ways, the same ways evil does its dance before you. As you see Jesus not just resisting but coming out holy, you'll learn how you can, too. You won't be able to do it perfectly like Jesus did, but his guidelines will bring you closer than you could ever get on your own.

# Sunday

> Jesus, full of the Holy Spirit, returned from the Jordan and was led by the Spirit in the desert, where for forty days he was tempted by the devil.
>
> Luke 4:1 – 2

Even though you may go to the dentist every six months, that doesn't guarantee that you won't get cavities—especially if you refuse to brush your teeth, you eat enough sugar to cause a coma, or you never go back to the dentist again. The dentist's work helps, but you have to keep up the cleaning to ensure healthy teeth.

Baptism isn't exactly like a cavity-prevention program, but it does guarantee that you are saved from having to suffer forever for your mistakes. However, it doesn't mean you won't ever be temped to do anything wrong. Take Jesus. He was no sooner out of the River Jordan after his baptism, for which God himself showed up, then the Spirit of God was leading him into the desert to prove that he could resist temptation. There wasn't even time for a party before he was out there facing evil.

Baptism didn't give even Jesus a temptation-resistant coating. He was going to come up against the teasing and the taunting of the evil one, and so are you. Thank goodness Jesus showed us how.

## Do That Little Thing: QUIZ

Check off any of these things that is tempting you right now. And hang in there. Resistance is on its way.

____ Food! I want sugar, junk food, McDonald's — anything that isn't good for me.

____ Stuff! I could so spend all of my allowance and birthday money right now.

____ Popularity. It wouldn't be that hard to be a cool chick — I'd just have to gossip, be bossy, and laugh at uncool kids.

____ Revenge. With the Internet, I could get back at the girls who bully me and nobody would ever know.

____ Fun!! I'm sick of doing homework and chores. I could just kick back for a few days.

# Monday

After fasting forty days and forty nights, he was hungry.

Matthew 4:2

Are you ravenous (like, practically starving) when you get home from school or after a sports practice? Could you eat everything that's not nailed down? It really does seem like you'll faint if you don't have food in your stomach in the next seven seconds, even though it's only been a few hours since lunch.

Imagine, then, how Jesus felt after forty days (and nights) without food. How was he even functioning? More of a mystery, why did he do that?

Fasting (going without food) is an ancient practice that helps some people cleanse themselves. We do spend a lot of time thinking about, planning for, and eating food, so when it's out of the picture, a person can focus more on other things, like God. Don't try this at home, by the way. Seriously. You have a young, growing body that needs regular nourishment. Fasting would not cleanse your soul; it would make you sick. Jesus, on the other hand, was an adult and he had a LOT of temptation to face. He wanted to be clean and ready.

The only trouble with fasting is that it makes a person vulnerable. As hungry as Jesus was, it would have been easy to take the devil up on his offer of a full banquet, anything he wanted. And he didn't even have to provide it. Jesus could have snapped his fingers and had spaghetti and meatballs. He didn't. He'd made himself weak in body so he had to rely on God to make him strong in spirit. No matter how hungry you get for popularity or stuff or even junk food that's going to rot your teeth — and even if all you have to do is reach for it, God can make you strong.

## Do That Little Thing: FIND OUT

Ask your God-loving grown-up friends what their biggest temptations were when they were your age. Get ready to laugh, or to relate. The world hasn't changed all that much!

# Tuesday

Man does not live on bread alone, but on every word that comes from the mouth of God.

Matthew 4:4

We've used being popular as an example of a temptation. What's so wrong with being popular anyway? Is there something evil about being well-known and well-liked, to have people want to be around us?

Not at all. If you're being the You God made you to be, people are going to like spending time with you. They may even want to be like you. That's a good thing, and most of us want it.

Being human, though, we can be tempted to use that popularity to serve ourselves. It's great being adored, so in order to have everybody love us, we stop being totally us and do a little manipulating, a little game-playing to make sure we stay on top. That's how evil works. It can look so attractive that we don't see what's wrong with it until we're in the middle of it, and maybe not even then.

In the desert, there would have been nothing wrong with Jesus calling out for a pizza, but he understood that wouldn't help him be strong. It wouldn't help him be the real Jesus. He trusted that God was giving him what he needed, which was his words, his wisdom. It may seem like you need popularity, but if you listen to God, you find out you only need to be liked for who you truly are. It's a temptation worth resisting.

## Do That Little Thing: JUST THINK

Go back to one of the temptations you checked off on Sunday's quiz and think about the ways it seems so attractive, so not-that-bad. What's one Oreo going to hurt? (Or the whole bag, even?) Wouldn't you just be Miss Thing if you had that pink cell phone? Doesn't that Mean Girl deserve to be put in her place by you? Wouldn't you be helping a lot of other future victims? Just think about it.

# Wednesday

Do not put the Lord your God to the test.

*Matthew 4:7*

Satan couldn't get to Jesus through food, so he tried fame. There's nothing like the promise of the spotlight to get somebody thinking that this one little lie, this tiny cheat, would be worth it. All Jesus had to do, Satan said, was test how faithful God really was. He even quoted Scripture, Psalm 91:11, to be exact. "He will command his angels concerning you to guard you in all your ways." If the Bible says it, how can it be wrong?

In the first place, Satan was twisting God's words—never a good idea. The Bible says God's angels will protect you from harm. It doesn't say go jump off the top of a temple and the angels will be there with a safety net. It's kind of scary, isn't it, that even God's Word can be used to tempt people? That's why it's so important to understand it.

And Jesus did. He came right back at Satan with, "Don't you dare put the Lord your God to the test." There would be none of that, "If you'll do this for me, then I'll know you're really God." Jesus—and God—would have gotten more than fifteen minutes of fame if Jesus had thrown himself off the temple and the angels had kept him from even stubbing his toe. But that wasn't the plan God had. We mess with that plan at our own risk.

## Do That Little Thing: GOD? CAN WE TALK?

Talk to God about how you can know he's really there, without asking him to "prove" himself to you. See if you get a thought or a feeling that assures you more than the miracle of a pony in your backyard ever would.

# Thursday

Away from me, Satan!

Matthew 4:10

Food didn't work and neither did fame, but Satan had saved his best temptation for last. He brought out the fun factor.

Wouldn't it be great, Satan said, if you could have the power to avoid this suffering that God has planned for you? What's up with that? If you fall down and worship me instead of him, he said, you can have a life of ease.

That *would* be tempting. You could go without the filet mignon and baked potato. You could even make it with a few friends rather than the Miss Popularity title. But if you could have a life without pain or sorrow or suffering of any kind so that every day was Disneyland, wouldn't it be just so easy to do whatever it took to have it?

Jesus knew that worshiping Satan wasn't going to give him a life without pain. Nobody can provide you with that, no matter what you do. Satan was promising something he couldn't deliver on because he didn't have the power to do it.

It was so ridiculous, Jesus didn't even argue with him. He just said, "Get away from me, dude." You can do that too. If someone promises you a pain-free path through drugs, alcohol, power-through-popularity, popularity-through-using, that person is lying to you. Just tell him or her to get away from you with that dog food, because you know better. Just do it—just say no. And then say yes to God.

## Do That Little Thing: LISTEN UP!

Listen for promises of perfection today. You'll hear them on TV commercials, see them in magazine ads. You might catch a kid telling other kids that something "totally rocks" and they should try it. One place you won't hear it is in church, and you won't see it in the Bible. The only promise you can believe is that God loves you and will keep you with him forever. All you have to do is believe.

# Friday

When the devil had finished all this tempting, he left [Jesus] until an opportune time.

Luke 4:13

It was over—for now. After resisting temptation three times, Jesus got rid of Satan, but only for the time being. He was too big a threat to the devil's hope of taking over for Satan to leave him alone. All through Jesus' ministry, the devil popped back up and tried to distract him.

Like the day Jesus was telling the disciples that he was going to be crucified. He wanted to warn them so they'd understand when it happened that it was God's doing. Peter just couldn't handle it. He said no—wasn't there some way to keep that from happening? Jesus said, "Get behind me, Satan." He wasn't really calling Peter the devil. He was talking to the temptation that wanted him to skip the crucifixion scene and go right to the glorious rising from the dead. "Get back," he said. Just as he did in the wilderness.

Just as you'll have to do almost every day. Temptation doesn't leave you alone once you've resisted it once. It will return to nag you and bug you and tease you over and over, hoping you'll someday give in. Be prepared to say, "Get back!" quite often. That part will get easier, because God's with you, helping you see what is wrong to do, what choice is bad to make. You'll become stronger with every "get away from me, dude!"

## Do That Little Thing: YOU CAN *SO* DO THIS!

Go back once again to the temptation you've been thinking about since Sunday. Get yourself prepared to tell it to "Get back!" the very next time it crooks its finger at you. You may not even have to wait until then. You can go straight to it and give it a shove — whether it's the entire bag of chips that could be yours for the taking, the yummy morsel of gossip you can practically taste, or the flawless plan to take down Miss Thing once and for all. Rip it up, tear it up, shove it into the closet, or just tell it no. You can so do this.

# Saturday

Angels came and attended him.

Matthew 4:11

Just in case all this talk of temptation-resisting is making you feel a little stressed, know this: you don't have to do it alone. In fact, you can't. Even Jesus didn't.

The minute he banished Satan, at least for the time being, there was space for God. He moved right in, feeding Jesus, taking care of him, getting him back to health after his forty days (and nights) in the desert. That's the way it works. You make room for God by getting rid of the evil in your life, and he is so there, giving you what you need to strengthen you so you can keep on resisting things like girl politics and getting stuff and being a couch potato. He will make you stronger for the bigger temptations that lie just around the corner as you get older. He'll help you see them for what they are and be ready for them and never take your own strength for granted. He'll put those words, "Get away from me!" right into your mouth, and his own love and caring right into your heart.

You're not alone in this. You've got angels, girl.

## Do That Little Thing: SHOUT-OUT

Has God been there for you this week as you've given temptation the slip? Tell somebody about that. Have you stumbled into a tempting situation you just couldn't pull yourself out of? Ask somebody to pray with you. That's a shout-out in itself, because it shows that you know just what God can do. And he will.

# The In-Crowd

> They pulled their boats up on shore, left everything and followed him.
>
> Luke 5:11

Let's say you were doing something that had your total attention, something you'd rather be doing than anything else. Could be watching the movie you'd been waiting to see for, like, ever — or playing a killer game of backyard soccer (and winning) — or even just savoring a giant bowl of strawberry shortcake with whipped cream.

What would it take to get you away from that? Fire? Earthquake? Threat of eternal groundation? An announcement that homework was banned forever?

The guys Jesus called to be his disciples were doing the work they'd been raised to do, living lives that took their total attention, when Jesus got them to drop it all and walk away. He didn't scare them or threaten them or even promise them the best time they'd ever had. He just asked them to follow him. Period.

Could Jesus get you to drop the movie, the soccer, the dessert if he called you? It's a good question to answer for yourself, because Jesus does ask us to stop what we're doing and focus on him all the time. This week will help you know what that sounds like and show you how to respond to it, just as the disciples did. So drop everything right now and start reading!

# Sunday

Go away from me, Lord; I am a sinful man!

Luke 5:8

What is your favorite success-dream? To be a world-class skater? Win the National Spelling Bee? Take center stage on Broadway?

How cool would it be to see the BEST of your dream category in person? An Olympic gold medalist. A national bee winner. The actor who walked away with all the Tony Awards last year.

And what if that person turned to you and said, "Come skate with me," or "Can you spell this?" or "How about we sing a song together?" Chances are you'd say — once you got your lips to actually move — "No! I'm not good enough!"

So you can understand why when Peter, big-time fisherman, saw Jesus fill his nets and his boats and even his friends' boats with seafood, he said, "I'm not even good enough for you to stand here next to me. Please go away."

Who *is* good enough to hang around with Jesus? That wasn't and still isn't the point. Jesus doesn't expect you to be "good enough" to follow him. He shows his power to you, like he did to Peter with the catch of the day, so you'll see that he's the one you *need* to follow. It's a good thing Jesus didn't listen to Peter and say, "Okay, I'll go away." He doesn't say it to you, either. He doesn't expect you to be "good enough." He just wants you to recognize the signs that he's the Lord, and follow.

## Do That Little Thing: QUIZ

Check off any of these you think makes you "not good enough" to hang out with Jesus:

_____ I don't think about God all the time.
_____ I would sometimes rather play than pray.
_____ I disobey my parents now and then.
_____ I'm not always that nice to other people.
_____ I have been known to tell a lie or two.
_____ I get lazy.

Now that you've admitted those things, know this: Jesus wants to hang out with you BECAUSE of those things. How else is he going to help you?

# Monday

Why does he eat with tax collectors and "sinners"?

Mark 2:16

Who has a reputation in your school for being the bad kids? They could be the ones who cheat and lie and steal, the ones who pick fights on the playground, the ones you hear adults whisper are sure to end up behind bars.

Those were the kinds of people Jesus was spending time with. A tax collector, like Levi, was an outcast. He couldn't serve as a judge or even a witness and definitely wasn't allowed to go into the synagogue (the Jewish church). Even members of his family were considered unclean, right down to the kids.

And Jesus wasn't just having coffee with Levi and others like him. He was eating with them, which in Jewish culture was a sign of friendship. Sitting down to a meal with Levi (also called Matthew, who became one of the disciples) and his friends meant Jesus wanted to be close to them. He liked them. It would be like going into a prison and having a pizza with the guys on Death Row.

Jesus didn't choose Matthew because he needed Matthew on his team. He chose Matthew because Matthew needed *him*. Jesus would gather those "bad kids" on the playground and start a game of dodgeball so he could get to know them. Whatever you checked off on yesterday's quiz draws you into Jesus' group. He wants to have a burger with you, talk about how you can change. After all, you need him.

## Do That Little Thing: FIND OUT

Ask your God-loving adult friends what things they did as kids that made them prime candidates for Jesus' table in the lunchroom. Share your own misfitness with them. If at all possible, include popcorn.

# Tuesday

Look, the Lamb of God!

John 1:36

Here's how it went down. John the Baptist was in Bethany with two of his disciples when he saw Jesus walking by. He did what he always did when he spotted his cousin. He said, "Look, the Lamb of God!" An odd way to identify somebody, but Andrew, one of the two disciples with John, figured it out. Lambs were important because they were special sacrifices people made to God. If this guy was good enough to be *God's* sacrifice, he must be pretty significant. So Andrew ditched John and took off after Jesus. He followed him all the way to where he was staying and sat with him all day.

Those same steps can work for you in following Jesus. When someone points our Lord out to you — a Sunday school teacher, your pastor, a friend, even this book — find out as much as you can about him. Read about him. Talk to him in prayer. Be taught by other people who know him well. It'll take time, but soak in everything, just like Andrew.

## Do That Little Thing: JUST THINK

Think about — and maybe make a list of — the people who have pointed Jesus out to you. You might include your parents, people at your church, friends — even somebody who just acts the way you think Jesus did in generosity and love. Those are people you'll want to hang out with if you want to follow Jesus to his house and spend your days with him.

# Wednesday

The first thing Andrew did was to find his brother Simon and tell him, "We have found the Messiah."

John 1:41

Whenever something exciting happens to you—especially if it involves somebody famous—what's the first thing you want to do? Tell your best friend, of course! Sometimes it doesn't even seem real until you share it with her, and when you do it's as if you're reliving it all over again through her eyes. It's the best.

It only made sense then that Andrew would run home from spending the whole day with the amazing Jesus and tell his brother. Jesus wasn't famous yet, but Andrew knew he was important—the most important person on earth—the person their people had been waiting so very long to see.

That's your next step in following Jesus, too. Once someone has pointed him out to you and you've gotten to know how amazing his presence is, run (don't walk) to the person you're closest to and share the news. Don't keep it to yourself, because we were meant to follow Christ together.

## Do That Little Thing: GOD? CAN WE TALK?

Feeling a little shy about sharing the news, even with your closest pal? God understands that it's a big risk. You could be laughed at, snorted at, told you're a geek. So talk to God about it first. Express your embarrassment. Ask for the words to say. Feel his encouragement. You can so do this.

# Thursday

His disciples came to him, and he began to teach them.

Matthew 5:1–2

A nd he taught them, and he taught them, and he taught them. What follows that verse in the Bible is known as the Sermon on the Mount, and it goes on for three whole chapters. It was packed with what Jesus wanted them, and wants us, to know as his disciples. We'll study it in detail later.

For now, just think about there being 104 verses worth of stuff you need to know about how Jesus wants us to live our lives. What you need to do at this point is simply get into the habit of paying attention, as the disciples had to do. Listen up — to the Bible, your pastors and Sunday school teachers, other adults who obviously follow Christ (including your parents), and to the things you learn in your own quiet time with God. Jesus wants you to know SO much.

## Do That Little Thing: LISTEN UP!

For this day, really keep your antennae up for messages Jesus wants you to get about him. Listen for them in your parents' love, in your teachers' caring, in your friends' warmth. In your quiet time with God, review those messages with him. Like a disciple, come to him.

# Friday

He called his twelve disciples to him and gave them authority
to drive out evil spirits and to heal every disease and sickness.

Matthew 10:1

Ever wonder why you have to get an education? Why you have to
do chores at your house? Why your parents are always all over
you about manners and stuff? Seriously, why can't everybody just
lighten up and let you be a kid?

The answer to that, of course, is that, hello, you're going to grow
up, and it's going to be your responsibility to take care of your own
life, and probably some other people's lives (like your kids). You
might even participate in the lives of the whole world. Where do
you think the future senators and scientists and ministers are going
to come from? You have to start learning now, because your parents
aren't always going to be there to coach you.

Jesus knew his time on earth was going to be short. When he
was gone it would be up to the disciples to continue the work he
started, the most important work there is. So not only did he teach
them; he gave them power.

You may think, how cool would it be to have the authority,
straight from Jesus, to drive out evil spirits and heal diseases? You
have the power to do something just as cool: whatever it is God has
put you here to do. All you have to do to tap into that power is what
the disciples did—go straight to Jesus when he's pointed out to you,
share him with other people, gather with them to be taught by him,
and obey what you learn. Be faithful to that and *you've got the power!*

## Do That Little Thing: YOU CAN *SO* DO THIS!

Choose one of these steps you can take today — the one that's closest
to where you are in following Jesus — and do that little thing.

- Decide you're already "good enough" to hang out with Jesus,
  because you are, and just sit down and talk to him.
- Ask somebody to point Jesus out to you.
- Tell somebody else about Jesus.
- Learn something new about Jesus.

# Saturday

Any of you who does not give up everything he has cannot be my disciple.

Luke 14:33

That's one of the scariest verses in the whole Bible, so let's just get right down to it. It does *not* mean you have to give up everything you own right now—cool bike, iPod, entire wardrobe. It *does* mean you must be willing to do whatever you have to in order to really follow Jesus.

- Maybe you need to give up gossiping, because when you're bad-mouthing other people you are going way off in a non-Jesus direction.
- Perhaps you have to give up a team that has practice or games on Sunday because they interfere with church.
- Could be you should give up a friendship that puts you in too many tempting situations.

Anything you do that steers you off the Jesus-path, that makes it way hard to follow what you've learned about him, has to go. It can feel like you're giving up everything you own. But once you do it, what a journey you'll be on. Don't miss it. Clean house.

## Do That Little Thing: SHOUT-OUT

You've made a step — even a baby step — this week in following after Jesus. Tell somebody what you did, what you learned, what you gave up. Getting there is half the fun, and fun is so much better when you share it.

# The Blessed-Are's

Blessed are those …

Matthew 5:6

Have you ever heard somebody say, "I was so blessed"? Usually it means something good is happening, something that makes that person happy. But in the verses you'll read this week, Jesus says things like, "Blessed are those who mourn," and "Blessed are the poor in spirit." If "blessed" means "happy," that doesn't make any sense at all. It's almost impossible to be happy when somebody you love dies, so how can you be blessed when you mourn?

"Blessed" doesn't mean "happy." It means "filled with God." Don't you think about praying more when you're sad or scared or in trouble than when everything is going your way? That's because you're more aware of God—you're more God-filled—when you know you need him.

In Jewish culture, people believed that if things were falling apart, it was because God was punishing them for something. Jesus was saying, "No way!" In the Beatitudes—the "blessed are's"—he let them know that just because they were having a hard time didn't mean God wasn't right there to help them. They didn't have to earn his presence in times like that. It was simply a gift, a blessing—all the time.

This week you'll learn about seven different times in a person's life when God is working the hardest inside her. It'll be a blessing for you.

# Sunday

Blessed are the poor in spirit, for theirs is the kingdom of heaven.

Matthew 5:3

You probably get what "poor" means. It's not how you feel when your mom says she can't afford that iPod you're dying for. Real poverty is having to do without the things the body needs. Very poor people don't have enough to eat, may not have shelter, are low on clothes to protect them from the weather.

"Poor in spirit" is being without the things that make the heart glad, like hope and joy and love. You may have been poor in spirit yourself when you had a fight with a friend, or felt left out at school, or needed time with your mom when she was too busy. And yet Jesus says you are blessed when you're totally bummed out. You're filled with God at times like that. How can that be? Ask yourself:

- Who do I go to when there's nobody around to understand?
- Who else hangs in there with me when everybody else thinks I should be over it?
- Who knows exactly how I feel in a way nobody else can?

That, of course, would be God—who never says he "can't afford" to give you what your spirit needs. He is, in fact, the only one who can. That's a blessing.

## Do That Little Thing: QUIZ

Choose the statement that fits you (and remember, there are no wrong answers!). To me, "blessed" means:

- God cares when I feel bad.
- God makes me feel better when I'm down.
- God aches right along with me when I'm hurting inside.

Carry your answer in your heart.

# Monday

Blessed are those who mourn, for they will be comforted.

Matthew 5:4

Think about the last time you were so upset you thought you'd *never* feel better.

Did your friends ditch you? Did your grandpa die? Did your parents get a divorce? Even things nobody else thinks are a big deal can leave you feeling that way—anything from getting an F on your report card to hurting the feelings of somebody you really love. Grieving is like an elephant sitting on your chest, squeezing out your hope.

Maybe somebody came along who said or did just the right thing to give you hope that maybe you *would* get over it. A new friend appeared. Your mom shared her grief and a plate of cookies with you. Your dad promised he would always be there for you. You could breathe again.

Chances are when you did feel happy once more, you felt better than you ever had before. That's why those who mourn are blessed—because they will be comforted by God, who knows all the right things to do and say. That feeling of hope in the future is worth the fear you had that it was lost forever. Every time God comforts you, you will feel a little safer, knowing that nothing can happen that will take away hope forever. And that's a blessing.

## Do That Little Thing: FIND OUT

Ask your mom (or another grown-up who has always known you) about the first time you experienced a loss as a little girl — anything from the death of a pet to the giving up of that special blankie. Have her tell you how she comforted you. Then imagine God doing that in an almighty way — for the next time you have to mourn.

# Tuesday

Blessed are the meek, for they will inherit the earth.

Matthew 5:5

Which of these would you LOVE to be voted as?

- Cutest
- Most Talented
- Most Likely to Succeed
- Most Popular
- Best All-Around

How cool would it be to have your picture above that title in the yearbook?

Actually, it might be cool for a while, until everybody forgot about it and went on to the next thing.

Jesus says that you're more God-filled when you're just happy to be who you are. There's nothing wrong with being drop-dead gorgeous or American-Idol talented or the girl everyone wants to be around. But you don't have to be that in order to be filled with God. You just have to be you. That's when you have everything on earth that's really worth anything. You will be:

- Miss Peaceful, who isn't always worried about what other people think of you.
- Happy Girl, because you're free to be.
- Way Loved, because people adore and respect you for being just yourself.

That's the inheritance God the Father wants you to have. It's the one that will last for always.

## Do That Little Thing: JUST THINK

Do you think the most popular (prettiest, smartest, blah, blah, blah) girl you know always feels like she's at the top? Do you think it's hard for her to do and be what it takes to stay there? Maybe it would be a good idea to pray for her today, you think?

# Wednesday

Blessed are those who hunger and thirst for righteousness, for they will be filled.

Matthew 5:6

What are you in the mood for right now? Domino's Pizza? Ben and Jerry's Ice Cream? Your mom's double-chocolate brownies? Let your mouth water. Can you almost taste and smell? Getting pretty hungry? What would you do to have just one bite at this moment?

Now imagine being that eager to understand what God wants you to do. Think of wanting to do the right thing so much you can almost taste it. Maybe you do feel that way. There might be something you'd give a lot to be able to change — like being nicer to your sister or arguing less with your mother or treating that handicapped girl more like a friend. You've tried on your own and you just can't do it and you SO want to because you love God.

Jesus says if you want God that much, you'll have God in every part of you. Letting him come in to work that change in you will be like finally biting into that cheese-dripping slice with pepperoni or taking the first lick from that double cone or dipping that brownie in a big glass of milk. Being God-filled is that satisfying — so start working up your appetite!

## Do That Little Thing: GOD? CAN WE TALK?

However close you feel to God right now (even if it's, uh, like you're in a separate universe), go to a quiet place, get still, and ask God to bring you closer. Ask the way you beg your mom to stop at Baskin-Robbins — only times one hundred. The asking might make you feel like God's nearer — all by itself.

# Thursday

Blessed are the merciful, for they will be shown mercy.

Matthew 5:7

Mercy sounds like something that happens in court. The judge shows mercy for the criminal and only puts him in jail for twenty years instead of for life—that kind of thing. We think of it as a big deal that only happens to adults.

You've experienced mercy yourself, though. What about that time you really messed up and your parents decided not to ground you for the rest of your life? Or the time your sister promised she wouldn't tell on you for something you SO did?

You even show mercy. It's what you do when you care so much about a friend, you forgive her for hurting your feelings. Or when your little brother flushes your math homework down the toilet, and you don't flush him down with it. God doesn't miss the mercy you show because he invented it. He likes it—so much that he has mercy on you when you need his forgiveness. It's nice how that works out, isn't it? It makes it definitely worth it to cut that home-work-flushing little brother some slack.

## Do That Little Thing: LISTEN UP!

Pay attention to the ways God has mercy — whether it's the spelling test the teacher forgets to give (just when you didn't study) or the feeling that God still loves you, even though you had a melt-down because you didn't get your way. The more you pay attention to God's mercy, the more you'll want to be merciful yourself. He's a great teacher.

# Friday

Blessed are the pure in heart, for they will see God.

Matthew 5:8

"Pure in heart?" you may be saying. "I guess *I* won't be seeing God!" Okay, so none of us is totally "pure" inside. The stuff going on around us—gossiping girls, annoying boys, teachers having bad days—makes it pretty hard to constantly think, feel, do, and say lovely things.

Jesus is saying you can only come close to that in two ways.

One, you have to work on it. Deliberately turn away from gossip, even when it's really juicy and could get you a lot of attention. Patch up a quarrel, even though you KNOW you're right and it kills you to give in. When you do that, you see a little bit of what God is like, because God is always pure that way. Doing the absolute right thing makes you purer in heart.

And two, Jesus says, let God work in you. Pray for purity. Make space inside yourself for God. Pay attention. He knows you can't do it all by yourself and he doesn't expect you to. Let him purify you. It's such a blessing.

## Do That Little Thing: YOU CAN *SO* DO THIS!

Nobody always knows the right thing to do — except God. If you're trying to figure out what action to take in a situation, write a letter to God, asking for directions. Then wait. You probably won't get a postcard in the mail, but someone or something will show you just how to handle that difficult friend or that funky dilemma. That's how God works.

# Saturday

Blessed are the peacemakers, for they will be called sons of God.

*Matthew 5:9*

Don't you love it when the whole family gets together for Christmas or Thanksgiving or just a big ol' reunion? It's so cool to sit at the table and look around and realize you're part of something special that nobody can take away from you. Nobody can gossip you out of *that* circle.

You're also part of God's family, an even bigger group which, frankly, doesn't always get along. If you really want to make God the Father happy, try teaching other members of God's family how to cooperate rather than fight. Help your brothers and sisters negotiate who gets the remote without drawing blood. Bring your girlfriends together to talk things out instead of joining in the drama. Stop the squabbling on the soccer team and convince the players to focus on teamwork.

In the middle of that, you're going to see who you are. While you're making peace, you'll see that you're strong and brave and loving and righteous. You've become God's Go-To Girl, the one he can count on. Talk about a blessing, huh?

## Do That Little Thing: SHOUT-OUT

Tell one person about a moment this week when you felt like God was right there with you. Maybe it was when you felt like God totally understood what nobody else was getting. Or when you felt comforted after crying your eyes out. When you realized God loved you just for being you, or when you craved God like you do a peanut butter sandwich. Maybe it was even when you cut somebody slack or just plain did the right thing. Tell your share-partner just how blessed you were.

## It's Like ...

You are ...

Matthew 5:13

Have you learned about *similes* and *metaphors* in language arts yet? Those are terms for the ways writers have of describing things so you know exactly what they're talking about. For example—

- "Willoughby looked like an egg about to crack open."
- "The waves tumbled over one another like puppies."
- "Every time Mama and Daddy were in the same room lately, they turned into popsicles."

Willoughby didn't actually have a white shell. She was just vulnerable and fragile at that moment, about to cry. The waves didn't have tails and wet noses. They just moved the way puppies do when they're playing. Mama and Daddy obviously weren't going to turn into frozen treats. They just acted cold and stiff around each other.

Those similes (the ones with "like" in them) and the metaphor (the one without "like" in it) compare two things that aren't alike and make them seem so alike that you see them in your head more clearly.

Because Jesus was an amazing storyteller, he used similes and metaphors to help us understand how he wants us to be as holy children of God. You're going to explore seven of them this week—and hopefully come out with a dazzling portrait of You. Get ready to use your imagination, like a bird uses its wings!

# Sunday

You are the salt of the earth.

Matthew 5:13

When somebody says, "Please pass the salt," you know that person wants a little more flavor on her hamburger or her french fries. Back in Jesus' day, salt was also used for preserving food, the way we put ours in the refrigerator to keep it from going bad. Salt was valuable because without it, supper would be a rotten affair.

When Jesus said, "You are the salt of the earth," he meant that you are important. You can give life "flavor," make it fun and interesting, show people love, be who you are. And you can also keep the good things going. By being honest and compassionate and brave, you preserve those values the way salt preserves beef jerky.

"But if the salt loses its saltiness," Jesus said, "how can it be made salty again?" In his day, the salt used in Israel was from the Dead Sea and was full of impure stuff that caused it to lose some of its flavor. The people then would have understood that Jesus was saying, "Don't be sinful and impure, or you can't be what you were put here to be — a giver of life and a saver of goodness."

It may be hard to think of yourself as a big ol' salt crystal coming out of the sea, but give it a shot. Imagine people reaching out to you to put some flavor into their lives or to help them hang onto the goodness that's so hard to find these days. Even one little grain of you can make a difference.

## Do That Little Thing: QUIZ

Check off one way that you could bring a little flavor to someone's life. Add your own "salt crystal" if you want.

____ Hug your mom or dad for no reason.
____ Pay your brother or sister an unexpected compliment.
____ Tell your teacher you think she's doing a good job.
____ Pass a fun note to the lonely girl.
____ Say thanks to the bus driver when you get off.

____ _____

Remember, it only takes a grain or two to add some zest.

# Monday

You are the light of the world.

Matthew 5:14

A re you ever afraid of the dark? Just about everybody is at some point — usually when there's a storm going on outside, or something makes a weird noise, or you wake up from a freaky dream. Darkness can be frightening, especially when it's that inside blackness you feel when you're sad or confused or hurt. You just want somebody to turn on a light, right?

Jesus knew about that, and at one point (John 8:12), he called himself the light of the world. All people had to do was turn to him and he would chase away the sadness and fear and confusion. In today's verse, he said we, too, are the light of the world. He expects us to carry on the work he started, rather than keeping the Message of his love and forgiveness to ourselves.

If Jesus were to use a modern-day metaphor, he might say, "Don't put your flashlight under your sweatshirt so nobody else can see the path in the dark." What would happen if you did that? You wouldn't be able to see *your* way either. If you whipped out that Maglight and sent its beam out, all of you could see where to go.

You see God so much better when you share him. You are, after all, the light the world needs.

## Do That Little Thing: FIND OUT

Ask your God-loving adult friends where they see a light in you. It isn't conceited to want to know that about yourself. If you aren't aware of how you shine, how can you turn on the light when someone needs to see? While you're at it, tell those grown-ups who have served you so well through this book how you see *them* casting their beams for you.

# Tuesday

In the same way, let your light shine before men, that they may see your good deeds and praise your Father in heaven.

Matthew 5:16

What do you think of when you hear the word "star"? After the ones in the sky, you probably go to "TV star," "movie star," "rock star." We name them after those twinkly heavenly bodies because they are somehow "above" ordinary people, and they seem to shine more. They have talent or beauty or knock-out personalities that make the rest of us want to bask in their "light."

Jesus said *all* of us need to let our lights shine. We're supposed to use our talents, share the beautiful parts of ourselves, make people happy. But there's a difference between that kind of light and the light movie and rock stars send out. The shining Jesus wants us to do is not for the praise and the fame and the adoring fans. It's for *God's* glory. He wants us to do shining things — like love and be generous and make sacrifices — so that God will get the praise and the fame and the adoring fans.

So don't hide who you are and what you can do. Hold it up like a candle, a Fourth of July sparkler, a spotlight — and let everyone know it's God, doing his thing through you.

## Do That Little Thing: JUST THINK

Think about your talents. Come on, you have tons. Can you make a baby laugh when nobody else can? Make a killer tuna fish sandwich? Add fractions in your head? Touch your nose with your tongue? Whatever those lights are, think of how you can shine them in a way that shows God to someone. HINT: Anybody in a bad mood will appreciate the nose-with-the-tongue trick.

# Wednesday

The eye is the lamp of the body.

Matthew 6:22

Have you ever noticed that when people are trying to explain something to you, they often say, "Do you see?" "Do you see how the government is set up?" the teacher says, when you aren't actually looking at it at all — you're just thinking about it.

In this section of the Sermon on the Mount (Matthew 6:19–24), Jesus was saying, "Do you *see* how ridiculous it is store up a bunch of 'stuff' instead of working on being the best person you can be?"

Why pray for your own cell phone instead of wisdom in a friend situation? Or try to get clothes like "everybody" has instead of the courage to be exactly who you were meant to be? Do you "see"?

Obviously, when you're physically seeing, you can't do it when your eyes aren't good, when they're darkened by disease or infection. You have to take care of them so you won't stumble over things. It's the same with mentally seeing, Jesus said. Fill your mind with light by taking care of it, by storing up good things in there so you'll be able to "see" where Jesus wants you to go in every step of your life.

But you have to make a choice, he says. You either have to keep those good eyes on God, or you keep them on "stuff." You can't "see" both at the same time. Where do you want to keep *your* eyes pointed?

## Do That Little Thing: GOD? CAN WE TALK?

Put all the "stuff" out of your mind, the physical things you want or the events you are dying to have happen. Instead, fill it up with questions for God about the path he wants you to take. You might talk to him about what he wants you to do about a floundering friendship, or how to confess something to your parents, or how to spend your free time this summer. Keep your eyes open while you're talking to him. You never know what you might "see."

# Thursday

Everyone who hears these words of mine and puts them into practice is like a wise man who built his house on the rock.

Matthew 7:24

They had some pretty big rainstorms in the land where Jesus lived. You may have seen some like them, where the rain comes down in sheets and washes away big chunks of dirt and sand. You might even have heard about mudslides, where whole houses tumble down a mountain when the big rains come.

Then, as now, it was best to build a house on a strong foundation — like rock. It wasn't going to move and it wasn't going to wash away. God is described as a rock sometimes, because he doesn't move away, and he's always there for protection. It also makes sense, then, to build your *life* on rock, the God-rock.

That means making your decisions based on God's ways. Think about God's love in the way you treat other people. Move forward with God's promises in your mind. If you do that, you won't be "washed away" when the "rains" come — the problems and the issues and the troubles and the temptations. There's no time like now to find that rock and start building.

## Do That Little Thing: LISTEN UP!

Listen to your life. Is it raining anywhere? Are you being washed away by problems in school? Other kids who tempt you to do bad stuff? Even your own attitude? Those rainy places will tell you where you need the God-rock. Get there, before the storm breaks.

# Friday

The one who received the seed that fell on good soil is the man who hears the word and understands it.

Matthew 13:23

This whole metaphor about the seeds was so complicated, even the disciples were confused. Read about it in Matthew 13:3–8, and maybe you'll see why. Because Jesus wanted them—and you—to really get it, he told them what it meant in Matthew 13:18–23.

Some people, he said, hear the Message of God's love and forgiveness but they don't really take it in, so the first time they're tempted to do something wrong, they forget all about God. That's like seed that falls on a path and gets trampled.

Others take in the Message with joy and go with it for a while, but then some big bad thing happens, like a death in the family, and they turn away because God "failed" them. That's like seed that falls among rocks.

Still others hear it and talk about it and almost look like they get it, but they don't really live it. Their faith gets choked out by worrying about and gathering "stuff." That's the seed that lands in the weeds.

But there are those people, Jesus said, who hear the Message, understand it, and live it, so that they produce all kinds of good things for God. They're like the seed that falls into good, well-prepared soil.

Jesus said to get your soil ready. Read on to find out how.

## Do That Little Thing: YOU CAN *SO* DO THIS!

Choose one or more of these things to do, soon. Pray. Talk to God like he's a Father and to Jesus like a friend. Read a Bible you can understand. Ask your God-loving adult friends questions. Ask for a Bible study group for girls your age.

Do everything you can to understand what God is saying. That will make good soil for his seeds.

# Saturday

No one sews a patch of unshrunken cloth on an old garment, for the patch will pull away from the garment, making the tear worse.

Matthew 9:16

Have you ever gotten a rip in your most favorite pair of jeans? Don't you hate that? If you try to patch the tear with a piece of cloth, the next time you wash your jeans the patch will shrink and pucker up and make the whole mess worse. It's totally time for new jeans.

Jesus was saying it was time for a whole new *life*. He said don't try to take a little bit of what he says here and a little bit of what he says there and stick it onto your old way of doing things, because that isn't going to work. Don't keep anything from the old life that isn't Jesus-like, he told them—he tells us. It won't fix the old you.

He meant things like people you hang out with who make fun of your Christianity. Old habits like watching hours of TV instead of devoting one of those hours to God. Continuing to yell at your sister when you've pledged your love to God.

Out with the old, he said. Or the new won't really work at all.

## Do That Little Thing: SHOUT-OUT

Do you feel God helping you to be one of these?

- the salt of the earth
- the light of the world
- a light for him
- a storer of heavenly treasures
- a rock foundation builder
- a pile of great soil
- a whole new pair of jeans

If so, tell somebody what that's like. Shout out a simile for God!

# Behind Enemy Lines

> You have heard that it was said, "Love your neighbor and hate your enemy."
>
> Matthew 5:43

Anytime you see Jesus saying, "You have heard that it was said," brace yourself. He's about to turn whatever you've heard upside down and inside out. That's what this week is about. You're going to get down to the nitty-gritty, where it's really hard to follow the rules, be wise, avoid temptation, be a disciple, feel like God is with you, and (big breath) be all God wants you to be.

In other words, you're going to learn about what to do with your enemies.

- the bullies
- the nasties
- the really mean girls

You may have heard that it was said, "Love your neighbor and hate your enemy." Stand by. Jesus has other plans for you.

# Sunday

I tell you: Love your enemies and pray for those who persecute you.

Matthew 5:44

*W*hat? Some RMG (Really Mean Girl) does dirty, rotten stuff to you, and you're supposed to *love* her? Yikes! Could Jesus make it just a little bit harder, maybe?

Before you decide you cannot possibly do that, Jesus isn't saying to go hang out with her (or anybody else you "hate"), or try to be her friend, or let her stomp all over you. Here's what he *is* telling you to do.

Pray for her. Not, "Father, please make her go cross-eyed and let a bushel of basketballs fall on her head." And not, "God, thank you that I'm a better person than she is." Simply pray that God will heal whatever is making this person treat you so badly, because nobody is just born to do that.

Have compassion for her. Being mean never gives a person joy, so whoever sets herself up as your enemy is actually pretty miserable. Be soft toward her in your heart, even though you can't trust her (or him) with your feelings.

Avoid telling everyone what a mean little brat this person is being. She may be doing that to you, but as a Christ follower, you don't get to do that to her.

Forgive her. Again, that doesn't mean to tell her it's okay that she's horrible to you, because it isn't. But holding hate for her inside you only makes you, well, full of hate—hateful. Let go of thoughts of wanting to get back at her. Otherwise, she still has control over you. Forgiveness sets you free. It'll be hard, but Jesus didn't promise easy.

## Do That Little Thing: QUIZ

Check the things that you do (or are tempted to do) when you have an enemy (boy or girl, though we've just used "her" for convenience). These are things you'll want to work with this week:

\_\_\_\_ Talk about her behind her back.
\_\_\_\_ Turn other people against her.
\_\_\_\_ Yell at her.
\_\_\_\_ Do something physical to her, like smack her.
\_\_\_\_ Destroy something of hers.
\_\_\_\_ Give her dirty looks.
\_\_\_\_ Wish something bad would happen to her.

# Monday

If you greet only your brothers, what are you doing more than others?

Matthew 5:47

Picture yourself walking down the hall at school or church. People you like pass by and you smile, wave, and holler something like "You rock!"

And then Miss Thing comes your way, that girl who thinks she's all that and you're nothing at all. You have no smile for her, no wave, no funny comment. You turn your head and keep on going. She has no time for you, so why waste yours on her?

It sounds reasonable. It just doesn't sound like Jesus.

He said anybody can do that, but you aren't just anybody. You're a holy child of God. More is expected of you. You can't just be nice to the people who are nice to you. You have to be nice to the people who treat you like scum.

That doesn't mean be a doormat. Just be the kind, loving, open person you are in God's eyes. Hold onto the power to be yourself (with all of the above qualities). Don't let some unhappy person take that away from you.

Picture the scene this way. Here comes Miss Thing. You smile and wave and say, "I think your dress is cute." She rolls her eyes and says, "Like I care what you think." Instead of the "Right back at ya, then," you'd love to reply with, you think of Jesus and say, "Oh, come on, you're so much better than to say something like that." What's she going to come back with, "No, I am not better than that!"? While she's mulling that over, smile again and go on your way. Your Jesus way.

## Do That Little Thing: FIND OUT

Ask your God-loving grown-up friends what they do when they're faced with somebody they don't get along with, somebody who's possibly hurt them. If they struggle with this issue, you might share what you've just read. It isn't just for kids.

Settle matters quickly with your adversary.

Matthew 5:25

You've seen it happen. You may even have been involved in it yourself. Two girls have a disagreement—usually over something totally lame—and Girl 1 runs to the restroom crying. Somebody else goes in after her. Maybe two or three somebodies. Somebody entirely different goes after Girl 2, with a few people to back her up. Within the half hour, sides have been taken and a full-scale drama is being staged. People who don't even know Girl 1 and Girl 2 get involved behind the scenes. It can go on for days. Weeks, even.

Why do girls do that? Probably because life can get pretty boring, especially at school, and you have to liven things up. Jesus would prefer you choose something else, like a rousing basketball tournament or a giant recycling project. As for girl drama, he doesn't want you dragging out fights and arguments. Sure, they're going to happen, but he wants you to get to the bottom of any disagreement immediately, settle it, and move on.

You want to do a production of *Cinderella*? He'll watch that and enjoy it. When it comes to the other kind of drama—he won't even buy a ticket.

## Do That Little Thing: JUST THINK

Think about the last "Girl Drama" you witnessed or were involved in. What started it? Whose side were you on? How did it get out of hand? How was it finally resolved — or was it? Think about what you could have done, or could still do, to get it settled. It'll be great practice for next time — and there will surely be a next time.

# Wednesday

If someone strikes you on the right cheek, turn to him the other also.

Matthew 5:39

Before you get all huffy at the idea of standing there letting somebody smack your face twice, understand exactly what Jesus was talking about.

More people are right-handed than left-handed, so Jesus was referring to a righty. If a right-handed person slaps a person facing him or her on the right cheek, the slapper has to do it with the back of his or her hand, not the palm. In Jesus' day, a back-handed slap was meant more to insult than to physically harm.

So—if someone insults you, Jesus said, don't insult her back—even if the best comeback ever springs right to your tongue. Instead, just look her right in the eye, not in a "bring it on" way, but with a gaze that clearly says, "You didn't hurt me with that; you can't hurt me."

She may keep on. That's okay. It's better to be insulted twice than to get into a big fight where somebody is really going to get hurt. If she can't get to you, she won't be back for more. Turn away from her, and take your cheek with you.

## Do That Little Thing: GOD? CAN WE TALK?

Of course it hurts when someone insults you. It's better not to let an enemy see that you're hurt, which is where God comes in. Take your bruised feelings to your Father and pour them all out. He saw the whole thing. He knows the truth. You can count on that.

# **Thursday**

First take the plank out of your own eye, and then you will see clearly to remove the speck from your brother's eye.

Matthew 7:5

It is way hard not to bad-mouth somebody who is making your life miserable. You're so angry, so frustrated, so hurt you can't think about anything else, so naturally every time you open your mouth, that's what comes out. It's human.

But before you speak out about your enemy, either behind her back or to her face, Jesus says you need to be sure you have your own act together. Do you have stuff in yourself you need to deal with, that might even be worse than what she's dishing out? After all, a plank is a whole lot bigger than a speck.

She might be spreading a rumor about you. You've never spread a rumor, right?

She might be saying all kinds of evil things about you. You have never said an unkind thing about anybody, have you?

Understanding your own not-so-good stuff can go a long way to helping you understand why that girl has done you dirty. It can also keep you from making a bigger mess out of things as you go around painting her as the one who's wrong. Take care of your own bad business, and let God take care of hers.

## Do That Little Thing: LISTEN UP!

If you ask God to bring your bad behavior out so you and he can look at it, he will, because he wants to help. Just ask, and then listen. Thoughts will come to you — thoughts some people might call your conscience. It's really God talking.

# Friday

Do not be afraid of those who kill the body but cannot kill the soul.

Matthew 10:28

Most of the enemies you will face at this time in your life are bullies—girls who try to scare you into thinking you're nothing or nobody. Jesus has great advice about them. He says to remember that there's nothing a bully can do to take away who you are. She doesn't even *know* who you are, so your power to be you is safe.

That comes in handy when she batters you with evil comments. Believing in that keeps you from running away crying, which only gives a bully a reason to pick on you some more. She's getting what she wants—your power. Keep it, and she's got nothin'.

Whatever a bully does to you—whether she excludes you, insults you, gossips about you, threatens you—remember that she can't take away who you are, a holy child of God. Go where you always go. Sit where you usually sit. Do what you're in the habit of doing. Do not let her think she can cut you off from your own life. Inside, keep saying, "I am free. I live my life the way I know is right. Nobody can stop me." That is the Jesus-truth.

## Do That Little Thing: YOU CAN SO DO THIS!

Are you being bullied, or do you know somebody who is? Make one of these small steps to take away the fear the bully is putting into hearts.

- Tell yourself (or the bullied girl) that no one can take another person's power to be herself.
- Face the bully without showing she's hurting you (or help the bullied girl do that).
- Walk away from the girl who is mean to you without saying a word (or go with the bullied girl as she does that).
- Go someplace the bully tries to keep you away from (or go with the bullied girl).
- Pray for her (or pray with the bullied girl).

# Saturday

If anyone will not welcome you or listen to your words, shake the dust off your feet when you leave.

Matthew 10:14

One last word about a bully: you are not likely to change her. It would be nice if you could. Can't you just imagine turning somebody from a gossiping, lying, really mean girl into a sweet, kind person?

Maybe you can't imagine it, probably because it isn't going to happen. A girl who bullies is hurting deep inside, and she needs more help than you can give her in order to change.

You can leave that part to God, by praying for her. As for your part, if a girl or her group makes fun of you or just shuts you out, quietly withdraw. As Jesus said, don't make a scene. Shrug your shoulders and be on your way. Your job is to let God heal the heart that she has hurt so you don't turn into her, and so that you become a strong example for other people.

That brings us back to changing her. There is a chance that when she sees how confident you are, how easy it is for you to refuse to let her take yourself away from you, she might get that her tricks aren't working anymore. She might pause. She might even stop. If she does, that's a God-thing. If she doesn't, it isn't your fault. Trust that God will see to her in his own time, in his own way. Just dust off those sandals and move on.

## Do That Little Thing: SHOUT-OUT

Gather some friends, as well as some kids being bullied who aren't necessarily your best buddies, and go over the things you've learned about enemies this week. Tell them this is the Jesus way to handle bullies. Suggest that you all practice it together. It'll be the best shout-out you can give the Lord.

## Talking to God about It

Lord, teach us to pray.

Luke 11:1

It must have been awesome for the disciples to watch Jesus pray, which he seemed to be doing constantly. He had the kind of connection with God no one had ever seen before. No wonder they said to him, "Lord, teach us to pray."

Has anyone actually taught you how to pray or have you just sort of done what you heard somebody else doing? You don't have to wing it anymore. When Jesus shared the way of prayer with the disciples, he put it out there for all of us, and that's what this week is about.

First you'll go through the prayer Jesus gave the twelve (what we call The Lord's Prayer), step by step. Then you'll hear two warnings he gave them about their talks with God. One thing you'll want to know going in—the more you talk to him, the closer you'll get to him and the more you'll understand. It's that way in any relationship. It's the most important in this one.

# Sunday

Father, hallowed be your name.

Luke 11:2

How do you start out your talks with God?
"Hi, God, how are ya?"
"Hey, God, it's me again."
"Dear Heavenly Father."

Those all work. As long as you're giving God your attention, you're praying. Jesus said, though, that it's best to start off praising God. Tell him the particular reasons why you love him today. Tell him where you've seen his amazing work show up in your world since the last time you talked. Just tell him he's awesome.

Jesus also means for us to pray that God's name will be "hallowed" by everybody else, too. To "hallow" is to make something holy and sacred. When you say, "Hallowed be thy name," you're hoping and praying that people will treat God and his name as something more special than anything else. The more people do that, the better the world will be. You're praying a pretty big prayer. That's why you're here.

## Do That Little Thing: QUIZ

Which of these greetings fits your way of talking to God? Try using it the next time you pray.

____ "Father, it's me again, lovin' you."

____ "Lord, you are the best, the best, the best. I can't wait to talk to you."

____ "Beautiful, powerful, loving God, I'm here to pour out my heart to you."

____ "Jesus? Could I just climb into your lap and cuddle because you're so safe and warm?"

# Monday

Your kingdom come.

Luke 11:2

You've probably read enough fairy tales — and seen enough Disney movies — to know what a kingdom looks like. Things like castles, moats, knights in shining armor, princesses trapped in towers probably come to mind.

Kingdoms — societies ruled by kings — weren't quite so romantic in Bible times. Many of them were run by selfish, cruel monarchs who couldn't have cared less about the needs of their people. While they dined in palaces, a lot of their subjects were scrounging for food.

When Jesus talked about the kingdom of God, he was helping people see that things could be different. If they saw God as their king and followed his directions, they would be taken care of on the inside. He asked his disciples to pray that such a kingdom would come about on earth and in each of them.

As you say, "thy kingdom come," you're praying that your life will look like a kingdom set up and run by God and for God in absolutely every way. You can also pray that prayer for other people, especially those whose lives don't look much like kingdoms of God right now. What if everybody prayed for that? What a kingdom we would have!

## Do That Little Thing: FIND OUT

Ask your God-loving grown-up friends how they picture the kingdom of God on earth. See if you can picture it in your mind — and decide if you want to pray for those exact things.

# Tuesday

Give us each day our daily bread.

Luke 11:3

With so many problems to deal with, not just in your life but in the whole world, doesn't it seem like a waste of time to be praying for something as small as bread? Come on. All you have to do is open the cupboard and there it is, sliced and ready for a sandwich, right?

First of all, in Jesus' time, nobody could take the day's supply of bread for granted. They had to pick the grain and grind it into flour and then combine it with yeast and other stuff and bake it. Some people were even too poor to afford the ingredients or too sick or weak to do all the work. Their daily bread had to be one of the first things they prayed for.

Whatever it is you need each day to do what you've been given to do for that day, that's the "daily bread" you can pray for. Ask for it in detail, whether it's a clear mind to take that social studies test or the patience to deal with your little sister asking you "Why?" seven thousand times.

And since Jesus said, "Give *us* this day our daily bread," pray for the things other people need too. Could your mom use some of that patience? Does your best friend need help curbing that sharp tongue? Does one of those really mean girls you learned about last week need to get a clue? God has it all to give. Just ask—every day.

## Do That Little Thing: JUST THINK

Think about all the things you have to do tomorrow. Do you have a test in school or a report due? Is there a discussion you need to have with a friend? Do you have some very-cool afternoon activity to look forward to? Now think about what you'll need for all those things. That ought to take up some significant prayer time!

# Wednesday

Forgive us our sins.

Luke 11:4

This is the part of praying people often ask about. If God knows everything you've thought, said, and done, why do you have to tell him?

Jesus told us to confess our sins to God, not because he's missed anything, but because he wants to know that we are aware of our sins and we know we need to be forgiven, big time. If you went around thinking, "It's okay that I messed up. God forgives me," you'd have an attitude God's not so crazy about. He has to make sure you see that without his forgiveness, you would carry that bad stuff around forever.

Here's the best part about that. When you confess to God and he forgives, he also forgets. Your sin is wiped out of his memory. You get to start over with a clean slate. You can move on with the good life the two of you are building together. It's definitely worth getting down on your knees and saying, "Father? I have really done it this time."

## Do That Little Thing: GOD? CAN WE TALK?

You guessed it — confession time. Don't be afraid. God won't be surprised by anything you tell him. He's going to be pleased to hear it from your lips. And the sooner you tell all, the sooner he forgets. How cool is that?

# Thursday

Lead us not into temptation.

Luke 11:4

Have you ever had to ask yourself, "How did I get into this mess?" Everybody has, because no one can always resist temptation. That's why this part of prayer is so important. If you get to thinking you're strong enough to say no to anything on your own, that's when you're sure to wind up in one of those "how did I get here?" situations.

There are several things to ask God in this part of prayer.

- Ask him to keep you away from anything that could cause you to sin, whether it's a person, an opportunity, or even a smell.
- Ask him to take away the urge to do the wrong thing. The itch to spread a rumor. The thought of cheating. The mysterious inside nudge to poke your little brother when he's minding his own business.
- Ask the Father to help you run like a freaked-out rabbit when you get the first sniff of trouble, be it the gossip gleam in your best friend's eye or the teacher's answer key lying right there on her desk.

All you have to do is pray, "God, don't take me there," and you're on your way — in the right direction.

## Do That Little Thing: LISTEN UP!

Listen for temptation. It's always whispering. When you hear those thoughts that say, "Who's gonna know?" take them straight to God. He'll steer you clear.

# Friday

How much more will your Father in heaven give the Holy Spirit to those who ask him!

Luke 11:13

If you asked your mom for a hamburger, would she put a snake on a bun and serve it to you?

If you told your dad you wanted scrambled eggs, would he put a big tail-swinging scorpion on your plate?

Hello! Your parents might not be perfect, but they would never do *that!*

That's what Jesus pointed out when he told the disciples how to pray. If mothers and fathers, who are not perfect, know how to give the right things to their kids, then surely God, who *is* perfect, does too.

And God doesn't just provide burgers and eggs. He gives the Holy Spirit to anyone who truly asks for it — the spirit that fills you with the desire to do good things, the courage to be who God made you to be, the energy to do the work he gives you to do.

Jesus says go big with your prayers. Don't just ask for a picnic lunch or a Grand Slam breakfast. Go for the gold. Ask to be filled with God's Holy Spirit.

## Do That Little Thing: YOU CAN *SO* DO THIS!

Go ahead. Sit before God and be bold. Ask for the ultimate gift — his holy and life-giving Spirit. Keep asking. Keep looking for it. Keep knocking on his door. You will receive. You will find. The door will be opened.

# Saturday

When you pray, go into your room, close the door and pray to your Father, who is unseen.

Matthew 6:6

Evidently some people in Jesus' time made a huge deal out of their praying. They'd stand up in the synagogues (Jewish churches) and go on and on, or hang out on street corners, flashing their prayer shawls and pretending to talk to God. They didn't do it because they loved God so much. It was all for show—and Jesus wasn't having it. People might pay a lot of attention to them, but that was the only reward they were going to get.

Jesus wanted his disciples, which includes you, to talk to God for real, not to show off. The best way to keep from performing when you pray is to go off by yourself, where there's no one to perform *for*. In the privacy of your room with the door closed, there's not a chance that you'll show off. The only thing to do is talk to God in an honest, natural, real way. You won't get attention from people, but you'll get plenty from God, and that's the best kind.

This doesn't mean that praying in pubic is bad. The Lord's Prayer is full of "our" and "us," so it's good for us to pray together. We just always need to keep it real, no matter where we are and who is with us. It's God you're talking to, so why do it any other way?

## Do That Little Thing: SHOUT-OUT

Do you know someone who seems to talk to God a lot? Share what you've learned about praying this week with that person. You might even pray together. Just remember to keep it real.

## All About Stuff

Store up for yourselves treasures in heaven.

Matthew 6:20

It's way hard to live like a Christian in a world that's always telling you that you need "stuff." If you're going to be accepted, the world says, you have to own the right clothes, the best bling, the trendiest toys. And not just what everybody else has, but *better*. The *best*. You get a lot of attention for what you own, and it can be hard to focus on anything else. Like God.

But as usual, hard as it is, Jesus has a way. Get ready to look at your stockpile of "stuff" this week and learn what's important to God—and what isn't.

Do not store up for yourselves treasures on earth.

Matthew 6:19

When you get money for your birthday or Christmas, or cash for making good grades comes in from your grandma, what's the first thing some grown-up says to you? "Be sure to save some of that." Then you read the Bible, and Jesus says, "Don't store up treasures." What's up with that?

Jesus wasn't saying that wealth and material things are bad. When he told people not to store up treasures on earth, he didn't mean everybody needs to take a vow of poverty. Remember, he was always talking about feeding the poor and giving them the stuff they needed.

He was referring to "hoarding," which is storing things up just to have them, as if that is going to make you happy. Did you ever know a kid who accumulated candy and just kept it in his room, but never ate it? Or a girl who had to have every Barbie doll and outfit and accessory, but never played with any of them? That's hoarding. Jesus said it's great to enjoy nice things, but if you have way more than you really need or can actually enjoy, you're going to focus on what you have and on getting more of it. Your prayers might even be for that fifteenth pair of jeans or about your resentment over the new girl having cuter shoes than you do. God doesn't want to hear about that stuff! He has more important things to talk to you about, like how you can be a great friend, and how you can figure yourself out. Stuff is fine and fun. It just can't be your focus.

## Do That Little Thing: QUIZ

What material things do you tend to focus on? Choose from this list, and add your own if you want. Remember, it isn't bad to like fun stuff. It's just dangerous to make it the center of your universe.

____ Clothes      ____ Jewelry

____ Toys      ____ Sports equipment

____ Music (iPod, CDs)      ____ Computer stuff

____ Art supplies      ____ Collections

____ _____

# Monday

Store up for yourselves treasures in heaven.

Matthew 6:20

What *are* these "treasures in heaven" you're supposed to be storing up? If somebody would just tell you what they were, you'd start saving right now, right?

You probably didn't have a hard time at all picking out your "treasures on earth" in yesterday's quiz. The "treasures in heaven" are harder to spot because they aren't things you *have*—they're things you *do* and things you *are*. A heavenly treasure is anything good in this life that lasts long after most "things" are gone.

Every time you do or say something genuinely loving to someone, you make a deposit in your heavenly bank account. You don't do it just to be "rich" when you get to heaven, but you will be rewarded by God there. So include the girl nobody else will talk to. The kid you saw cheating on the math test? Help him understand how to do the problems. Don't argue with your mom when you can see she's already having a bad day. Those things will last forever in their hearts, and in God's.

## Do That Little Thing: FIND OUT

Ask your God-loving grown-up friends what treasures in heaven they're trying to store up. What heavenly treasures have other people shared with them? They might even include you in that group. You may have made deposits you didn't even know about!

# Tuesday

I tell you, do not worry about your life, what you will eat...
what you will wear.

Matthew 6:25

So does that translate as, "Don't plan for your science project (or rehearse for your piano recital or go to soccer practice) — just kind of let it happen"?

Uh, no. There's a difference between *planning* and *worrying*. Planning, looking ahead, being sure you have what you need — those are all good things to do. If nobody planned, life would basically be chaos (as in, there wouldn't be food in your kitchen, you'd never go on a family vacation ...).

Worrying is when you get stressed out because you don't have the Crocs everybody else in your group has, and you nag your mom until there's a big argument. If you want those Crocs, do extra chores, save your money, and buy them. That's planning. Don't freak out because you think that without them *today*, you are a total loser. That's worrying, the kind of worrying Jesus warned against. God has the important things handled, and those have nothing to do with what shoes you wear.

## Do That Little Thing: JUST THINK

Think about the things that make you chew your nails or lie awake in bed or create flocks of butterflies in your stomach. Do they include grades, friend issues, family stuff? Are they along the lines of getting things, having stuff, being the best at something? Try to sort out which of those things require some planning so they'll turn out the best way possible, and which you just plain stew over and can't really do anything about. This could do wonders for your fingernails.

# Wednesday

Do not be afraid, little flock, for your Father has been pleased
to give you the kingdom.

Luke 12:32

When Christmas or your birthday is getting close, do you make a list of the things you want, just to make shopping easier for your gift-givers? How nice of you.

What about making another kind of list—a list of all that you already have? It might include things like:

- parents who love you
- sisters and brothers who, though they drive you nuts, are part of you
- a best friend who's more loyal than your golden retriever
- as much food as you want
- a strong body that does anything you tell it to

You could probably fill up a whole book with the blessings in your life. And they just keep coming. If every night before you went to bed you wrote down five things you were grateful for in the day you'd just lived, you would see that God is giving you absolutely everything. He's giving you his kingdom.

### Do That Little Thing: GOD? CAN WE TALK?

Make that gratitude list and share it with God. Tell him how much you appreciate everything you have — even if you sometimes whine to him about getting more. Ask him to help you remember to be grateful for being a princess in the kingdom.

# Thursday

Sell your possessions and give to the poor.

Luke 12:33

Does that mean *everything*? The cool jeans you waited so long for? The books you've been collecting since kindergarten? Gulp — the computer-of-your-own your dad just bought you? Relax. Jesus wasn't even telling his disciples to sell absolutely everything. He was simply saying that good fortune should be shared.

For instance, do you have twelve sweaters? That's more than you can wear in a week. Do you know somebody who only has one, or maybe none? Could you give one or two of yours to her?

Do you have a pool in your backyard? Do you only invite the "popular" girls over to swim? Are there girls who know you don't get to go anywhere or do anything fun? Could you have them over for a game of water volleyball?

There are plenty of "poor" people around you who could sure use some of what you have to share, whether it's "stuff" or just a little piece of you. And as you're figuring out this week, the sharing is a heavenly treasure, a deposit in your back account with God. It's going to come back to you someday in ways you can't even imagine.

## Do That Little Thing: LISTEN UP!

Listen today for the cries of the poor. Someone may have a puny lunch or seem embarrassed because she's outgrown her jeans. Is there something you can share that might help? Listen for the answer to that question too. God will put just the right thing in your mind.

# Friday

Use worldly wealth to gain friends for yourselves.

Luke 16:9

Whoa! Back that truck up! Is Jesus saying you can buy friends? If that were the case, only the rich would have BFFs, and you know that isn't the case. Girls with a lot of stuff may also be popular, but they aren't necessarily surrounded by real friends who love them for who they are (not what they have).

Jesus means that if you help somebody in need, she may be grateful and forever consider you a friend. If that one girl on your soccer team who never has any money with her is mega-thirsty after a game, buy her a soda if you can. Or share yours. Chances are from then on, if you are down, she'll be the first one there to ask what's wrong. She'll share whatever she has, including her fun giggle. You've created a bond, and God loves that.

Jesus does *not* mean that you should share your wealth just so people will like you. Do it because it's a God-thing. Do it because she's your sister in God's family. Do it even though some people won't be all that grateful. There are those who have too much pride to accept help, or who have been hurt so much they don't trust anyone and may take what you give them and run. But God appreciates what you do for his other children, and that's a treasure you store up in heaven.

## Do That Little Thing: YOU CAN *SO* DO THIS!

Keep your eyes open for one small thing you can do for someone else today. Don't *expect* that it will result in instant friendship, but *know* it will bring you closer to God.

# Saturday

Whoever can be trusted with very little can also be trusted with much.

Luke 16:10

When you receive an expensive and sort of grown-up gift, like an iPod or a computer or a porcelain doll, someone always says, "Now you be careful with that." It's sort of annoying—like you don't *know* that you have to take care of it—but it's actually good advice. It's the same counsel Jesus is giving in today's verse: whatever you have, no matter how little, you have to take care of it.

What does that mean in God's kingdom, where you're storing up the good stuff? It might mean tithing your allowance—putting one tenth of it into the collection plate at church. Or spending wisely. Or sharing. Or taking time each day to be grateful for what you have.

Doing that shows character, and that's what counts. It really does. Just try it, and you will see how people respect you more and trust you more with more important things. It might not happen in fourth grade or in middle school, but it will happen. That's the way it works with God.

## Do That Little Thing: SHOUT-OUT

Tell somebody how good God's been to you. In fact, throw a party for God Appreciation Day. Share what you have with friends who'll understand that being grateful for the non-stuff treasures is the key to the kingdom.

# WEEK 49

## When Sorry Is Enough

If your brother sins against you ...

Matthew 18:15

It's really not a matter of "if" someone sins against you. It's more like "when"—because somebody is *always* doing or saying something to make you feel lame, unpopular, unlovely, or you-name-it, when all you're doing is trying to be your child-of-God self.

Jesus says that when someone does that to you, he wants you to forgive. That's about the *last* thing you feel like doing. But, once again, Jesus never promised easy. What he did promise is help, and that's what you'll get this week as Jesus explains what forgiveness really is and how to forgive all the time, every time. Those are good things to know, because it isn't a matter of if; it's a matter of when.

# Sunday

If you forgive men when they sin against you, your heavenly
Father will also forgive you.

Matthew 6:14

If you dare to walk past her, she curls her lip and sniffs the air like she's smelling rotten eggs. Yet you're supposed to forgive her? *Why?*

Jesus knew we'd need to understand the reason for forgiving people who treat us like pond scum. He explained that if we don't forgive other people, no matter what they do, God won't forgive *us* no matter what we do. He used a story (Matthew 18:22–35) which, in modern terms, goes something like this:

A girl hasn't turned in her money—thirty dollars—for the class field trip. It's the last day and she's forgotten again. The teacher says she's sorry, but Late Girl can't go. Late Girl cries and begs and the teacher gives her one more day. Happy again, Late Girl dashes out of class that afternoon and runs into a friend.

"Hey," she says to Friend. "You owe me a dollar for that Coke I bought you last week."

When Friend asks for more time to get the money, Late Girl says, "No way. Give it to me now, or we're not friends any more."

The teacher overhears that conversation and tells Late Girl she can forget about going on the field trip. If she can't forgive Friend a debt of one measly dollar, she doesn't deserve an extra day to get her thirty bucks in. End of discussion.

That's how it works with God too.

## Do That Little Thing: QUIZ

This could be tough (but remember, Jesus doesn't do easy). Make a list of people you haven't quite forgiven for doing hurtful things to you or somebody you love. Think about grudges you're holding, people you refuse to speak to ever again, memories that make you mad all over again, just thinking about them. Don't worry if your list is longer than your arm. By the end of the week, it may be erased completely.

# Monday

Do good to those who hate you, bless those who curse you, pray for those who mistreat you.

Luke 6:27–28

Does Jesus mean that when some girl tells a lie about you to the whole school, you're supposed to say to her, "Oh, that's okay. I'm over it"?

That's isn't what today's verse says. Jesus only tells you to do three things for that rumor-spreading little woman.

Step One: do good to her. Don't spread a rumor about *her* because she did it to you. Don't trip her in the hall because she deserves it. In fact, if she's crying in the restroom because somebody else hurt her, give her a Kleenex. That's an act of forgiveness.

Step Two: bless her. If she sneezes, she gets a "God bless you" just like anybody else. When she walks past you, smile at her. And if she represents your class in the school spelling bee or your school on the soccer field, support her. Those are the blessings of forgiveness.

Step Three: pray for her. Who needs prayer more than someone who is so unhappy she has to make other people miserable to feel better herself? God is, in fact, the first one you should talk to about her dirty deeds. That's the prayer of forgiveness.

So, no, it isn't okay that she's hurt you. You're just too good to hurt her back. Instead, forgive.

## Do That Little Thing: FIND OUT

Ask your God-loving grown-up friends what they do when they forgive someone. To get the conversation started, put the three things Jesus talked about out there: (1) do good to them, (2) bless them, and (3) pray for them.

# Tuesday

Lord, how many times shall I forgive my brother when he sins against me?

Matthew 18:21

Jesus' answer to that question when the disciples asked him was, "Seventy times seven," which, in case you haven't gotten that far in math, is 490 times. Even though that's a lot, Jesus really meant, "As many times as he sins."

That always brings up the question, "How is somebody supposed to learn a lesson if you keep forgiving them?"

First of all, remember that forgiving isn't the same as saying "That's okay," and letting the person do the same thing to you again. People do sometimes learn from lost friendships and the fact that their bullying no longer works.

But that isn't the point of forgiveness. When you forgive, the person who has hurt you doesn't necessarily change — but you do. Our job isn't to fix her; it's to become closer and closer to the person God made you to be. Sure, you can try to work things out, but the person who has done you wrong may not be willing to do what it takes for that to happen. Meanwhile, as you pray and bless and avoid getting revenge, you grow. You soften. You become a holy child of God. It almost makes being put down worth it, doesn't it?

## Do That Little Thing: JUST THINK

Bring to the center of your mind a person who has really hurt you. How many times have you forgiven him or her? If that number isn't the same as the number of times she's tromped on your feelings, see if you can even that out. It may not change her, but it will sure change you — for the better.

# Wednesday

Forgive your brother from your heart.

Matthew 18:35

"Tell Sister you're sorry," says Mom.

Brother rolls his eyes and says, in a decidedly un-remorseful voice, "Okay. I'm *sor*-ry."

If you've ever been the Sister in that kind of conversation, you know that Brother's apology is about as satisfying as brown wax would be if you needed chocolate. When somebody isn't really sorry for what they've done, it's hard to forgive.

And yet Jesus says forgiveness doesn't count unless it's the real thing. It has to come from way down inside as you clean out every trace of bitterness, every leftover of revenge. How do you know when you've forgiven someone that deeply?

You know when you can think about the person without the word "hate" coming to mind. When you don't wish something heavy would fall on her. When you have a chance to get back at her by doing something equally evil to her — and you don't do it.

Don't expect it to happen the minute you decide it's time to forgive. It takes a lot of talking to God about it. It requires a great deal of sorting things out in your head and keeping yourself from saying ugly things and returning over and over to Jesus' words, "forgive … from your heart." But eventually you will think of other things, move on to better stuff. Your heart will be clean again.

## Do That Little Thing: GOD? CAN WE TALK?

This is the perfect time to have a conversation with the Father about any clinging hate and revenge and ugliness you have in your heart. Invite him to come in with the scouring pad and help you get all that out of there so you can enjoy being your forgiving self.

# **Thursday**

When you stand praying, if you hold anything against anyone, forgive him.

Mark 11:25

Have you ever been to a sleepover where before the night was over everybody was snapping at each other? When you all woke up the next morning, was it funky? Did it seem as if everyone was tip-toeing around their words? It can be hard to get back to being comfortable with each other when there are still unfixed arguments in the silent air.

That's the way it is with God. If you go to him for a talk, and you're holding a major grudge against somebody in your heart, you and God are going to have an uneasy conversation. Your unforgiveness will hang in the air between you, making it impossible to discuss anything else until that's cleared up.

Jesus says if you start to pray and you realize your thoughts are filled with, "She's so hateful," and "I'm never speaking to her again," take care of that first. Make a decision to let go of your hurt. Tell God you'd like him to bless her and heal her. Shake off the need to get her good and focus on what God has for you next. With the air clear, you can have a good talk with your Father.

## Do That Little Thing: LISTEN UP!

Listen to your feelings today — the ones that tell you if you're holding a grudge or nursing a hurt or gritting your teeth when a certain somebody comes into the room. Let your heart-reactions show you what you need to take to God for help in letting go.

# Friday

Receive the Holy Spirit. If you forgive anyone his sins, they are forgiven.

John 20:22

She has committed the ultimate fifth grade sin — whatever that happens to be this week. That's it — forget it — she can never be trusted again. She might as well just change schools because her life here is basically over.

And yet you can make sure that she is forgiven. You have the power.

That doesn't mean you make a speech in the cafeteria that will change the hearts of every fifth-grader and return Outcast Girl to popularity. That means you can go to her and tell her that Jesus already took the punishment for her sins in God's eyes. The other kids may take a while to get past what she's done, but God has already forgotten about it. All she has to do is believe Jesus has done that for her.

If she gets it, she's forgiven. If she refuses to see it, she's not. But if she doesn't know she has that choice, she can't make it. You can put that decision before her. God gives you the gift of forgiveness. Share it.

## Do That Little Thing: YOU CAN SO DO THIS!

If you know anyone who has no clue about the gift of forgiveness, take a small step today to fill him or her in. Here are some suggestions to get you started:

- Pray for the person, that she'll be open to this present from Jesus.
- Invite her to go to Sunday school with you.
- Ask her if she's ever heard of Jesus.
- Make her a card with your favorite Bible verse on it.
- Forgive her for something she may have done to you.

# Saturday

*Father, forgive them, for they do not know what they are doing.*
Luke 23:34

W hat was she *thinking?*"
"Doesn't he know any better?"
"I can't believe somebody is that clueless!"

It's hard to understand why a person does the things she does that are so hurtful to other people. You would never dream of doing such a thing, because you know better. That person doesn't.

Some people really aren't taught right from wrong. They don't see good behavior modeled at home. No one has shown them how to treat other people. We aren't born knowing how to behave decently. We have to be molded and shaped. When that doesn't happen in a person's life, she might do any number of hateful things and not even know what she's doing.

Maybe the girl who is constantly poking at your feelings hasn't been taught how to be sensitive to other people. Perhaps the boy who is mean to you has never experienced anything but meanness at home. That doesn't make it all right for them to do what they're doing, but it makes it important for you to forgive. This hurting person doesn't need your hatred and revenge added to the problems she already has.

## Do That Little Thing: SHOUT-OUT

Go back to your "Quiz" from Sunday. Have you let go of any of those grudges, those angry memories, those thoughts of "I'll never speak to her again"? If you have, tell somebody what God's doing in you. Announce how clean-hearted you feel!

# It All Comes Down to This

> Teacher, which is the greatest commandment in the Law?
> Matthew 22:36

Each day in this book you've received a small piece of instruction. At this point, that's 343 commandments. When you think of all the ones in the Bible that aren't here—it boggles the mind. That's why Jesus gave an easy-to-remember summary, which he learned from Scripture (Deuteronomy 6:5) as a young boy: "Love the Lord your God with all your heart and with all your soul and with all your strength."

This, he said in Matthew 22:38, was the first and greatest commandment. He pointed out in Matthew 22:39 that the second was like it: "Love your neighbor as yourself."

The entire Old Testament upholds these two things, he said. So if you can't remember all those laws and rules, focus on these, and you'll be close to God. That's what we're going to do this week. Get ready—this may be some of the most important work you ever do in the Bible.

# Sunday

Love the Lord your God with all your heart and with all your soul and with all your mind. This is the first and greatest commandment.

Matthew 22:37–38

Why do you follow the rules at home—because you would get in trouble if you didn't or because you want your mom and dad's approval? It may be a little of both, but if you never received a hug or a smile or a "You are wonderful" for anything you did, the threat of punishment wouldn't be enough to keep you obedient. It's love that keeps you wanting to do the right thing. St. Augustine, a great Christ-follower, even said, "Love God. Then do what you want."

Even if you could remember all the rules and regulations given in the Old Testament, you couldn't possibly follow them if you didn't love God with everything that was in you. It's not about following rules. It's about totally committing to God so that you want to do what he asks of you. It's about being so into God that everything you feel and think and are deep inside is about him.

That takes a lot of energy and focus. It's big stuff. That's why it's the first and greatest commandment.

## Do That Little Thing: QUIZ

Check all that are true for you.

I love God so much, I sometimes:

____ feel all filled up with joy.

____ want to cry happy tears.

____ feel peaceful inside.

____ stop myself from doing the wrong thing.

____ do the right thing even though it's hard.

____ realize I've done the right thing without thinking about it.

____ think about him at random moments.

____ pray before I even know I'm doing it.

____ just know he's there.

# Monday

The second is like it: Love your neighbor.

Matthew 22:39

S he makes me so mad."

"Every time he comes near me I want to smack him."

"Why can't everybody just leave me alone?"

How many times have you said things like that? We all have, because people can be so annoying. It would be way easier to be good if others didn't make it so hard, right?

But they're here with us all the time, because we were created to live in community with the rest of God's family. Not only that, but we have to love them, whether it's easy or not. No wonder there are only two great commandments. We could spend our whole lives just trying to follow this one.

And follow it we must. We have to forgive. We have to be generous. We have to cry and laugh and eat and work together. We have to love. It's the law.

## Do That Little Thing: FIND OUT

Ask your God-loving grown-up friends how they manage to love everybody in God's family. Give them a scene, like a grocery store line or a traffic jam — how do they show love to everybody there? You'll find out that following the second great commandment isn't easy for even the most mature Christians. It's a good thing we're all in it together.

# Tuesday

Love your neighbor as yourself.

Matthew 22:39

If someone were teaching you how to whistle, he might say, "Pucker up like you've been sucking on a lemon." That wouldn't help much if you'd never tasted that sour little fruit.

The second great commandment works that way too. You are to love your neighbor (that's everybody else on the planet) the way you love yourself. If you don't know how to love yourself, you really can't love anyone else very well either.

Isn't loving yourself conceited?

Not at all. It simply means:

- taking care of yourself.
- doing nice things for yourself.
- encouraging yourself.
- giving yourself chances to do good things.

None of that is selfish as long as you don't brag about how wonderful you are or only do those things for yourself and not for anyone else. In fact, it's quite unselfish, because the only way you can be loving is to be the person God made you to be, and you can only be that by doing those four things. Ya gotta love YOU!

## Do That Little Thing: JUST THINK

Which of the four things could you do for yourself right now? Take care of yourself by eating something that's good for you? Treat yourself to a bubble bath and a good book? Tell yourself how much you've improved in swimming or spelling or getting along with your sister? Think about it. Make a list if you want. Self-love needs attention.

# Wednesday

He asked Jesus, "And who is my neighbor?"

Luke 10:29

Jesus answered the question the way he usually did: with a story. In today's terms it might go something like this.

A girl is walking home from school and some bullies take her backpack, empty its contents into the middle of the street, and knock her into the gutter. Laughing like a pack of hyenas, they run off and leave her there.

Two of the most popular girls in school happen along. When they see Bullied Girl in the gutter, they get all uncomfortable and cross to the other side of the street. The same goes for the three really smart kids who always make straight A's.

Then along comes Outcast Girl, the one everybody makes fun of because she gets her clothes at a thrift store and snorts when she laughs and is always about three steps behind everybody else in math. Seeing how upset Bullied Girl is, Outcast gathers up all the stuff lying around on the ground and puts it back into B.G.'s pack. She helps her up and brushes the litter off of her jeans and walks her the rest of the way home so no more bullies can humiliate her.

Which of these do you think is Embarrassed Girl's neighbor? That's what Jesus asked. The answer, of course, is the one who had mercy on her. Anyone who needs you is your neighbor, and vice versa. As Jesus says, you are to go and do likewise.

## Do That Little Thing: GOD? CAN WE TALK?

Chat with God about neighbors you may be overlooking, people who need your mercy, even if you don't feel like you're the person for the job. After all, Samaritans were despised by the people Jesus was talking to, and yet to be a Good Samaritan now means to deserve a medal.

# **Thursday**

In everything, do to others what you would have them do to you.
Matthew 7:12

Jesus obviously believed in having great friends, because he hung around with twelve of his for three straight years, not to mention all the other people he befriended along the way. Jesus didn't just party at weddings and go on boat rides with them. He was constantly talking to them about how to treat each other. Things like: "Ask yourself what you want people to do for you, then ... do it for *them*."

You might know that as The Golden Rule. He expects us to follow it just as he did back then. Talk to other people the way you want them to talk to you, without put-downs and mean teasing, and with lots of kindness and encouragement. Do the things for other people you want them to do for you, like listen when they have a problem, stand up for them when somebody's unfair to them. Think of them the way you want them to think about you — without judgment or criticism.

"In everything," Jesus said. Whether you like your neighbor or not. Even if she drives you nuts. Love her as you do yourself. Love her as you do God.

## Do That Little Thing: LISTEN UP!

Listen to your own hopes for yourself today. What do your thoughts tell you about how you want to be treated? When those thoughts speak to you, put them into action for someone else. Do you want someone to notice your cute outfit? Compliment your classmate on hers. Do you need a hug? Offer one to a friend who looks lonely. Listen to what you want. Then give it to someone else. That's neighbor love.

# Friday

Love does no harm to its neighbor.

Romans 13:10

She is an R.M.G., a Really Mean Girl, and as far as you can tell her meanness goes all the way down to her core. You have prayed for her, forgiven her, and done to her as you wish she'd do for you. But you just can't love her.

Give yourself a break. Love isn't just that feeling you have when you want to hug somebody. Sometimes it isn't a feeling at all. Sometimes it just comes down to this: don't do that person any harm. So don't tell everybody how mean she is. Don't plan how you'll give her a dose of her own meanness. Don't even daydream about seeing her go down once and for all.

That may be all the love you can show for that R.M.G. If it is, it's enough.

## Do That Little Thing: YOU CAN *SO* DO THIS!

Today, love by not-doing. Think about situations where you could have harmed some unlovable person, but didn't. You held back that sharp remark. Curbed that hateful expression. Pulled back that ready-to-strike hand. That's love.

# Saturday

The commandments ... are summed up in this one rule: "Love your neighbor as yourself."

Romans 13:9

Even after Jesus left the earth, his followers continued to use his "summary" to help people remember the most important part of his message. Just to make sure you remember it, let's put it into very You words. If at any time you face a "girl politics" kind of problem, just do this: love with everything you have. That means:

- If a friend is careless with your feelings, love her enough to tell her how you feel. Wouldn't you want her to tell you if it were the other way around?
- If a girl looks lonely, love her enough to ask her how she's doing. Wouldn't you want somebody to do that to you if you were alone?
- If somebody bullies you, love her enough not to spit right back in her face. Wouldn't you want somebody to control herself if you had a bully moment?
- If you see somebody having a hard time with a Really Mean Girl, love her enough to stand up for her. Wouldn't you be just so grateful if someone saved you from humiliation?
- If bullying becomes a problem at your school, love your generation enough to do what you can to stop it. Don't you want somebody to make your school a safe place to be?
- Most of all, don't let anyone forget that it's all about love. Keep that message alive for yourself, for your neighbors, and for God.

## Do That Little Thing: SHOUT-OUT

Love. After thinking about love for a whole week, what comes to mind? Are you loving God more? Being kinder to yourself? Treating other people — even your enemies — the way you want to be treated? Whatever is happening in your love department, tell someone about it. Let them know that the God who *is* love is doing a good work in you.

## What Do I Do Now?

> When they saw him, they worshiped him; but some doubted.
>
> Matthew 28:17

It's easy for us to say that if *we* had been disciples of Jesus, we would never have doubted him for a moment. As soon as he rose from the dead, we'd have been all over it, ready to do whatever we were told.

Evidently it wasn't that simple, because some of the disciples did doubt this was really Jesus. They saw him die. They witnessed his burial. How could he now be walking and talking with them? Jesus didn't let them wonder for long. He did what he always did with his followers; he simply told them what to do next.

Jesus gives us the same job, even though it may look different for each person. This week you'll learn the basics that apply to all of us as we take what we've learned from our Lord and put it to work — so that we never have to wonder "Is this really God?"

# Sunday

Go into all the world and preach the good news to all creation.

Mark 16:15

There it was, their job description. And yours.

"But how am I supposed to do that?" you may be asking. "I'm just a kid!"

Here's the deal. Right now you're in Phase One of that job. You're learning the Good News so that, when you're a more mature Christian, you'll be ready to spread the Word in whatever way God wants you to. But you don't have to wait until you know it all (because nobody ever totally does). Right now you can show Christ to the people in your little piece of the world by doing and being all that you've learned about in this book. If someone asks why you're so happy or where you get the courage to stand up to people or how you always seem to know the right thing to do, you can tell them it's all about your relationship with God.

That's the preaching part. As for the go into all the world part, remember that the world is made up of millions of classrooms, soccer fields, households, church halls, school buses, dance studios, and backyards. As you go into the ones in your world, spread the word by what you say and do and are. Even a kid can do that.

## Do That Little Thing: QUIZ

Check off any of these parts of the world that you go into in a week's time. Add your own if you want.

_____ my house

_____ my friends' houses

_____ my bus

_____ my classroom(s)

_____ the school lunchroom

_____ the schoolyard

_____ the soccer field, baseball diamond, basketball court, or other sports arena

_____ a dance or gymnastics studio

_____ a church

# Monday

He who is not with me is against me, and he who does not gather with me scatters.

Matthew 12:30

There are some things you can't just "sort of" do. You can't "sort of" be on a soccer or softball team. You can't "sort of" do your homework. You can't "sort of" obey your parents. Well, you can, but it isn't going to get you very far!

One thing you definitely can't "sort of" do is be a Christ-follower. You can *try* following just the commandments that aren't that hard, or loving only the neighbors who are easy to get along with—but that "sort of Christianity" isn't going to get you very close to God. In fact, Jesus said if you aren't with him all the way, on everything he says, you really aren't with him at all. You could mess things up by giving somebody the impression that a follower of Christ doesn't have to be totally honest or completely loving or always obedient to God.

So before you set out to spread the Good News in your little world, be sure you aren't just "sort of" ready or "kind of" committed. Get yourself ready to be with Jesus in every way. He doesn't just "sort of" expect it.

## Do That Little Thing: FIND OUT

Ask your God-loving grown-up friends if there is anything "sort of" about their belief in God and what he wants for their lives. By this time, they'll surely be honest with you, and you can be the same with them. Talk to them about any "sort ofs" you have. They can help with that — because they've been there.

# Tuesday

I tell you the truth, whatever you did for one of the least of these brothers of mine, you did for me.

Matthew 25:40

Wouldn't you hate to be considered "the least"? That would mean you were somehow less than everybody else—less smart, less cute, less popular, less tall. Maybe you do feel like the least in some way, which means you know how it feels. How cool would it be if somebody did something to make you feel like "the most"—or even just a little more than you are?

That's part of the job Jesus gives us as we go about spreading the Good News. Find "the least" and make them more. Tutor the less smart. Compliment the less cute. Include the less popular. Make the less tall feel big inside. When you do it for them, you do it for Jesus. He is, after all, in each of us, waiting to be recognized. He is the most.

## Do That Little Thing: JUST THINK

Have ever felt like "the least" — or do you feel like that in some way now? Is anyone helping you be more? Think about how you could do that for someone who may be experiencing some "leastness." Remember, when you do it for her, you do it for God.

# Wednesday

These signs will accompany those who believe: In my name they will drive out demons.

Mark 16:17

You're supposed to drive out demons? What demons?

When we think of Jesus driving out demons, they're usually evil spirits that are driving somebody crazy. But those aren't the only kind of demons around. There are plenty that present themselves right in your own experience.

Take bullying, for example. That's an evil spirit if there ever was one. It turns otherwise nice girls into Bully Princesses who rule as if they were possessed by the need for power. Do you take down the R.M.G.s ? No, you drive out bullying itself. Refuse to participate. Don't put labels on people—popular kids, girly girls, wannabes, freaks, losers, even "bully." Treat everyone as an individual with some good qualities. Make it clear that you will not repeat a rumor. Walk away when girls start gossiping. Better yet, announce that you won't even listen to it. If you're there, you're part of it. If you're not, who are they gonna gossip to?

Those are only two demons you can help drive out. Others might be jealousy, race-hatred, and disrespect. If you believe, God will give you what you need for the fight. Do it in his name.

## Do That Little Thing: GOD? CAN WE TALK?

Talk to God about any demon he wants you to help drive out. Is it bullying? Disrespect for the teachers at your school? A wave of cheating? You can't even begin it without God. But with him you can be the driving force that takes it down.

# Thursday

He opened their minds so they could understand the Scriptures.
Luke 24:45

Learn the Good News. Spread what you know now, in your own little pieces of the world. Commit yourself to it totally. Take it to "the least." Drive out their demons.

That's what you've learned so far this week: things that apply to all those who believe in God as Christ showed him to us and who want to do what he told us to do. There's so much more, all of it packed into the Bible. You've been studying it for almost a whole year now, and you've barely made a dent in it.

It's okay. Even though you have a lot more to learn, Jesus opens the minds of all who want to follow him so they can understand the Scripture as they continue to read and study it. Amazing, isn't it? You don't even have to "get it" on your own. Jesus opens your mind, makes space for the new God-stuff that will sometimes pour and sometimes trickle in over the years ahead of you. Just keep showing up at the page. There's so much there for you.

## Do That Little Thing: LISTEN UP!
Choose the verse from this week that you've liked the best and read it out loud. Close your eyes and hear it again in your mind. Listen to it as if God himself were speaking to you — because he is.

# Friday

Feed my lambs ... Take care of my sheep ... Feed my sheep.
John 21:15, 16, 17

If you ask a bunch of grown-ups if they knew when they were kids that they were going to grow up to be whatever they are—doctor, lawyer, fireman, rock star—most of them would probably say no. It was revealed to them much later, maybe even while it was happening!

It was the same way for Peter. He started off as a fisherman. Then he was chosen to be one of Jesus' disciples. At one point Jesus said he was going to be a rock, but even that was a little vague. Not until Jesus was about to ascend into heaven did he give Peter his complete job description. He was going to be the head of the new church that would worship God in the ways Jesus had taught. He was to treat the new believers as a faithful shepherd would a flock, a flock that belonged to God. He had to "feed" them the Good News, whether they were tender young'uns (lambs) or just clueless grown-ups who needed someone to guide them to God (sheep).

Peter didn't get all of that right at the beginning. And you won't get what God has for you to do for his kingdom right away either. Like Peter, though, stay with Jesus. Ask his forgiveness if you get off track. Let him know you love him. You'll get your job description when the time is right.

## Do That Little Thing: YOU CAN *SO* DO THIS!

If there are any of these things you aren't doing yet, see if you can at least make a start on one of them.

- Love God more than you love anything or anyone else, with everything that's in you.
- Read and study the Bible so you can learn the Good News.
- Show the message of Jesus in your little world.
- Be more than a "sort of" Christian.
- Help the least feel like more.
- Drive out the demons you see.

If you keep doing those things, God will show you, just as he did Peter, what your job for him is.

# Saturday

You will receive power when the Holy Spirit comes on you; and you will be my witnesses.

Acts 1:8

Do you ever get a nervous tummy or sweaty palms when someone you love is leaving? That's called separation anxiety, and, man, did the disciples have it when Jesus was getting ready to ascend into heaven and leave them on earth without him. They asked him all kinds of anxious questions, which is understandable. He was leaving them alone with a big job to do.

But just as he'd always done, Jesus comforted them when they started to freak out. He said they weren't really going to be alone because the Holy Spirit was going to be in them, giving them the power to do everything he was asking them to do.

They weren't the only ones to get this powerful Spirit. Everyone who decides to be more than a "sort of" follower of Christ is filled with it. That means you too. You don't have to worry that you can't pull it off, that you're not good at spreading the Good News, that you'll bomb in the job God gives you. Being filled with the Holy Spirit means God will give you everything you need to do this work for him. He will spur you on to do things you can't even imagine now. You will be God's witness that he is alive and real and at work in the world.

## Do That Little Thing: SHOUT-OUT
The Holy Spirit is at work in you right now, planting seeds for the future. Celebrate that with someone who will know exactly what you're talking about. Wear red, the Spirit's traditional color, and share the joy. He is the best, the best, the best.

## Body Talk

> Every day they continued to meet together ... with glad and sincere hearts.
>
> Acts 2:46

Think of all the things you do absolutely all by yourself, with no one around, nobody helping you, not a single person involved but you.

Your list is probably pretty short. Except for sleeping and going to the bathroom, there aren't many things a person does totally alone. God planned it that way from the beginning when he said in Genesis 2:18, "It is not good for the man to be alone," and, of course, created a woman for him.

From then on, people have lived, worked, and played together. There are very few important things that can be accomplished by a single person, especially in God's kingdom. Jesus chose not one but twelve people to start his church, which he called the Body of Christ. He was the head, he said, and everyone else who believed made up the body, eyebrows to toenails.

You can't be a holy child of God all by yourself. You're a member of Christ's body, and without the other parts, you're like a floating finger or a lost elbow. This week, as you finish your year with God's Word, you'll discover what that means through six body care tips. Get ready for a workout.

# Sunday

We have different gifts, according to the grace given us.

Romans 12:6

Remember when you lost a baby tooth? You couldn't keep your tongue out of the hole it left. Chewing was funky, and certain words came out with a spray of spit. Your body was missing a small part of itself, and that affected the rest of you.

As a member of the body of Christ, you have a special job, assigned to you by God. You may feel like you're just a heel or only an armpit, but without you, the body can't stand up straight or cool itself with sweat. The best part of having your own unique gift—no matter what it is—is that you don't have to compare yourself to other people ever again. Miss Thing may be the body's drop-dead-gorgeous smile, but you don't have to try to be her, because YOU are the body's I-can-hear-a-pin-drop ears.

Jealousy can disappear as you get so focused on using your flair for storytelling in the primary class, you don't notice that Miss Thing is getting a lot of attention for her performance on the worship team. A thigh bone will never be an eyelash, but who cares? The parts are assigned by God, and everybody gets the benefits of all of them. So do your thing, because nobody else can do it like you can.

## Do That Little Thing: QUIZ

Which of these gifts from Romans 12:7–8 do you think you have? Remember, it isn't conceited to know what God has given you. How can you use your gifts if you don't know what they are?

\_\_\_\_ I can sense what God is saying to me.
\_\_\_\_ I am a born helper.
\_\_\_\_ I can explain things almost as well as my teacher does.
\_\_\_\_ I know how to cheer people up.
\_\_\_\_ It's natural for me to share.
\_\_\_\_ Friends look to me to be the leader.
\_\_\_\_ I'm very good at forgiving.

# Monday

> The Gentiles are heirs together with Israel, members together of one body.
>
> Ephesians 3:6

Don't you love it when you look at the circle of giggling girls at your birthday party and realize that you all belong to something special? You share funny sayings and wear each other's clothes and sometimes even think the same things at the same times. It's so wonderfully freaky.

But what happens when somebody from the "outside" tries to move into the circle? She doesn't know your unique language. She wears the wrong kind of shoes. She doesn't understand why you all burst out laughing when no one has even said anything. She just isn't a member of the body.

That's what it felt like to the Jews from Israel when the disciples of Jesus announced that non-Jews—Gentiles—were part of the body of Christ too. What? They didn't know the customs or the rules. Their ancestors hadn't traveled through the desert with Moses. How could they possibly be God's heirs too?

It's hard for any of us to accept that God wants everyone in the body, but we don't get to decide who's in and who's out. That girl you think is too trampy to come to Sunday school may be just the tooth or the nostril or the cheekbone the body needs. Your job? Be open to anyone who wants to be part of the body of Christ. You are heirs together.

## Do That Little Thing: FIND OUT

Ask your God-loving grown-up friends if they have ever doubted whether someone belonged to the body of Christ, or if they themselves have ever felt like they weren't welcome as members. How did they feel in that situation? What did they do? You might decide together what to do from now on when it comes to "outsiders."

# Tuesday

Make every effort to keep the unity of the Spirit through the bond of peace.

Ephesians 4:3

Whether you are a kneecap or a little toe, it is your responsibility to keep the body of Christ working together. It's *every* member's job.

"What can I do?" you may be thinking. "I'm just a kid." (Or a navel or a tonsil!)

You can do plenty, because wherever people gather, there's a chance the peace will be disturbed. In your own class at school, you can bring kids together by making a pledge to be more sensitive to other kids' feelings and encourage others to do the same. You can stand up for anyone who's being mistreated. You can allow people to be who they are. You can be part of the generation that stops hateful behavior.

What you can't do is wait for somebody else to do it, somebody older or smarter or more popular. Make every effort, the Bible says. The Holy Spirit will do the rest.

## Do That Little Thing: JUST THINK

Think about what parts of the body you belong to might have splintered off and need to be brought back in. Is there a girl you haven't seen in church for a while? An old friend who has started cussing or disrespecting teachers? A group that's making "outsiders" feel like losers? What might you do to bring unity again? Just think about it.

# Wednesday

Prepare God's people for works of service, so that the body of
Christ may be built up.

Ephesians 4:12

When you were born, you had all the body parts you have now,
but you couldn't do everything you can do today. It took a
year before you could walk, another year or two before you could
talk and actually make sense, and several more before you were able
to skip, jump rope, and send your first text message. It will be years
from now before you even think about using your body to drive a car
or train for a marathon or have a baby.

It's the same with the body of Christ. You are born with the
gifts God has given you that you'll use for the body someday, but
you have to get in shape before then. God provides people to help
you prepare for the work you will someday do, personal trainers for
your spirit. They might be your parents, your Sunday school teacher,
a youth pastor. They may also include the school maintenance guy
who fixes your broken locker and your bummed-out mood, the cross-
ing guard who gives you a daily you-can-do-it smile, the art teacher
who says your outside-the-lines painting lifts her spirit. They are all
part of your training for service to other people, who will need your
fixing and smiling and praising.

So start warming up. The trainers are on their way. Your spiritual
self is about to get a workout.

## Do That Little Thing: GOD? CAN WE TALK?

Ask God who your spiritual trainers might be. Tell him who has
already shown up for the job and ask him to keep your eyes, mind,
and heart open for more, unexpected teachers who will appear at
just the right moments to get you in shape. Most of all, pray that he
will make you willing to do the workouts they'll require of you so you
don't become a spiritual couch potato.

# **Thursday**

Let the peace of Christ rule in your hearts, since as members of one body you were called to peace.

Colossians 3:15

Che has an attitude," somebody says — and everyone listening
Oknows what that means. A 'tude announces without words —

- "I will disagree with everything you say just because I can."
- "Whatever it is, I already hate it."
- "I do what I want, when I want, so don't bother me with what you think I should do."

Nobody is just born with an attitude. It usually happens when Attitude Girl is constantly disagreed with and made fun of and neglected by someone else with an attitude — maybe even her own family. Your job as part of the body of Christ is (1) not to look at the world that way yourself, and (2) to make peace with the people who do.

How do you do that? In his letter to the Colossians, which is where today's verse is found, Paul says instead of pulling attitude, give thanks. Rather than blow that girl off because she's negative and snotty, show her what she has to be grateful for — like having you as a friend. It's not our natural reaction, but it works. When you're busy pointing out what you and she do have, it will be almost impossible to have an argument. It's a call to peace.

## Do That Little Thing: LISTEN UP!

Keep your ears open for "attitudes" in the next day or two. Whenever you hear someone being bitter or picking a fight or saying something negative, see if you can slip in something grateful, something peaceful. You might be laughed at — or you may not. It's worth a try.

# Friday

What causes fights and quarrels among you?

James 4:1

What makes you cranky? Your first answer might be, "When my little sister gets into my stuff," or "When I have to do stupid story problems in math."

If you dig a little deeper, you may discover that it isn't your little sister or the math problems themselves that get you whining and breaking pencils. It's the stuff that's doing battle inside you. Your tantrum over your little sister getting into your diary and your art supplies drawer is really about your need for privacy, for something that belongs to just you. Your issues with story problems has everything to do with your fear that you're way stupid in math and you have to take pre-algebra next year and you're scared you'll fail and never get into college and—

Anger and fear doing battle *inside* you cause most of the fights you have *outside*, with other people in the body of Christ. To get along, to help the body work the way God wants it to, you need to deal with the stuff that's bothering you deep down. The first step in doing that is to go to God and ask for help. It will come in many forms—just the right grown-up to talk to, the perfect conversation with a friend who's going through the same thing, a Sunday school lesson that convinces you the teacher has been peeking into your diary. Your inner work will be part of your training, and it'll sure show on the outside.

## Do That Little Thing: YOU CAN *SO* DO THIS!

What is one thing you're always arguing with a particular person about? Do you and your mom "discuss" your slowness at getting ready for school every single morning? Do you and your best friend disagree over who else gets to hang out with you two? Whatever it is, try to figure out what's going on inside you that makes it hard for you to let go of your side. If you can't make sense of it, go to a grown-up you trust for some help. Stopping the battle on the inside may make the one on the outside go away too.

# Saturday

Now the dwelling of God is with men, and he will live with them. They will be his people, and God himself will be with them and be their God.

Revelation 21:3

You have this body of Christ thing *down*, girl.

You're finding out what your special gifts are and you're learning to use them for the whole. You're open to anyone who wants to be part of the body, and you're helping them to do that peacefully. You know you need trainers to get you in shape, and you're working on your attitude by giving thanks and dealing with your deep-down-inside issues. Whatever your function is in the body of Christ, from hair follicle to right index-finger knuckle, you're giving it your all.

Why? Because God has promised that as part of his body you will be with him. He will live *in* you, so that you will always know the kind of love and belonging and peace and joy and understanding that only God can give you. You will be his, and he will be yours. All the things you've learned as you've used this book to study God's Word come together in this final thought: you are God's own girl, part of his very-holy-self.

That is SO you.

## Do That Little Thing: SHOUT-OUT

You did it. You stuck with God's message to you about yourself for a WHOLE YEAR! Shout it out to everyone you know who will understand what that means. Celebrate what God has done in you — and what he will continue to do, forever and ever. Amen.

# Introduce your mom to Nancy Rue!

Today's mom is raising her 8-to-12-year-old daughter in a society that compels her little girl to grow up too fast. *Moms' Ultimate Guide to the Tween Girl World* gives mothers practical advice and spiritual inspiration to guide their mini-women into adolescence as strong, confident, authentic, and God-centered young women; even in a morally challenged society and without losing their childhoods before they're ready.

Available wherever books are sold.

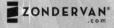
ZONDERVAN
.com